CONGRESSIONAL POLICIES, PRACTICES AND PROCEDURES

A CLOSER LOOK AT THE 2020 CENSUS

Congressional Policies, Practices and Procedures

Additional books and e-books in this series can be found
on Nova's website under the Series tab.

CONGRESSIONAL POLICIES, PRACTICES AND PROCEDURES

A CLOSER LOOK AT THE 2020 CENSUS

SILLE M. SCHOU
EDITOR

Copyright © 2019 by Nova Science Publishers, Inc.

All rights reserved. No part of this book may be reproduced, stored in a retrieval system or transmitted in any form or by any means: electronic, electrostatic, magnetic, tape, mechanical photocopying, recording or otherwise without the written permission of the Publisher.

We have partnered with Copyright Clearance Center to make it easy for you to obtain permissions to reuse content from this publication. Simply navigate to this publication's page on Nova's website and locate the "Get Permission" button below the title description. This button is linked directly to the title's permission page on copyright.com. Alternatively, you can visit copyright.com and search by title, ISBN, or ISSN.

For further questions about using the service on copyright.com, please contact:
Copyright Clearance Center
Phone: +1-(978) 750-8400 Fax: +1-(978) 750-4470 E-mail: info@copyright.com.

NOTICE TO THE READER

The Publisher has taken reasonable care in the preparation of this book, but makes no expressed or implied warranty of any kind and assumes no responsibility for any errors or omissions. No liability is assumed for incidental or consequential damages in connection with or arising out of information contained in this book. The Publisher shall not be liable for any special, consequential, or exemplary damages resulting, in whole or in part, from the readers' use of, or reliance upon, this material. Any parts of this book based on government reports are so indicated and copyright is claimed for those parts to the extent applicable to compilations of such works.

Independent verification should be sought for any data, advice or recommendations contained in this book. In addition, no responsibility is assumed by the Publisher for any injury and/or damage to persons or property arising from any methods, products, instructions, ideas or otherwise contained in this publication.

This publication is designed to provide accurate and authoritative information with regard to the subject matter covered herein. It is sold with the clear understanding that the Publisher is not engaged in rendering legal or any other professional services. If legal or any other expert assistance is required, the services of a competent person should be sought. FROM A DECLARATION OF PARTICIPANTS JOINTLY ADOPTED BY A COMMITTEE OF THE AMERICAN BAR ASSOCIATION AND A COMMITTEE OF PUBLISHERS.

Additional color graphics may be available in the e-book version of this book.

Library of Congress Cataloging-in-Publication Data

ISBN: 978-1-53616-508-1

Published by Nova Science Publishers, Inc. † New York

CONTENTS

Preface		**vii**
Chapter 1	The Decennial Census: Issues for 2020 *Jennifer D. Williams*	**1**
Chapter 2	The 2020 Decennial Census: Overview and Issues *Jennifer D. Williams*	**35**
Chapter 3	Commerce Department Announces Citizenship Question on 2020 Census and Lawsuits Filed *L. Paige Whitaker*	**43**
Chapter 4	The Supreme Court Temporarily Blocks Citizenship Question on the 2020 Census *Mainon A. Schwartz and Benjamin Hayes*	**49**
Chapter 5	Department of Commerce – Memorandum Regarding a Citizenship Question on the 2020 Decennial Census Questionnaire *United States Government Accountability Office*	**61**
Chapter 6	2020 Census: Additional Actions Needed to Manage Risk *United States Government Accountability Office*	**69**

Chapter 7	2020 Census: Bureau Is Making Progress Opening Offices and Recruiting, but Could Improve Its Ability to Evaluate Training *United States Government Accountability Office*	139
Chapter 8	2020 Census: Bureau Has Made Progress with Its Scheduling, but Further Improvement Will Help Inform Management Decisions *United States Government Accountability Office*	183
Chapter 9	2020 Census: Census Bureau Improved the Quality of Its Cost Estimation but Additional Steps are Needed to Ensure Reliability *United States Government Accountability Office*	211
Chapter 10	2020 Census: Additional Steps Needed to Finalize Readiness for Peak Field Operations *United States Government Accountability Office*	249
Chapter 11	2020 Census: Actions Needed to Improve In-Field Address Canvassing Operation *United States Government Accountability Office*	287
Chapter 12	2020 Census: Continued Management Attention Needed to Address Challenges and Risks with Developing, Testing, and Securing IT Systems *United States Government Accountability Office*	319

Index	**363**
Related Nova Publications	**371**

PREFACE

The U.S. Constitution requires a population census every 10 years for apportioning seats in the House of Representatives. Decennial census data are used, too, for within-state redistricting and in certain formulas for distributing more than $450 billion annually in federal funds to states and localities. Census counts also are the foundation for estimates of current population size between censuses and projections of future size. Businesses, nonprofit organizations, researchers, and all levels of government are steady consumers of decennial and other census data. The bureau's task in conducting the enumeration can be summarized in very basic terms: count each person whose usual residence is in the United States (the aim of complete census coverage); and count that person only once, at the right location, where the person lives all or most of the time (the goal of census accuracy). This book highlights key issues pertaining to the 2020 Census.

Chapter 1 - The U.S. Constitution—Article I, Section 2, clause 3, as modified by Section 2 of the 14th Amendment—requires a population census every 10 years for apportioning seats in the House of Representatives. Decennial census data are used, too, for within-state redistricting and in certain formulas for distributing more than $450 billion annually in federal funds to states and localities. Census counts also are the foundation for estimates of current population size between censuses and projections of future size. Businesses, nonprofit organizations, researchers, and all levels of government are steady consumers of decennial and other census data. The Constitution stipulates that every enumeration is to be conducted "in such Manner as they [Congress] shall by Law direct." Congress, through Title 13 of the *United States Code*, has delegated this responsibility to the Secretary of Commerce and, under the Secretary's purview, the Bureau of the Census (Census Bureau). Title 13 U.S.C., Section 221, requires compliance with the census and provides for a fine of up to $100 for nonresponse. In accordance with provisions of the Sentencing Reform Act of 1984, Title 18 U.S.C., Sections 3559 and 3571, the possible fine has been adjusted to not more than $5,000. The 2020 census questionnaire, like that in 2010, will collect only the most basic population and housing information. Detailed socioeconomic data that formerly were gathered from a population sample in conjunction with the decennial census now are collected by the American Community Survey, which the bureau conducts separately from the census and at more frequent intervals. April 1, 2020, the official date of the 24th decennial census, will mark the culmination of extensive census planning, testing, and other preparations. A key objective, as Congress has directed, is to make the census more cost-effective without jeopardizing coverage and accuracy. The total life-cycle cost of the 2010 census was about $13 billion, reportedly an all-time high. To hold the 2020 cost to approximately $12.3 billion, the Census Bureau is focusing on four innovations:

- using governmental administrative records and satellite imagery to eliminate some of the fieldwork involved in updating census addresses and maps, which are the basis for an accurate enumeration;
- maximizing early census responses, especially online, to reduce the number of nonrespondents left for the bureau to contact by telephone or personal visits after the initial census phase;
- further limiting nonresponse follow-up by using administrative records to help fill gaps in census information; and
- better using technology to streamline fieldwork.

At the same time, the bureau has a mandate to obtain the best possible accounting of all U.S. residents, regardless of their race, ethnicity, or living circumstances. The tension between funding the census sufficiently to produce good results and controlling census costs is apparent. Concerns as the 2020 census approaches include whether the bureau's enacted appropriations have been and will be sufficient to permit complete testing and implementation of the census plan; whether technology, notably the new Census Enterprise Data Collection and Processing system, will be ready on schedule and will perform well; and whether information security will be adequate to deter cybercrimes against data, respondents, and bureau employees. This chapter will be updated as developments warrant.

Chapter 2 - The census is a count, as nearly complete and accurate as possible, of every person whose usual residence is in the United States. Article I, Section 2, clause 3 of the U.S. Constitution, as modified by Section 2 of the 14th Amendment, requires a population census every 10 years, conducted "in such Manner as they [Congress] shall by Law direct." Congress, in Title 13, *U.S. Code*, has delegated this responsibility to the Secretary of Commerce and, within the U.S. Department of Commerce (DOC), the Census Bureau. The first census took place in 1790; the next will be in 2020. The constitutional reason for taking a census is to have an updated basis for apportioning seats in the U.S. House of Representatives. Census data also are used to redraw legislative boundaries within states; to produce population estimates and projections; in formulas that help allocate more than $675 billion in federal funds annually to states and localities; and by subnational governments, businesses, nonprofit organizations, and researchers for myriad purposes.

Chapter 3 - This is an edited, reformatted and augmented version of Congressional Research Service Publication No. LSB10114, dated April 6, 2018.

Chapter 4 - This is an edited, reformatted and augmented version of Congressional Research Service Publication No. LSB10319, Updated July 5, 2019.

Chapter 5 - This is an edited, reformatted and augmented version of the United States Government Accountability Office Publication No. B-330288, dated February 7, 2019.

Chapter 6 - With less than 1 year until Census Day, many risks remain. For example, the Bureau has had challenges developing critical information technology systems, and new innovations—such as the ability to respond via the internet—have raised questions about potential security and fraud risks. Fundamental to risk management is the development of risk mitigation and contingency plans to reduce the likelihood of risks and their impacts, should they occur. GAO was asked to review the Bureau's management of risks to the 2020 Census. This chapter examines (1) what risks the Bureau has identified, (2) the risks for which the Bureau has mitigation and contingency plans, (3) the extent to which the plans included information needed to manage risk, and (4) the extent to which the Bureau's fraud risk approach aligns with leading practices in GAO's Fraud Risk Framework. GAO interviewed officials, assessed selected mitigation and contingency plans against key attributes, and assessed the Bureau's approach to managing fraud risk against GAO's Fraud Risk Framework.

Chapter 7 - The decennial census is a crucial, constitutionally mandated activity with immutable deadlines. To meet these statutory deadlines, the Bureau carries out thousands of activities that need to be successfully completed on schedule for an accurate, cost-effective head count. These activities include opening area census offices, recruiting and hiring a large temporary workforce, and training that workforce. GAO was asked to review the Bureau's plans for critical logistical support activities. This chapter (1) assesses the Bureau's progress in opening area census offices; (2) determines the extent to which the Bureau is following its field hiring and recruiting strategy for the 2020 Census; and (3) determines the extent to which the Bureau has followed its plans for training field staff, and whether this training approach is consistent with selected leading practices. To assess the extent to which the Bureau is following its plans for opening area census offices, recruiting and hiring, and training, GAO reviewed current Bureau planning documents and schedules, and interviewed Bureau officials, including officials at the Bureau's six regional offices. GAO used its guide to training (GAO-04-546G) as criteria for selected leading practices.

Chapter 8 - The Bureau is required by law to count the population as of April 1, 2020; deliver state apportionment counts to the President by December 31, 2020; and provide redistricting data to the states within 1 year of Census Day, April 1, 2021. To meet these statutory deadlines, the Bureau carries out hundreds of projects, which it manages with an integrated master schedule. Because census operations need to proceed in concert with one another, significant delays could propagate to other activities resulting in increased costs, reduced operational quality, or changes to the design of the census in order to compensate for lost time. This chapter determines the extent to which the Bureau is using leading practices for scheduling key projects. GAO selected three projects for review based on their cost and in-progress status. GAO analyzed schedules and their supporting documents against GAO's Schedule Assessment Guide. GAO also spoke with relevant Bureau officials regarding the three selected projects. GAO provided a draft of this chapter to the Department of Commerce, which agreed with the findings.

Chapter 9 - In October 2017, the Department of Commerce (Commerce) announced that the projected life-cycle cost of the 2020 Census had climbed to $15.6 billion, a more than $3 billion (27 percent) increase over its 2015 estimate. A high-quality, reliable cost estimate is a key tool for budgeting, planning, and managing the 2020 Census. Without this capability, the Bureau is at risk of experiencing program cost overruns, missed deadlines, and performance shortfalls. GAO was asked to evaluate the reliability of the Bureau's life-cycle cost estimate. This chapter evaluates the reliability of the Bureau's revised life- cycle cost estimate for the 2020 Census and the extent to which the Bureau is using it as a management tool, and compares the 2015 and 2017 cost estimates to describe key drivers of cost growth. GAO reviewed documentary and testimonial evidence from Bureau officials responsible for developing the 2020 Census cost estimate and used its cost assessment guide (GAO-09-3SP) as criteria.

Chapter 10 - The cost of the decennial census has steadily increased over the past several decades, with self-response rates declining over the same period. The largest and costliest operation that the Bureau undertakes, NRFU is the Bureau's attempt to enumerate households not initially self-responding to the census. GAO was asked to review NRFU implementation during the 2018 Census Test as well as the Bureau's overall readiness for peak field operations, which cover the actual enumeration of residents. This chapter examines (1) how peak field operations, including NRFU, were implemented during the test; and (2) the extent to which prior test implementation issues have been addressed. GAO reviewed test planning and training documentation, as well as production and payroll data. At the test site, GAO observed and interviewed enumerators, field supervisors, and managers conducting peak operations.

Chapter 11 - The success of the decennial census depends in large part on the Bureau's ability to locate every household in the United States. To accomplish this monumental task, the Bureau must maintain accurate address and map information for every location where a person could reside. For the 2018 End-to-End Test, census workers known as listers went door-to-door to verify and update address lists and associated maps in selected areas of three test sites—Bluefield-Beckley-Oak Hill, West Virginia; Pierce County, Washington; and Providence County, Rhode Island. GAO was asked to review in-field address canvassing during the End-to-End Test. This chapter determines whether key address listing activities functioned as planned during the End-to-End Test and identifies any lessons learned that could inform pending decisions for the 2020 Census. To address these objectives, GAO reviewed key documents including test plans and training manuals, as well as workload, productivity and hiring data. At the three test sites, GAO observed listers conducting address canvassing.

Chapter 12 - One of the Bureau's most important functions is to conduct a complete and accurate decennial census of the U.S. population. The decennial census is mandated by the Constitution and provides vital data for the nation. The Bureau plans to significantly change the methods and technology it uses to count the population with the 2020 Census, such as by offering an option for households to respond to the survey via the Internet. In preparation for the 2020 Census, the Bureau is conducting a test of all key systems and operations (referred to as the 2018 End-to-End Test), which began in August 2017 and runs through April 2019. GAO was asked to review the Bureau's IT readiness for the 2020 Census. This chapter (1) determines the Bureau's progress in developing and testing systems for the 2018 End-to-End Test and (2) describes the challenges and risks that the Bureau has faced in implementing and securing these systems. To do this, GAO reviewed key documentation, including plans for system development and testing, and outcomes of key IT milestone reviews and security assessments.

In: A Closer Look at the 2020 Census
Editor: Sille M. Schou

ISBN: 978-1-53616-508-1
© 2019 Nova Science Publishers, Inc.

Chapter 1

THE DECENNIAL CENSUS: ISSUES FOR 2020[*]

Jennifer D. Williams

SUMMARY

The U.S. Constitution—Article I, Section 2, clause 3, as modified by Section 2 of the 14th Amendment—requires a population census every 10 years for apportioning seats in the House of Representatives. Decennial census data are used, too, for within-state redistricting and in certain formulas for distributing more than $450 billion annually in federal funds to states and localities. Census counts also are the foundation for estimates of current population size between censuses and projections of future size. Businesses, nonprofit organizations, researchers, and all levels of government are steady consumers of decennial and other census data.

The Constitution stipulates that every enumeration is to be conducted "in such Manner as they [Congress] shall by Law direct." Congress, through Title 13 of the *United States Code*, has delegated this responsibility to the Secretary of Commerce and, under the Secretary's

---

[*] This is an edited, reformatted and augmented version of a Congressional Research Service publication R44788, prepared for Members and Committees of Congress dated March 16, 2017.

purview, the Bureau of the Census (Census Bureau). Title 13 U.S.C., Section 221, requires compliance with the census and provides for a fine of up to $100 for nonresponse. In accordance with provisions of the Sentencing Reform Act of 1984, Title 18 U.S.C., Sections 3559 and 3571, the possible fine has been adjusted to not more than $5,000.

The 2020 census questionnaire, like that in 2010, will collect only the most basic population and housing information. Detailed socioeconomic data that formerly were gathered from a population sample in conjunction with the decennial census now are collected by the American Community Survey, which the bureau conducts separately from the census and at more frequent intervals.

April 1, 2020, the official date of the 24th decennial census, will mark the culmination of extensive census planning, testing, and other preparations. A key objective, as Congress has directed, is to make the census more cost-effective without jeopardizing coverage and accuracy. The total life-cycle cost of the 2010 census was about $13 billion, reportedly an all-time high. To hold the 2020 cost to approximately $12.3 billion, the Census Bureau is focusing on four innovations:

- using governmental administrative records and satellite imagery to eliminate some of the fieldwork involved in updating census addresses and maps, which are the basis for an accurate enumeration;
- maximizing early census responses, especially online, to reduce the number of nonrespondents left for the bureau to contact by telephone or personal visits after the initial census phase;
- further limiting nonresponse follow-up by using administrative records to help fill gaps in census information; and
- better using technology to streamline fieldwork.

At the same time, the bureau has a mandate to obtain the best possible accounting of all U.S. residents, regardless of their race, ethnicity, or living circumstances. The tension between funding the census sufficiently to produce good results and controlling census costs is apparent.

Concerns as the 2020 census approaches include whether the bureau's enacted appropriations have been and will be sufficient to permit complete testing and implementation of the census plan; whether technology, notably the new Census Enterprise Data Collection and Processing system, will be ready on schedule and will perform well; and whether information security will be adequate to deter cybercrimes against data, respondents, and bureau employees.

This chapter will be updated as developments warrant.

INTRODUCTION

The U.S. Constitution—Article I, Section 2, clause 3, as modified by Section 2 of the 14th Amendment—requires a population census every 10 years to serve as the basis for apportioning seats in the House of Representatives. Decennial census data are used, too, for within-state redistricting and in certain formulas that determine the annual distribution of more than $450 billion in federal funds to states and localities.[1] Census counts are, in addition, the foundation for constructing intercensal estimates of current population size and projections of future size.[2] Businesses, nonprofit organizations, researchers, and all levels of government are steady consumers of decennial and other census data.

The Constitution stipulates that the once-a-decade enumeration is to be conducted "in such Manner as they [Congress] shall by Law direct." Congress, through Title 13 of the *United States Code*, has delegated this responsibility to the Secretary of Commerce and, within the Department of Commerce, the Bureau of the Census (Census Bureau). As specified in

---

[1] Testimony of then-Census Bureau Director Robert M. Groves in U.S. Congress, House Committee on Oversight and Government Reform, Subcommittee on Health Care, District of Columbia, Census, and the National Archives, *The Pros and Cons of Making the Census Bureau's American Community Survey Voluntary*, hearing, 112th Cong., 2nd sess., March 6, 2012, at http://oversight.house.gov/wp-content/uploads/2012/03/3-6-12-Census-Groves.pdf.

[2] U.S. Census Bureau, "Population and Housing Unit Estimates, Methodology," at http://www.census.gov/programs- surveys/popest.html; and U.S. Census Bureau, "Population Projections," at http://www.census.gov/topics/population/ population-projections/about.html.

Title 15 U.S.C., Section 1501, and Title 13 U.S.C., Section 21, both the Commerce Secretary and the director of the Census Bureau are appointed by the President, by and with the advice and consent of the Senate.

The bureau's task in conducting the enumeration can be summarized in very basic terms: count each person whose usual residence is in the United States (the aim of complete census coverage); and count that person only once, at the right location, where the person lives all or most of the time (the goal of census accuracy).[3] Title 13 U.S.C., Section 221, requires compliance with the census and provides for a fine of up to $100 for nonresponse. In accordance with provisions of the Sentencing Reform Act of 1984, Title 18 U.S.C., Sections 3559 and 3571, the possible fine has been adjusted to not more than $5,000.

The resources committed to each decennial census, measured not only in large sums of public money but in years of planning, testing, and related efforts as well, serve one chief purpose: to obtain the best possible accounting of all U.S. residents, regardless of their race, ethnicity, socioeconomic characteristics, or living circumstances. To the extent that the census falls short of this goal, the allocation of House seats, other political representation, and federal dollars may be less than equitable, particularly for those whom the census is most likely to miss, and census data with myriad uses may be flawed. The tension between funding the census sufficiently to produce good results and controlling census costs is apparent. Much of this chapter will discuss past and recent calls for cost containment, the bureau's response for the 24th decennial census in 2020, and factors like technology and funding that could affect the census. The report also will compare estimates of coverage in the previous two censuses and note some sociodemographic factors that could complicate the count in 2020.

Table 1 shows the dates for selected major 2020 census activities and several legal deadlines the Census Bureau must meet for finalizing the census questionnaire, conducting the census, and delivering apportionment

---

[3] See, for example, the testimony of then-Census Bureau Director Steve Murdock, in U.S. Congress, House Committee on Appropriations, Subcommittee on Commerce, Justice, Science, and Related Agencies, *The Fiscal Year 2009 Budget*, hearing, 110th Cong., 2nd sess., April 3, 2008 (Washington, DC: 2008), p. 4.

and redistricting data. The 2020 questionnaire is not yet available, but, as mentioned below in the discussion of the 2015 national content test, the questionnaire will ask for only the most basic demographic, household, and housing data. The same was true in 2010. Long-form data—detailed data that formerly were collected from a population sample in conjunction with the decennial census—now are gathered by the American Community Survey (ACS). The bureau conducts the ACS separately from the census and at more frequent intervals.[4]

Table 1. Timeline for the 2020 Census

Date	Activity or Legal Deadline
September 2015-July 2019	In-office address canvassing period
April 1, 2017	Deadline for providing the 2020 census topics to Congress (13 U.S.C. §141(f)(1))
December 2017	Regional census centers scheduled to open
April 1, 2018	Deadline for providing the 2020 census questions to Congress (13 U.S.C. §141(f)(2))
January 2019	Census field offices scheduled to open
August 2019-December 2019	In-field address canvassing period
April 1, 2020	Official 2020 Census Day (13 U.S.C. §141(a))
April-August 2020	Nonresponse follow-up period
December 31, 2020	Deadline for transmitting to the President the official state population counts for House apportionment (13 U.S.C. §141(b))
March 31, 2021	Deadline for delivering redistricting data to the states (13 U.S.C. §141(c))
April 2023	End date for releasing remaining 2020 census data products

Source: U.S. Census Bureau, *2020 Census Operational Plan*, version 2.0, September 2016, pp. 50-51, at http://www2.census.gov/programs-surveys/decennial/2020/ program-management/planning-docs/2020-oper- plan2.pdf.

THE GOALS OF CENSUS COST CONTROL AND COMPLETE, ACCURATE COVERAGE

The following discussion focuses on repeated calls for cost containment in the decennial count and the sociodemographic factors

---

[4] See CRS Report R41532, *The American Community Survey: Development, Implementation, and Issues for Congress*, by Jennifer D. Williams.

tending to drive up census costs as well as impede a complete, accurate enumeration.

The Need to Contain Census Costs

The Government Accountability Office (GAO) stated in a 2016 report that, at a total life-cycle cost of about $13 billion, the 2010 census was the most expensive in U.S. history. The expense exceeded by more than 50% the 2000 census total of $8.1 billion, in 2010 dollars.[5] Indeed, as GAO pointed out, the average amount spent to count each housing unit in the United States increased "from $16 in 1970 to $94 in 2010," in 2010 dollars.[6] Earlier GAO reports and testimony, such as in 1986,[7] 1990,[8] 1992,[9] 2001,[10] 2002,[11] 2008,[12] 2011,[13] 2012,[14] 2013,[15] and 2015,[16] also noted

---

[5] U.S. Government Accountability Office, *2020 Census: Census Bureau Needs to Improve Its Life-Cycle Cost Estimating Process*, GAO-16-628, June 2016, p. 1.

[6] Ibid.

[7] Testimony of Gene L. Dodaro, U.S. General Accounting Office, in U.S. Congress, House Committee on Post Office and Civil Service, Subcommittee on Census and Population, *The Census Bureau's Preparations for the 1990 Decennial Census*, hearing, 99th Cong., 2nd sess., May 14, 1986 (Washington, DC: GPO, 1986), pp. 1-5.

[8] U.S. General Accounting Office, *Decennial Census: Preliminary 1990 Lessons Learned Indicate Need to Rethink Census Approach*, GAO/T-GGD-90-18, August 8, 1990, p. 4.

[9] U.S. General Accounting Office, *Decennial Census: 1990 Results Show Need for Fundamental Reform*, GAO/GGD-92-94, June 1992, pp. 2-4, 23-26.

[10] U.S. General Accounting Office, *2000 Census: Significant Increase in Cost Per Housing Unit Compared to 1990 Census*, GAO-02-31, December 2001, pp. 5-7.

[11] U.S. General Accounting Office, *2000 Census: Lessons Learned for Planning a More Cost-Effective 2010 Census*, GAO-03-40, October 2002, pp. 6, 14-17, 22.

[12] U.S. Government Accountability Office, *2010 Census: Census Bureau Should Take Action to Improve the Credibility and Accuracy of Its Cost Estimate for the Decennial Census*, GAO-08-554, June 2008, pp. 1-8.

[13] Testimony of Robert Goldenkoff, U.S. Government Accountability Office, in U.S. Congress, Senate Committee on Homeland Security and Governmental Affairs, Subcommittee on Federal Financial Management, Government Information, Federal Services, and International Security, *2010 Census: Preliminary Lessons Learned Highlight the Need for Fundamental Reforms*, hearing, 112th Cong., 1st sess., April 6, 2011, pp. 1, 5-7, at http://www.hsgac.senate.gov/subcommittees/federal-financial-management/hearings/census-learning-lessons-from-2010-planning-for-2020.

[14] U.S. Government Accountability Office, *Decennial Census: Additional Actions Could Improve the Census Bureau's Ability to Control Costs for the 2020 Census*, GAO-12-80, January 2012, pp. 1, 22-24.

[15] U.S. Government Accountability Office, *2020 Census: Progress Report on the Census Bureau's Efforts to Contain Enumeration Costs*, GAO-13-857T, September 11, 2013, pp. 1-2.

the steadily rising price of the census after the mid-20th century and usually called for cost containment.

Congress, likewise, repeatedly has directed the Census Bureau to control its spending for the census, as in the instances cited below.

- A conference report on legislation to fund the Departments of Commerce, Justice, and State, the Judiciary, and related agencies (CJS) in FY1993 stated that "the 2000 Census Research and Development Office should direct its resources toward a cost-effective census design that will produce more accurate results than those from the 1990 census." This design should "focus on realistic alternative means of collecting data, such as the use of existing surveys, rolling sample surveys or other vehicles," and "cost considerations should be a substantial factor in evaluating" these alternatives.[17]

- In reporting legislation to fund the CJS entities for FY1995, the Senate Committee on Appropriations "strongly" recommended that the bureau use "more cost-effective means of conducting the next census." The committee observed that "Clearly, the budgetary caps and strict employment ceilings adopted by the President and Congress will not accommodate a repeat of the process used in 1990."[18]

---

[16] U.S. Government Accountability Office, *2020 Census: Recommended Actions Need to Be Implemented before Potential Cost Savings Can Be Realized*, GAO-15-546T, April 20, 2015, p. 1.

[17] U.S. Congress, Conference Committee, Making Appropriations for the Departments of Commerce, Justice, and State, the Judiciary, and Related Agencies for the Fiscal Year Ending September 30, 1993, and for Other Purposes, conference report to accompany H.R. 5678, 102nd Cong., 2nd sess., H.Rept. 102-918 (Washington, DC: GPO, 1992). See also conference report, Congressional Record, vol. 138, part 19 (September 28, 1992), p. 28313.

The American Community Survey, which the Census Bureau developed in the 1990s, is the sort of rolling sample survey the conferees advised the bureau to use. See CRS Report R41532, *The American Community Survey: Development, Implementation, and Issues for Congress*, by Jennifer D. Williams.

[18] U.S. Congress, Senate Committee on Appropriations, Departments of Commerce, Justice, and State, the Judiciary, and Related Agencies Appropriations Bill, 1995, and Supplemental Appropriations Bill, 1994, report to accompany H.R. 4603, 103rd Cong., 2nd sess., S.Rept. 103-309 (Washington, DC: GPO, 1994), p. 82.

- A conference report on FY1996 CJS appropriations legislation expressed "the conferees' continuing concerns with the inability of the Census Bureau to recognize budgetary realities." The report further noted that the House and Senate Appropriations Committees had "for several years cautioned the Bureau that the cost of the Year 2000 Census had to be kept in check, and that only through early planning and decision making could costs be controlled."[19]
- The Senate Appropriations Committee's report on FY2012 CJS appropriations legislation directed the bureau to examine "seriously" the lessons learned from the 2010 census "to create more cost-effective operations."[20] The committee then directed the bureau "to consider budgeting for the 2020 decennial census at a level less than the 2010 Census and to further consider spending less than the 2000 Census, not adjusting for inflation."[21] The committee's reports on the FY2013,[22] FY2014,[23] FY2015,[24] FY2016,[25] and FY2017[26] CJS appropriations bills reiterated the substance of this directive.

---

[19] U.S. Congress, Conference Committee, Making Appropriations for the Departments of Commerce, Justice, and State, the Judiciary, and Related Agencies for the Fiscal Year Ending September 30, 1996, and for Other Purposes, conference report to accompany H.R. 2076, 104th Cong., 1st sess., H.Rept. 104-378 (Washington, DC: GPO, 1996), p. 108.

[20] U.S. Congress, Senate Committee on Appropriations, *Departments of Commerce and Justice, and Science, and Related Agencies Appropriations Bill, 2012*, report to accompany S. 1572, 112th Cong., 1st sess., S.Rept. 112-78, September 15, 2011, p. 16, at http://www.gpo.gov/fdsys/pkg/CRPT-112srpt78/pdf/CRPT-112srpt78.pdf.

[21] Ibid., p. 17.

[22] U.S. Congress, Senate Committee on Appropriations, *Departments of Commerce and Justice, and Science, and Related Agencies Appropriations Bill, 2013*, report to accompany S. 2323, 112th Cong., 2nd sess., S.Rept. 112-158, April 19, 2012, p. 16, at https://www.gpo.gov/fdsys/pkg/CRPT-112srpt158/pdf/CRPT-112srpt158.pdf.

[23] U.S. Congress, Senate Committee on Appropriations, *Departments of Commerce and Justice, and Science, and Related Agencies Appropriations Bill, 2014*, report to accompany S. 1329, 113th Cong., 1st sess., S.Rept. 113-78, July 18, 2013, p. 17, at https://www.gpo.gov/fdsys/pkg/CRPT-113srpt78/pdf/CRPT-113srpt78.pdf.

[24] U.S. Congress, Senate Committee on Appropriations, *Departments of Commerce and Justice, and Science, and Related Agencies Appropriations Bill, 2015*, report to accompany S. 2437, 113th Cong., 2nd sess., S.Rept. 113-181, June 5, 2014, p. 20, at https://www.gpo.gov/fdsys/pkg/CRPT-113srpt181/pdf/CRPT-113srpt181.pdf.

[25] U.S. Congress, Senate Committee on Appropriations, *Departments of Commerce and Justice, and Science, and Related Agencies Appropriations Bill, 2016*, report to accompany H.R.

- In reporting FY2013 CJS funding legislation, the House Appropriations Committee cited a need for the bureau to establish 2020 census procedures that would "increase response rates while containing costs," and expressed its expectation that the total life-cycle cost of this census would not exceed the approximately $13 billion spent on the 2010 census.[27]

The Census Bureau, in turn, has acknowledged that it is seeking to control the cost of the next enumeration while preserving census quality. In 2012 congressional testimony, then-bureau director Robert M. Groves stated that "the rising cost of the decennial census" is unsustainable. Census expenditures per housing unit were 38% greater in 2010 than in 2000 and 76% more in 2000 than in 1990. Without design changes to the 2020 census, its cost is projected to increase "at a similar rate," which he called "untenable."[28]

Early in 2015, current bureau director John H. Thompson testified that "as we began this decade, the Census Bureau, with the guidance of Congress, established an important goal to design and conduct the 2020 Census in a manner that costs less per housing unit than the 2010 Census and to maintain quality."[29]

2578, 114th Cong., 1st sess., S.Rept. 114-66, June 16, 2015, p. 17, at https://www.gpo.gov/fdsys/pkg/CRPT-114srpt66/pdf/CRPT-114srpt66.pdf.

[26] U.S. Congress, Senate Committee on Appropriations, *Departments of Commerce and Justice, Science, and Related Agencies Appropriations Bill, 2017*, report to accompany S. 2837, 114th Cong., 2nd sess., S.Rept. 114-239, April 21, 2016, pp. 14-15, at https://www.gpo.gov/fdsys/pkg/CRPT-114srpt239/pdf/CRPT-114srpt239.pdf.

[27] U.S. Congress, House Committee on Appropriations, *Commerce, Justice, Science, and Related Agencies Appropriations Bill, 2013*, report to accompany H.R. 5326, 112th Cong., 2nd sess., H.Rept. 112-463, May 2, 2012, p. 14, at https://www.gpo.gov/fdsys/pkg/CRPT-112hrpt463/pdf/CRPT-112hrpt463.pdf.

[28] Testimony of then-Census Bureau Director Robert M. Groves, in U.S. Congress, Senate Committee on Homeland Security and Governmental Affairs, Subcommittee on Federal Financial Management, Government Information, Federal Services, and International Security, *Census: Planning Ahead for 2020*, hearing, 112th Cong., 2nd sess., July 18, 2012, p. 6, at http://www.hsgac.senate.gov/subcommittees/federal-financial-management/hearings/census-planning-ahead-for-2020.

[29] Testimony of Census Bureau Director John H. Thompson, in U.S. Congress, Senate Committee on Homeland Security and Governmental Affairs, *2020 Census: Challenges Facing the Bureau for a Modern, Cost-Effective Survey*, hearing, 114th Cong., 1st sess., April

Testifying later the same year, he referred to the past several decades of census history to explain the decennial design and cost problem the bureau now faces.

> The 1970 Census was a breakthrough for its time. We built an address list and mailed questionnaires to each housing unit on the list. We asked respondents to complete and return the questionnaires through the mail. We developed automated processes to capture the information on the returns. However, the task of collecting information from those households that did not self-respond required recruiting and managing an army of enumerators using paper and pencil. For each census since 1970, this paper-based process has been the standard, and it has been increasingly challenged by the growing diversity and complexity of our nation. We do not believe that a paper and pencil approach to the Census is sustainable for the 2020 or future censuses.[30]

The Goal of Complete, Accurate Census Coverage

Attempting to Reach the Goal in the Past Two Censuses[31]

The Census Bureau's goal of complete, accurate population coverage in the 2020 census is elusive, as it was in 2010 and 2000, not only because the U.S. population is large, tends to be mobile, and is distributed over a wide geographic area, but also because the nation is increasingly heterogeneous, or, in words of the bureau director quoted above, has more "diversity and complexity"[32] than in 1970. Many households consist of

---

20, 2015, p. 1, at http://www.hsgac.senate.gov/hearings/2020-census-challenges- facing-the-bureau-for-a-modern-cost-effective-survey.

[30] Testimony of Census Bureau Director John H. Thompson, in U.S. Congress, House Committee on Oversight and Government Reform, Subcommittee on Government Operations and Subcommittee on Information Technology, *Preparing for the 2020 Census: Will the Technology Be Ready?*" hearing, 114th Cong., 1st sess., November 3, 2015, p. 1, at https://oversight.house.gov/hearing/preparing-for-the-2020-census-will-the-technology-be-ready/.

[31] The information under this heading is from CRS Report R40551, *The 2010 Decennial Census: Background and Issues*, by Jennifer D. Williams, which cited the U.S. Census Bureau, "Census Bureau Releases Estimates of Undercount and Overcount in the 2010 Census," press release CB12-95, May 22, 2012.

[32] Testimony of Census Bureau Director John H. Thompson, in U.S. Congress, House Committee on Oversight and Government Reform, Subcommittee on Government Operations and Subcommittee on Information Technology, *Preparing for the 2020 Census: Will the Technology Be Ready?*" hearing, 114th Cong., 1st sess., November 3, 2015, p. 1, at

racial and ethnic minorities; multiple families; low-income people; inner-city residents; those whose living circumstances are atypical; international migrants to the United States who may lack English language proficiency, lack legal status in this country, or distrust governmental activities; or various combinations of these attributes. Any of them can make enumeration difficult, and some of them contribute markedly to recurrent undercounts of racial and ethnic minorities. Overcounts of some population groups, on the other hand, can occur to the extent that the Bureau receives multiple census forms from the same people or households, then does not capture and eliminate the duplications. A husband and wife, for example, might own a vacation home and fill out a questionnaire at that address as well as at their usual residence. Another example would be parents who erroneously list a child on the form for their household when the child actually is away at college and has been correctly enumerated there.[33]

The bureau's 2010 Census Coverage Measurement (CCM) program showed the 2010 census to have been roughly, but not entirely, comparable to the 2000 census in net percentage undercount and overcount estimates.[34] Both censuses continued the historic tendency toward unintentionally overcounting the majority non-Hispanic white population and undercounting racial minorities and Hispanics. The estimates indicated a net percentage overcount of

- 0.01% for the total population (compared with the net overcount estimate of 0.49% in the 2000 census);
- 0.84% for non-Hispanic whites (compared with their 1.13% estimated net overcount in 2000); and
- 1.95% for American Indians off reservations (versus their 0.62% estimated net undercount in 2000).

---

https://oversight.house.gov/hearing/preparing-for-the-2020-census-will-the-technology-be-ready/.

[33] See U.S. Census Bureau, "The 2020 Census Residence Criteria," at https://www.census.gov/programs-surveys/decennial-census/2020-census/about/residence-rule.html.

[34] Estimated net percentage undercount or overcount pertains to "the difference between the true, but unknown, population count and an original census count." Kirk M. Wolter, "Accounting for America's Uncounted and Miscounted," *Science*, vol. 253 (July 1991), p. 12.

Every other racial category was undercounted to some extent in 2010, the CCM estimates suggested:

- non-Hispanic blacks by 2.07% (compared with their 1.84% estimated net undercount in 2000);
- non-Hispanic Asians by 0.08% (versus their 0.75% estimated net overcount in 2000);
- native Hawaiians or other Pacific Islanders by 1.34% (compared with their 2.12% estimated net undercount in 2000); and
- American Indians on reservations by 4.88% (versus their 0.88% estimated net overcount in 2000).

The CCM estimates indicated a net percentage undercount of 1.54% for Hispanics in 2010; their estimated net undercount in 2000 was 0.71%.

Among all racial groups and people of Hispanic ethnicity, only American Indians on reservations showed a statistically significant difference in estimated census coverage from 2000 to 2010.

GAO testified to Congress in July 2012 that "the 2010 Census generally accurately counted the total population of the country as well as each state."[35]

The Sociodemographic Challenge for 2020

Sociodemographic profiles of the population in 1970 and 2015 indicate how great a challenge the Census Bureau may face in 2020 when trying to obtain a high-quality, yet cost-controlled, count of all U.S. residents. In 1970, the United States had 203,302,031 residents[36] and 63,449,747 households,[37] compared with an estimated 321,418,820 residents[38] and

---

[35] U.S. Government Accountability Office, *2020 Census: Sustaining Current Reform Efforts Will Be Key to a More Cost-Effective Enumeration*, GAO-12-905T, July 18, 2012, p. 2.
[36] U.S. Census Bureau, *Statistical Abstract of the United States: 2012* (Washington, DC: GPO, 2011), p. 8.
[37] U.S. Census Bureau, *1970 Census of Population*, vol. 1, *Characteristics of the Population*, part 1, *United States Summary* (Washington, DC: GPO, 1973), p. 1-261.
[38] U.S. Census Bureau, "Annual Estimates for the Resident Population of the United States, Regions, States, and Puerto Rico: April 1, 2010 to July 1, 2015," at http:// www.census.gov/ data/tables/2015/demo/popest/nation-total.html.

134,789,180 households[39] in 2015. So not only did the population grow by 58.1%, but the number of households the bureau will have to locate, contact, and count also more than doubled. In addition, several overlapping categories of people who were generally easier to find and enumerate in 1970 constituted smaller proportions of the population in 2015 than in 1970. They include whites (87.5% of the population in 1970[40] and 77.1% in 2015),[41] the native-born (95.3% in 1970[42] versus 86.5% in 2015),[43] and married-couple families (69.2% of all households in 1970[44] versus 48.0% in 2015).[45] Moreover, poll data presented by the Pew Research Center show a pronounced shift in attitudes toward the federal government since 1970, when 54.0% of respondents said that they trusted it "just about always" or "most of the time." By 2015, only 19.0% of those polled gave this response.[46] The erosion of public trust in the lead-up to 2020 is of concern because the Census Bureau is a federal agency; it conducts the decennial census under constitutional authority and federal law. Even though compliance with the census is mandatory, it is arguably more likely when trust in government is higher than when it is lower.

---

[39] U.S. Census Bureau, "Annual Estimates of Housing Units for the United States and States: April 1, 2010 to July 1, 2015," at http://www.census.gov/data/tables/2015/demo/popest/total-housing-units.html.

[40] U.S. Census Bureau, *1970 Census of Population*, vol. 1, *Characteristics of the Population*, part 1, *United States Summary* (Washington, DC: GPO, 1973), p. 1-262.

[41] U.S. Census Bureau, "Annual Estimates of the Resident Population by Sex, Race, and Hispanic Origin: April 1, 2010 to July 1, 2015," at http://www.census.gov/data/tables/2015/demo/popest/nation-detail.html.

[42] U.S. Census Bureau, *1970 Census of Population*, vol. 1, *Characteristics of the Population*, part 1, *United States Summary* (Washington, DC: GPO, 1973), p. 1-361.

[43] U.S. Census Bureau, "Selected Social Characteristics in the United States, 2015 American Community Survey 1- Year Estimates," at http://factfinder.census.gov/faces/tableservices/jsf/pages/productview.xhtml?pid= ACS_13_1YR_DP02&prodType=table.

[44] U.S. Census Bureau, *1970 Census of Population*, vol. 1, *Characteristics of the Population*, part 1, *United States Summary* (Washington, DC: GPO, 1973), pp. 1-380, 1-957.

[45] U.S. Census Bureau, "Selected Social Characteristics in the United States, 2015 American Community Survey 1- Year Estimates," at http://factfinder.census.gov/faces/tableservices/jsf/pages/productview.xhtml?pid= ACS_13_1YR_DP02&prodType=table.

[46] Pew Research Center, "Public Trust in Government: 1958-2015," at http://www.people-press.org/2015/11/23/public-trust-in-government-1958-2015/.

INNOVATIONS FOR 2020 CENSUS COST CONTROL

As the Census Bureau prepares for the next enumeration, it is focusing on cost-control innovations in the four key areas discussed below. The bureau estimates that these innovations, if successful, could "save approximately $5.2 billion compared to repeating the 2010 design in the 2020 Census."[47] The estimated cost to repeat the 2010 design is $17.5 billion, compared with $12.3 billion for a reengineered census.[48]

More Efficiently Updating Census Addresses and Maps

Before the bureau can conduct the 2020 census, it must verify and update census addresses and maps—technically called the "Master Address File" (MAF) and the "Topologically Integrated Geographic Encoding and Referencing" (TIGER) system—through an address canvassing operation. The bureau director has stated that the "foundation of an accurate census is an accurate address frame, which includes both the address and geospatial location" of every housing unit in the United States.[49] Indeed, as the bureau noted before the 2010 census, MAF/TIGER "creates the universe for all other [bureau] operations that collect information from the public."[50] According to the operational plan for the 2020 census, address canvassing in the past several decades involved having census employees "walk and

---

[47] U.S. Census Bureau, *U.S. Census Bureau's Budget, Fiscal Year 2017*, p. CEN-3, at http://osec.doc.gov/bmi/budget/ FY17CBJ/ Census%20FY%202017%20CBJ% 20final%20not508.pdf.
[48] Ibid., p. CEN-110.
GAO has cautioned that the bureau's cost estimate is not reliable and does not "adequately account for risks that could affect the 2020 Census costs." U.S. Government Accountability Office, *Information Technology: Uncertainty Remains about the Bureau's Readiness for a Key Decennial Census Test*, GAO-17-221T, November 16, 2016, p. 3.
[49] Testimony of Census Bureau Director John H. Thompson, in U.S. Congress, Senate Committee on Homeland Security and Governmental Affairs, *2020 Census: Challenges Facing the Bureau for a Modern, Cost-Effective Survey*, hearing, 114th Cong., 1st sess., April 20, 2015, p. 2, at http://www.hsgac.senate.gov/hearings/2020-census-challenges- facing-the-bureau-for-a-modern-cost-effective-survey.
[50] U.S. Census Bureau, *United States Census 2010, High Risk Improvement Plan*, version 7-2, November 4, 2008, p. 2.

physically check 11 million census blocks,"[51] or roughly every block in the United States.[52] For 2020, the bureau intends to replace some of this activity with in-office canvassing that will, if successful, continually update

> the address list based on data from multiple sources, including the U.S. Postal Service, tribal, state, and local governments, satellite imagery, and third-party data providers. This office work will also determine which parts of the country require fieldwork to verify address information. While fieldwork began in 2016 on a small scale for address coverage measurement, the bulk of the In-Field Address Canvassing will begin in 2019 and is anticipated to cover approximately 25 percent of all addresses, a significant reduction from the 100 percent that were reviewed in the field during the 2010 Census.[53]

Maximizing Responses in the Initial Phase of the Census

As mentioned above, the 1970 through 2010 censuses were primarily mail-out, mail-back operations. Most U.S. households received their census forms by mail, with instructions to respond the same way. After this initial phase of the census, the bureau attempted to contact, by telephone or personal visits, households from which it had not received completed forms and persuade them to respond. The nonresponse follow-up (NRFU) phase was the most expensive, labor-intensive part of the census.[54]

---

[51] U.S. Census Bureau, *2020 Census Operational Plan*, version 2.0, September 2016, p. 15, at http://www2.census.gov/programs-surveys/decennial/2020/program-management/planning-docs/2020-oper-plan2.pdf.

[52] The bureau has "established blocks covering the entire nation." A "block is the smallest geographic unit for which the Census Bureau tabulates decennial census data." Blocks often "correspond to individual city blocks bounded by streets," but, especially in rural areas, blocks "may include many square miles and may have some boundaries that are not streets." U.S. Census Bureau, *Glossary*, "Block," at http://www.census.gov/glossary/#term_Block.

[53] U.S. Census Bureau, *2020 Census Operational Plan*, version 2.0, September 2016, p. 8, at http://www2.census.gov/programs-surveys/decennial/2020/program-management/planning-docs/2020-oper-plan2.pdf.

[54] From May through July 2010, for example, about 565,000 enumerators contacted approximately 47 million households that either had not received their 2010 census forms or had not completed and returned them. U.S. Census Bureau, "$1.6 Billion in 2010 Census Savings Returned," press release CB10-CN.70, August 10, 2010, p. 1; and U.S. Census

For 2020, the bureau proposes reducing its reliance on nonresponse follow-up in several ways, the first of which will be maximizing the public's cooperation with the initial census phase. The bureau will conduct an outreach campaign to promote the census and will offer multiple response options to facilitate answering it.

Public Outreach

The bureau's communications strategy for 2020 will be, as it was for the 2010 and 2000 enumerations,[55] to publicize and gain support for the census before it begins and while it is in progress. The strategy will involve advertising on television and radio, in print, and on social media (blogs, Facebook, Twitter, etc.), and partnering with outside organizations, especially those trusted by population groups who have tended to be harder to count in past censuses.[56] Partnership activities will include providing census-promotional information to "government agencies and hosting events at community, recreation, and faith-based organizations."[57]

Multiple Response Options, Featuring Online Responses

In a marked change from the past, the 2020 census will replace as much of the standard mail operation as possible with an Internet response option. The bureau believes that this option will save money, modernize census-taking, and better engage the public by making cooperation more convenient. Forms will be accessible online in multiple languages.[58] Help for online respondents is to be available by telephone, also in multiple languages, from the bureau's questionnaire assistance centers and via web

---

Bureau, "Nation Achieves 74 Percent Final Mail Participation in 2010 Census," press release CB10-CN.81, October 21, 2010, p. 1. GAO estimated the cost of 2010 census field data collection and related support systems at almost $9.1 billion, in 2010 dollars. U.S. Government Accountability Office, *Decennial Census: Additional Actions Could Improve the Census Bureau's Ability to Control Costs for the 2020 Census*, GAO-12-80, January 2012, p. 8.

[55] See CRS Report R40551, *The 2010 Decennial Census: Background and Issues*, by Jennifer D. Williams.

[56] U.S. Census Bureau, *2020 Census Operational Plan*, version 2.0, September 2016, p. 93, at http://www2.census.gov/programs-surveys/decennial/2020/program-management/planning-docs/2020-oper-plan2.pdf.

[57] Ibid., p. 18.

[58] Ibid., p. 19.

chat. The bureau estimates that 47% of households "in mailout areas" will respond by Internet.[59] Other options, for people unable or reluctant to provide their census information online, will include paper forms and responses entirely by telephone, through calls to the questionnaire assistance centers.[60]

Using Administrative Records to Limit Nonresponse Follow-Up

Addresses from which the bureau does not receive responses by web, mail, or telephone during the first phase of the 2020 census "will form the initial universe of addresses" for nonresponse follow-up.[61] Before it begins, the bureau will try to identify and remove the addresses of vacant housing units from this universe and thus reduce the NRFU workload. Governmental administrative records, chiefly "Undeliverable-as-Addressed" information from the U.S. Postal Service, will be the basis for identifying vacant units.[62]

The bureau's plan calls for making one attempt to contact nonresponding households, then further reducing the NRFU workload by using "administrative records and third-party data to enumerate occupied housing units where it makes sense and is feasible."[63] The "core administrative records" for this enumeration "will come from the Internal Revenue Service, the Centers for Medicare and Medicaid Services, the Indian Health Service and the Social Security Administration, as well as existing Census Bureau information and third-party data."[64] The bureau has

---

[59] Ibid., p. 95.
[60] Ibid.
[61] Testimony of Census Bureau Director John H. Thompson, in U.S. Congress, House Committee on Oversight and Government Reform, *Census 2020: Examining the Readiness of Key Aspects of the Census Bureau's 2020 Census Preparation*, hearing, 114th Cong., 2nd sess., June 9, 2016, p. 3, at https://oversight.house.gov/wp-content/uploads/2016/06/Thompson-Census-Statement-2020-Census-6-9.pdf.
[62] Ibid.
[63] U.S. Census Bureau, *2020 Census Operational Plan*, version 2.0, September 2016, p. 114, at http://www2.census.gov/programs-surveys/decennial/2020/program-management/planning-docs/2020-oper-plan2.pdf.
[64] Testimony of Census Bureau Director John H. Thompson, in U.S. Congress, House Committee on Oversight and Government Reform, *Census 2020: Examining the Readiness of Key*

acknowledged that it continues "to look for additional administrative data sets to use in the NRFU effort."[65]

Throughout the nonresponse follow-up period, as the bureau receives late census responses from some households, it will remove the addresses of these households from the NRFU workload.[66]

Using Technology to Streamline Fieldwork

The bureau plans to rely on technology for managing 2020 census fieldwork "efficiently and effectively."[67] As in past censuses, most of the fieldwork for 2020 will occur during nonresponse follow-up. The bureau intends for field staff to perform their duties "completely remotely," using handheld devices for "all administrative and data collection tasks." Supervisors, likewise, will use the devices to "work remotely" and communicate with staff.[68] According to the bureau, the new capabilities will greatly reduce the physical space and staff necessary to support fieldwork. For the 2010 census, the bureau opened 12 regional census centers and almost 500 area census offices and hired more than 516,000 NRFU enumerators. The design for 2020 envisions only six regional census centers and no more than 250 centers for administrative support. The bureau expects, too, that easier monitoring and management of staff will reduce the number of supervisors needed for fieldwork.[69]

Aspects of the Census Bureau's 2020 Census Preparation, hearing, 114th Cong., 2nd sess., June 9, 2016, p. 3, at https://oversight.house.gov/wp-content/uploads/2016/06/Thompson-Census-Statement-2020-Census-6-9.pdf.

[65] Ibid.
[66] U.S. Census Bureau, *2020 Census Operational Plan*, version 2.0, September 2016, p. 114, at http://www2.census.gov/programs-surveys/decennial/2020/program-management/planning-docs/2020-oper-plan2.pdf.
[67] Ibid., p. 26.
[68] Ibid.
[69] Ibid.

CENSUS ENTERPRISE DATA COLLECTION AND PROCESSING SYSTEM

The bureau's overarching Census Enterprise Data Collection and Processing (CEDCaP) initiative dates from 2014. CEDCaP, in the bureau's words, "will create an integrated and standardized system of systems that will offer shared data collection and processing across all censuses and surveys," including, prominently, the 2020 census. The initiative is intended to "consolidate costs by retiring unique, survey-specific systems and redundant capabilities" and bring a much larger share of the bureau's total information technology (IT) expenditures under one "centrally managed program." The bureau's plan is to "put in place a solution that will be mature and proven for the 2020 Census."[70]

GAO testified to Congress in 2016 that the 2020 census "relies heavily on CEDCaP to deliver key systems to support its redesign."[71]

TESTS AND RELATED ACTIVITIES TO SUPPORT THE 2020 PLAN

2013 Test

The 2013 census test explored using administrative records to remove the addresses of vacant housing units from the NRFU workload and reducing the number of attempts to contact nonrespondents, especially through personal visits. The test involved 2,077 housing units in Philadelphia. Data collection was completed in December 2013.[72]

---

[70] U.S. Census Bureau, *U.S. Census Bureau's Budget, Fiscal Year 2017*, p. CEN-7, at http://osec.doc.gov/bmi/budget/ FY17CBJ/ Census%20FY%202017%20CBJ%20final%20not508.pdf.

[71] U.S. Government Accountability Office, *Information Technology: Uncertainty Remains about the Bureau's Readiness for a Key Decennial Census Test*, GAO-17-221T, November 16, 2016, p. 8.

[72] U.S. Census Bureau, *United States Census 2020, 2020 Research and Testing: 2013 Census Test Assessment*, at https://www.census.gov/content/dam/Census/programs-surveys/decennial/2020-census/2013_Census_Test_Assessment_Final.pdf.

2014 Test

In 2014, the bureau tested strategies to encourage prompt census responses, especially via the Internet, and limit reliance on paper questionnaires. Also tested were mobile devices for use by NRFU field staff, various means of contacting nonrespondents, and different methods for managing assignments to field staff. In addition, the test involved identifying the addresses of housing units that could be removed from the NRFU workload because administrative records were determined to be adequate for enumeration. The test covered about 200,000 housing units in the District of Columbia and Montgomery County, Maryland. Data collection took place from late June through September 2014.[73]

2015 Tests

Address Validation Test

The address validation test took place from September 2014 through January 2015. One component of the test, a "full-block canvass" covering 10,100 nationally representative blocks, assessed how well different statistical models could predict which blocks had address changes that the Master Address File had not captured. Another part of the test involved having geographic specialists find previously unrecorded address changes and identify parts of blocks where changes were likely to have occurred. In this way, the bureau could conduct a "partial- block canvass" that could reduce the extent and cost of address canvassing.[74]

Census Tests

A census test officially dated April 1, 2015, used "digital, targeted advertising methods" to increase awareness of the test and encourage

---

[73] U.S. Census Bureau, "2014 Census Test," at https://www.census.gov/programs-surveys/decennial-census/2020- census/research-testing/testing-activities/2014-census-test.html.

[74] U.S. Census Bureau, "2015 Census Tests, Address Validation Test," at https://www.census.gov/programs-surveys/decennial-census/2020-census/research-testing/testing-activities/2015-census-tests/address-validation.html.

prompt responses, whether by web, on paper, or by telephone. Those who chose to respond online could do so without having bureau-assigned identification (ID) numbers.[75] The test included 407,000 housing units in the Savannah, Georgia, media market, with a sample of 120,000 nonresponding units. [76]

A 2015 census test of 165,000 housing units in Maricopa County, Arizona, also had an official date of April 1. The test examined the bureau's effort to streamline and control the cost of nonresponse follow-up.[77] The bureau considered whether training fieldworkers by computer was as effective as classroom instruction, looked at new technology for more efficiently assigning work to field staff, tested the collection of NRFU data by smartphone versus on paper, assessed whether enabling fieldworkers to collect data on their own electronic devices saved money and was effective, and examined how well administrative records could fill data gaps caused by missing census responses.[78]

National Content Test

The national content test, conducted from August through October 2015, covered a representative sample of about 1.2 million households, mostly in in the 50 states; 20,000 of the households were in Puerto Rico.

---

[75] U.S. Census Bureau, "2020 Census, February 2016 Monthly Status Report," p. 6, at http://www2.census.gov/programs-surveys/decennial/2020/program-management/monthly-status-reports/2016-02-msr.pdf.

[76] U.S. Census Bureau, *2020 Census Operational Plan*, version 2.0, September 2016, p. 41, at http://www2.census.gov/programs-surveys/decennial/2020/program-management/planning-docs/2020-oper-plan2.pdf; and U.S. Census Bureau, "2015 Census Tests, Frequently Asked Questions," at http://www.census.gov/programs-surveys/decennial-census/2020-census/research-testing/testing-activities/2015-census-ests/savannah/about.html.

The Savannah-area media market includes, besides Savannah and the rest of Chatham County, the neighboring Georgia counties of Appling, Bacon, Bryan, Bulloch, Candler, Effingham, Evans, Jeff Davis, Liberty, Long, McIntosh, Montgomery, Screven, Toombs, Tattnall, and Wayne; as well as, in South Carolina, Beaufort, Hampton, and Jasper Counties.

[77] U.S. Census Bureau, *2020 Census Operational Plan*, version 2.0, September 2016, p. 42, at http://www2.census.gov/programs-surveys/decennial/2020/program-management/planning-docs/2020-oper-plan2.pdf.

[78] U.S. Census Bureau, "2015 Census Tests, The Purpose of the 2015 Census Test in Maricopa," at http://www.census.gov/programs-surveys/decennial-census/2020-census/research-testing/testing-activities/2015- census-tests/maricopa.html.

The test considered alternative wording of the census questions,[79] examined various strategies for prompting respondents to answer the questions in the initial census phase, encouraged online responses, and provided estimates of response rates for Internet and other response options.

2016 Tests

2016 Census Test

The broad objective of this test was to refine methods for obtaining prompt census responses, especially online, and conducting nonresponse follow-up. The bureau continued its attempts to engage historically harder-to-count population groups. Outreach efforts included offering questionnaire assistance by telephone in English and several other languages: Arabic, Chinese (Cantonese and Mandarin), French, Korean, Spanish, Tagalog, and Vietnamese.[80] The bureau further assessed the possible use of administrative records and commercial information to

---

[79] Each test household was asked to report a telephone number and an email address for the household; the number of people living in the housing unit; whether the unit was rented or owned; and each household member's name, sex, age, race, Hispanic or non-Hispanic ethnicity, and relationship to the person completing the test form. U.S. Census Bureau, "What Specific Questions Are Asked on the 2015 National Content Test?" at https://www.census.gov/programs- surveys/decennial-census/2020-census/research-testing/testing-activities/2015-census-tests/national-content-test/ faqs.html.

Alternative wording of the questionnaire included combining the questions on race and Hispanic or non-Hispanic ethnicity versus keeping them separate, as has been past practice; and adding a new ethnic category, Middle East and North African (MENA), versus not doing so. The white racial category currently encompasses people with "origins in any of the original peoples of Europe, the Middle East, or North Africa." The checkbox for the new category shows, as examples, Lebanese, Iranian, Egyptian, Syrian, Moroccan, and Algerian. The change would align with the Office of Management and Budget's proposed addition of a MENA category to its standards for defining race and ethnicity. U.S. Office of Management and Budget, "Standards for Maintaining, Collecting, and Presenting Federal Data on Race and Ethnicity," 81 *Federal Register* 67398-67401, September 30, 2016, at https://www.gpo.gov/fdsys/pkg/FR-2016-09-30/ pdf/2016-23672.pdf; and U.S. Census Bureau, *2020 Census Operational Plan*, version 2.0, September 2016, p. 44, at http://www2.census.gov/programs-surveys/decennial/2020/program-management/planning-docs/2020-oper-plan2.pdf.

[80] U.S. Census Bureau, "Census Bureau Reaches Milestone on the Road to 2020 Census," press release CB16-61, April 1, 2016, at http://census.gov/newsroom/press-releases/2016/cb16-61.html.

reduce the NRFU workload, and reexamined the technology for assigning cases to NRFU field staff and collecting NRFU data. Also examined were the integration and performance of IT systems, IT security, and cloud computing technology, as well as how to process and validate responses submitted without bureau-assigned identification codes. The test took place from March through August 2016 in Harris County, Texas, and Los Angeles County, California. Each site included about 225,000 housing units. The sites were chosen as being representative of large metropolitan areas with demographic and language diversity, different levels of Internet usage, and high housing vacancy rates—characteristics that can present enumeration challenges.[81]

Address Canvassing Test

From August through December 2016, the bureau conducted an address canvassing test in Buncombe County, North Carolina, and St. Louis, Missouri. The goal of the test was to produce a complete, accurate address list and "spatial database," and determine the address characteristics of each housing unit in the test areas. The bureau examined the effectiveness of in-office canvassing, as compared with canvassing done in the field, and sought to refine the methods for both. In-office canvassing included the use of geographic information systems and aerial imagery to add addresses to MAF/TIGER. In-field canvassing analyzed the performance of an address listing and mapping application on a mobile device. Examined, too, were the effectiveness of online field supervisor and staff training and "reengineered methods for quality assurance."[82]

2017 Test

The 2017 census test is scheduled for April 1, 2017, to cover a nationwide sample of about 80,000 housing units. The emphasis again will

---

[81] Ibid.
[82] U.S. Census Bureau, "Address Canvassing Test," at http://census.gov/content/dam/Census/programs-surveys/decennial/2020-census/2016/address%20canvassing/address_canvassing_factsheet.pdf.

be on prompt responses, especially by web, with a Spanish-language response option. The test will involve integrating operational control systems with census questionnaire assistance and "non-ID" processing, and will continue to assess cloud computing.[83]

The bureau had planned, additionally, 2017 tests of field operations in Puerto Rico, the Standing Rock Indian Reservation in North and South Dakota, and the Colville Indian Reservation and off- reservation trust land in Washington. In October 2016, however, the bureau announced its decision to discontinue preparations for these tests due to uncertainty about FY2017 funding.[84] The bureau director noted at the time that proceeding "amid such uncertainty would all but guarantee wasted efforts and resources." Instead, the bureau "will consider" incorporating these operations into the 2018 test, discussed below.[85]

2018 Test

In July 2016, the bureau selected the sites where it will conduct its largest test in preparation for the 2020 census, the 2018 "end-to-end" test of 2020 "systems and operations."[86] The primary objective will be "to

---

[83] Testimony of Census Bureau Director John H. Thompson, in U.S. Congress, House Committee on Oversight and Government Reform, Subcommittee on Government Operations, *2020 Census: Outcomes of the 2016 Site Test*, hearing, 114th Cong., 2nd sess., November 16, 2016, p. 11, at https://oversight.house.gov/wp-content/uploads/2016/11/ Thompson-Statement-Census-Site-Test-11-16.pdf.

[84] The bureau was funded until December 9, 2016, at the FY2016 level, with a 0.496% reduction, under the Continuing Appropriations and Military Construction, Veterans Affairs, and Related Agencies Appropriations Act, 2017, and Zika Response and Preparedness Act, H.R. 5325, P.L. 114-223, Division C. The Further Continuing and Security Assistance Appropriations Act, 2017, H.R. 2028, P.L. 114-254, was enacted on December 10, 2016. Division A funds the bureau at the FY2016 level, minus a 0.1901% reduction, through April 28, 2017, but under Section 152, the bureau may draw on money from the Periodic Censuses and Programs account at the rate necessary to conduct operations to maintain the 2020 census schedule. See CRS Report R44567, *FY2017 Appropriations for the Census Bureau and Bureau of Economic Analysis*, by Jennifer D. Williams.

[85] U.S. Census Bureau, "U.S. Census Bureau Announces Changes to 2017 Field Tests," October 18, 2016, at http://directorsblog.blogs.census.gov/2016/10/18/u-s-census-bureau-announces-changes-to-2017-field-tests/.

[86] U.S. Census Bureau, "Census Bureau Selects Sites for 2018 End-to-End Census Test in Preparation for 2020 Census," at https://www.census.gov/newsroom/press-releases/2016/cb16-126.html.

confirm key technologies, data collection methods, outreach and promotional strategies, and management and response processes" that will support the 2020 census.[87] Although the test has an official date of April 1, 2018, it is to begin in August 2017 with address canvassing field operations.[88] It will cover more than 700,000 housing units in Pierce County, Washington; Providence County, Rhode Island; and nine West Virginia counties[89] that include the cities of Beckley, Bluefield, and Oak Hill. The bureau chose these locations for their diversity: a test population that varies by age, race, language spoken at home, and other sociodemographic characteristics, with different levels of access to and use of the Internet; housing that has conventional, rural, and other types of addresses; and housing variety that includes group quarters,[90] vacant units, multiple units, and mobile homes.

After reviewing the end-to-end test results, the bureau expects to incorporate "any lessons learned" and "finalize plans for all operations and make any necessary adjustments to ensure readiness for the 2020 Census."[91]

---

[87] Ibid.

[88] Testimony of Census Bureau Director John H. Thompson, in U.S. Congress, House Committee on Oversight and Government Reform, Subcommittee on Government Operations, *2020 Census: Outcomes of the 2016 Site Test*, hearing, 114th Cong., 2nd sess., November 16, 2016, p. 11, at https://oversight.house.gov/wp-content/uploads/2016/11/ Thompson-Statement-Census-Site-Test-11-16.pdf.

[89] The counties are Fayette, Greenbrier, McDowell, Mercer, Monroe, Pocahontas, Raleigh, Summers, and Wyoming. U.S. Census Bureau, "Census Bureau Selects Sites for 2018 End-to-End Census Test in Preparation for 2020 Census," at https://www.census.gov/newsroom/press-releases/2016/cb16-126.html.

[90] In Census Bureau terminology, "group quarters" are places "where people live or stay, in a group living arrangement." These quarters are "owned or managed by an entity or organization providing housing and/or services for the residents." Examples include "college residence halls, residential treatment centers, skilled nursing facilities, group homes, military barracks, correctional facilities, and workers' dormitories." U.S. Census Bureau, *Glossary*, "Group Quarters," at http://www.census.gov/glossary/ #term_GroupQuartersGQ.

[91] Testimony of Census Bureau Director John H. Thompson, in U.S. Congress, House Committee on Oversight and Government Reform, Subcommittee on Government Operations, *2020 Census: Outcomes of the 2016 Site Test*, hearing, 114th Cong., 2nd sess., November 16, 2016, p. 12, at https://oversight.house.gov/wp-content/uploads/2016/11/ Thompson-Statement-Census-Site-Test-11-16.pdf.

Contracts Awarded or Planned

The following discussion highlights the Census Bureau's considerable reliance on contractors to perform many of the functions supporting the 2020 census. They include communicating the importance of the census, helping respondents understand and respond to the census questionnaire, and performing various IT operations.

Census Questionnaire Assistance

In July 2016, the bureau awarded a contract to General Dynamics Information Technology for 2020 census questionnaire assistance. Assistance will consist of providing information to respondents about "specific items on the census form and answering general questions related to the census," as well as enabling respondents to submit their census information via telephone interview.[92]

Communications

The bureau pursued its outreach strategy by contracting in August 2016 with the Young & Rubicam advertising agency "to design, plan, produce, integrate, and implement an integrated communications program" for the 2020 census.[93] The contract covers, among other activities, research, marketing, advertising, public relations, and support for census partners.[94] Young & Rubicam also led the bureau's first-ever paid advertising campaign, for the 2000 census.[95]

---

[92] Ibid., p. 16.
[93] U.S. Census Bureau, "2020 Census Integrated Communications Contract," at https://www.census.gov/about/business-opportunities/opportunities/vendor-opps/2014-10-15-2020-comm.html.
[94] Testimony of Census Bureau Director John H. Thompson, in U.S. Congress, House Committee on Oversight and Government Reform, Subcommittee on Government Operations, *2020 Census: Outcomes of the 2016 Site Test*, hearing, 114th Cong., 2nd sess., November 16, 2016, p. 17, at https://oversight.house.gov/wp-content/uploads/2016/11/ Thompson-Statement-Census-Site-Test-11-16.pdf.
[95] U.S. Census Bureau, "Census 2000 Advertising Campaign," at http://www.census.gov/dmd/www/advcampaign.html.

Technical Integration

Another contract awarded in August 2016 went to the T-Rex corporation, to support "all design and architecture engineering and integration activities" for the 2020 census, including "infrastructure planning and design for the data center capability," the regional and area census offices, "and any other designated locations"; "disaster recovery solutions"; and expertise in areas "such as fraud detection and security." According to the bureau director, "the management team of T-Rex has demonstrated experience on prior censuses," both in the United States and internationally.[96]

Census Schedule a Human Resources Payroll System

In October 2016, the bureau awarded a contract to the CSRA corporation "to automate the recruiting, hiring, onboarding and separation" of Schedule A staff, the temporary fieldworkers who will do address listing and enumeration for the 2020 census. The new system is expected to be an improvement, in that it "will replace decades-old manual processes."[97]

Decennial Device as a Service

The bureau plans to award, at a yet-to-be-determined date in 2017, a contract that will enable it "to lease smartphones as the predominant mobile device for enumeration and address canvassing," from the 2018 end-to-end census test through the completion of 2020 census field operations.[98]

EMERGING CHALLENGES

The census could receive greater congressional attention as 2020 approaches; the bureau requests larger appropriations leading up to the

---

[96] Testimony of Census Bureau Director John H. Thompson, in U.S. Congress, House Committee on Oversight and Government Reform, Subcommittee on Government Operations, *2020 Census: Outcomes of the 2016 Site Test*, hearing, 114th Cong., 2nd sess., November 16, 2016, p. 17, at https://oversight.house.gov/wp-content/uploads/2016/11/ Thompson-Statement-Census-Site-Test-11-16.pdf.

[97] Ibid., p. 18.

[98] Ibid.; and information provided to the author by the Census Bureau, March 10, 2017.

count; and issues like House apportionment, within-state redistricting, federal funds distribution, and other uses of the decennial data gain prominence. The bureau is asking Congress to make substantial investments in census operations, particularly those related to information technology, which could invite increasing scrutiny of them. The discussion below notes concerns raised thus far about IT and IT security for the census, the status of census testing and findings from tests of nonresponse follow-up operations in two sites, and funding for census preparations.

Technology

General Concerns About 2020 Census Technology

In congressional testimony toward the end of 2016, GAO observed that 2020 census operations will depend on about 50 IT systems, including 11 CEDCaP "enterprise systems." With respect to CEDCaP, the bureau "developed several pilot systems to provide and test different capabilities" but in May 2016 decided to acquire six of them "from a vendor, using a commercial-off-the-shelf IT platform, rather than continue to develop the capabilities in-house."[99]

GAO questioned whether the bureau would be ready for the 2018 end-to-end census test, which, as previously mentioned, is scheduled to begin in August 2017. By October 2016, according to GAO, only 3 of the 50 systems for the test had been delivered; the remaining 47 systems were in various stages of development.[100] Moreover, the bureau had not "identified

---

[99] U.S. Government Accountability Office, *Information Technology: Uncertainty Remains about the Bureau's Readiness for a Key Decennial Census Test*, GAO-17-221T, November 16, 2016, p. 5. The bureau, in the words of its director, will take a "hybrid approach" to CEDCaP, which will integrate the commercial-off-the-shelf platform "with select Census Bureau custom solutions." Testimony of Census Bureau Director John H. Thompson, in U.S. Congress, House Committee on Oversight and Government Reform, Subcommittee on Government Operations, *2020 Census: Outcomes of the 2016 Site Test*, hearing, 114th Cong., 2nd sess., November 16, 2016, p. 3, at https://oversight.house.gov/ wp-content/ uploads/2016/11/Thompson-Statement-Census-Site-Test-11-16.pdf.

[100] U.S. Government Accountability Office, *Information Technology: Uncertainty Remains about the Bureau's Readiness for a Key Decennial Census Test*, GAO-17-221T, November 16, 2016, p. 11.

the entire infrastructure (i.e., cloud solutions and/or data centers)" for the end-to-end test or 2020 operations, and "did not yet have a time frame for the implementation of the infrastructure."[101]

GAO further questioned whether the bureau was "effectively managing its significant contractor support," such as for "the technical integration" of all "key systems and infrastructure, and the development of many of the data collection systems"; "development of the IT platform" that will be used for most data collection; "procurement of the mobile devices and cellular service" for nonresponse follow-up; and "development of the IT infrastructure in the field offices." Adding to the uncertainty is the fact that, as GAO noted, the 2020 census will be the first time the bureau relies on "contractor support" for this kind of technical integration, collects data nationwide online, and employs mobile devices for NRFU.[102]

The bureau's "past efforts to acquire and implement new approaches and systems have not always gone as planned," [103] GAO cautioned, citing the 2010 census to illustrate the point.[104] The bureau intended "to use handheld mobile devices to support field data collection," including for NRFU, in 2010. It switched from trying to develop the devices in-house to contracting for them, then encountered "significant problems" when it tested the devices. "Cost overruns and schedule slippages" were additional problems noted by GAO. The bureau thus abandoned its plan to use the handhelds for NRFU and "reverted to paper-based processing, which increased the cost of the 2010 Census by up to $3 billion" and greatly heightened "the risk of not completing the Census on time."[105] GAO accordingly "designated the 2010 Census a high-risk area in March 2008."[106]

---

[101] Ibid., p. 12.
[102] Ibid., pp. 12-13.
[103] Ibid., p. 6.
[104] For further discussion of the bureau's innovative, but partially failed, technology initiative in the 2010 census, see CRS Report R40551, *The 2010 Decennial Census: Background and Issues*, by Jennifer D. Williams.
[105] U.S. Government Accountability Office, *Information Technology: Uncertainty Remains about the Bureau's Readiness for a Key Decennial Census Test*, GAO-17-221T, November 16, 2016, p. 6.
[106] Ibid.

Because of government-wide IT challenges, GAO cited "improving the management of IT acquisitions and operations as a key area" in its 2015 high-risk report and similarly named CEDCaP as "one of nine programs across the federal government in need of the most attention."[107]

GAO's February 2017 update to the high-risk list included the 2020 census, largely due to the bureau's complex innovations for 2020; the need for improved "ability to manage, develop, and secure its IT systems"; and, related to both of these factors, the need for "better oversight and control over its cost estimation process."[108]

Information Security Concerns

The crucial role assigned to technology for the 2020 census, with the associated emphasis on web responses, heightens the need for information security in many interrelated areas. Areas identified by GAO include ensuring that only those authorized to see respondents' personal data have access to such data and that all bureau employees, both permanent and temporary, are aware of the need for security; protecting data on roughly 300,000 mobile devices that will be used for nonresponse follow-up; minimizing the threat of cybercrimes against data, respondents, and bureau employees; ensuring that those hired to fill key IT positions have expertise in information security; controlling "security performance requirements in a cloud environment"; and having "contingency and incident response plans" in place for all IT systems that will support the census.[109]

The end-to-end test could enable the bureau to determine whether it can "adequately secure" its IT systems for the census and deal with security breaches if they occur. Because most systems to be tested are not yet in place, however, the bureau "has not finalized" and assessed all the

---

GAO's high-risk series "calls attention to agencies and program areas that are high risk due to their vulnerabilities to fraud, waste, abuse, and mismanagement, or are most in need of transformation." Ibid., p. 7.

[107] Ibid.

[108] U.S. Government Accountability Office, *High-Risk Series: Progress on Many High-Risk Areas, While Substantial Efforts Needed on Others*, GAO-17-317, February 2017, pp. 221-223.

[109] U.S. Government Accountability Office, *Information Technology: Uncertainty Remains about the Bureau's Readiness for a Key Decennial Census Test*, GAO-17-221T, November 16, 2016, p. 10.

security controls that are to be implemented, developed plans for remediating any weaknesses in them, and determined whether it has time for remediation before the test begins.[110]

GAO's Observations about Certain Census Tests

2016 Test of NRFU Operations

In January 2017, GAO reported on its evaluation of nonresponse follow-up operations (NRFU, as previously noted) in the bureau's two 2016 census test sites, Harris County, Texas, and Los Angeles County, California.[111] GAO observed that although NRFU in both sites generally took place as planned, about 30% of the NRFU cases in Harris County and 20% in Los Angeles County were coded as "non-interviews." In these cases, the bureau collected "no data or insufficient data," either because it tried unsuccessfully to visit nonresponding households, a maximum of six tries per household, or because problems such as "language barriers or dangerous situations" prevented the bureau from completing visits.[112] Bureau officials, GAO reported, were "not certain" what accounted for so many non-interviews and were "researching potential causes."[113] One possible cause cited by GAO was enumerators' apparent lack of uniform understanding that proxy interviews are important in NRFU and their inconsistent adherence to "procedures for completing interviews with proxy respondents." GAO noted that a proxy is a "non-household member, at least 15 years old, and knowledgeable about the NRFU address."[114] Proxy data, as GAO pointed out, can make the difference between completed interviews and non-interviews, and thus are "important to the success of the census." The bureau informed GAO that it will "continue to refine procedures" for collecting proxy data in 2020.[115] The 2016 test

---

[110] Ibid., p. 13.
[111] U.S. Government Accountability Office, *2020 Census: Additional Actions Could Strengthen Field Data Collection Efforts*, GAO-17-191, January 2017, p. 1.
[112] Ibid., pp. 4-5.
[113] Ibid., p. 5.
[114] Ibid., pp. 6-7.
[115] Ibid., p. 7.

showed as well, according to GAO, a certain lack of flexibility in the automated case management system for fieldwork during nonresponse follow-up and inadequate training for enumerators in using the system. Enumerators, for example, had "difficulty accessing recently closed, incomplete cases."[116] In addition, GAO's field visits disclosed instances when

> enumerators had been told by a respondent or otherwise learned that returning at a specific time on a later date would improve their chance of obtaining an interview from either a household respondent or a property manager. According to the Bureau, while there was a mechanism for capturing and using this information, it was not uniformly available to the enumerators, nor did the enumerators always use the mechanism when appropriate.[117]

Decision to Cancel Some 2017 Census Tests

GAO expressed concern about the bureau's decision, for budgetary reasons, not to conduct 2017 tests of field operations in Puerto Rico, the Standing Rock Indian Reservation in North and South Dakota, and the Colville Indian Reservation and off-reservation trust land in Washington.[118] GAO cited, again with concern, the bureau's intention to consider incorporating these test sites into the 2018 test of all 2020 systems and operations.[119] Doing so, in GAO's assessment, will put "more pressure on the 2018 Test to demonstrate that enumeration activities will function as needed for 2020."[120]

Funding

As discussed above, the Census Bureau's uncertainty about FY2017 appropriations led it to stop work on some of the tests it intended to

---

[116] Ibid., p. 11.
[117] Ibid., p. 9.
[118] U.S. Government Accountability Office, *High-Risk Series: Progress on Many High-Risk Areas, While Substantial Efforts Needed on Others*, GAO-17-317, February 2017, p. 226.
[119] Ibid.
[120] Ibid.

conduct in 2017. The decision illustrates a problem the bureau has encountered throughout the ramp-up phase of the 2020 census, when heightened preparations for the count have required steady increases in funding. The bureau director testified to Congress in late 2016 that enacted appropriations for the census were "significantly" less than requested from FY2013 through FY2016.[121] In FY2013, the budget request was $131.4 million;[122] the enacted amount was $94.4 million.[123] In FY2014, the requested and enacted amounts were $244.8 million[124] and $232.7 million,[125] respectively; in FY2015, $443.2 million[126] and $344.8 million;[127] and in FY2016, $662.6 million[128] and $625.3 million.[129]

The 2020 census request for FY2017 was $778.3 million.[130] FY2017 appropriations legislation was not enacted by the end of FY2016. Instead, the Continuing Appropriations and Military Construction, Veterans Affairs, and Related Agencies Appropriations Act, 2017, and Zika Response and Preparedness Act, H.R. 5325, P.L. 114-223, Division C, provided funds for the bureau, including the 2020 census, at the FY2016 level, with a 0.496% reduction, from October 1, 2016, through December 9, 2016. The Further Continuing and Security Assistance Appropriations Act, 2017, H.R. 2028, P.L. 114-254, was enacted on December 10, 2016.

---

[121] Testimony of Census Bureau Director John H. Thompson, in U.S. Congress, House Committee on Oversight and Government Reform, Subcommittee on Government Operations, *2020 Census: Outcomes of the 2016 Site Test*, hearing, 114th Cong., 2nd sess., November 16, 2016, pp. 4-5, at https://oversight.house.gov/wp-content/uploads/2016/11/Thompson-Statement-Census-Site-Test-11-16.pdf.

[122] U.S. Census Bureau, *Fiscal Year 2013 Budget Estimates*, p. CEN-73, at http://www.osec.doc.gov/bmi/budget/fy13cbj/Census_FY2013_CongressionalJustification-FINAL.pdf.

[123] U.S. Census Bureau, *Fiscal Year 2015 Budget Estimates*, p. CEN-119, at http://osec.doc.gov/bmi/budget/FY15CJ/ CensusFY2015CJFinal508Compliant.pdf.

[124] U.S. Census Bureau, *Fiscal Year 2014 Budget Estimates*, pp. CEN-87, CEN-90, at http://osec.doc.gov/bmi/budget/ FY14CJ/Census_FY_2014_CJ_Final_508_Compliant.pdf.

[125] Information provided to the author by the Census Bureau, December 9, 2016.

[126] U.S. Census Bureau, *Fiscal Year 2015 Budget Estimates*, p. CEN-119, at http://osec.doc.gov/bmi/budget/FY15CJ/ CensusFY2015CJFinal508Compliant.pdf.

[127] Information provided to the author by the Census Bureau, December 9, 2016.

[128] U.S. Census Bureau, *Fiscal Year 2016 Budget Estimates*, p. CEN-83, at http://osec.doc.gov/bmi/budget/FY16CJ/ Census_2016_CJ.pdf.

[129] Information provided to the author by the Census Bureau, December 9, 2016.

[130] U.S. Census Bureau, *U.S. Census Bureau's Budget, Fiscal Year 2017*, p. CEN-87, at http://osec.doc.gov/bmi/budget/FY17CBJ/Census%20FY%202017%20CBJ%20final%20not508.pdf.

In general, Division A of the legislation funds the bureau at the FY2016 level, minus a 0.1901% reduction, through April 28, 2017. Under Section 152, however, the bureau may draw on money from the Periodic Censuses and Programs account—which includes the decennial census and other major programs, such as the economic census, the census of governments, and intercensal demographic estimates, together with geographic and data-processing support—at the rate necessary for conducting operations to maintain the 2020 census schedule. The bureau director stated that the bureau still requires "the timely appropriation of the remainder of the 2017 President's Budget request in order to stay on track" for the 2018 census test. Nevertheless, the level of funding for the rest of FY2017 remains unclear.

In: A Closer Look at the 2020 Census ISBN: 978-1-53616-508-1
Editor: Sille M. Schou © 2019 Nova Science Publishers, Inc.

Chapter 2

THE 2020 DECENNIAL CENSUS: OVERVIEW AND ISSUES[*]

Jennifer D. Williams

WHAT THE CENSUS IS AND HOW THE DATA ARE USED

The census is a count, as nearly complete and accurate as possible, of every person whose usual residence is in the United States. Article I, Section 2, clause 3 of the U.S. Constitution, as modified by Section 2 of the 14th Amendment, requires a population census every 10 years, conducted "in such Manner as they [Congress] shall by Law direct." Congress, in Title 13, *U.S. Code*, has delegated this responsibility to the Secretary of Commerce and, within the U.S. Department of Commerce (DOC), the Census Bureau. The first census took place in 1790; the next will be in 2020. The constitutional reason for taking a census is to have an updated basis for apportioning seats in the U.S. House of Representatives. Census data also are used to redraw legislative boundaries within states; to produce population estimates and projections; in formulas that help

---

[*] This is an edited, reformatted and augmented version of Congressional Research Service Publication No. IF11015, Updated April 22, 2019.

allocate more than $675 billion in federal funds annually to states and localities; and by subnational governments, businesses, nonprofit organizations, and researchers for myriad purposes.

ENGAGING THE POPULATION

The Census Bureau's mission for 2020 is complicated. It must cover a population that is large, tends to be mobile, is distributed over a wide geographic area, and, in the words of a former bureau director, has more "diversity and complexity" than in past decades. The need to avoid census miscounts, such as overcounts of people with more than one residence and undercounts of racial and ethnic minorities, makes the bureau's public outreach efforts before and during the census particularly important.

INNOVATIONS FOR 2020

Congress has directed the bureau to control the ever-rising cost of the census, now estimated at about $15.6 billion for 2020. The bureau has responded with four innovations designed to save money.

IN-OFFICE ADDRESS CANVASSING

The Census Bureau's goal is to have the correct address and geospatial location of every housing unit in the United States. Accurate addresses and maps are essential for contacting the public initially and during nonresponse follow-up (NRFU). In the past, census workers had to walk and check about 11 million census blocks. For 2020, the bureau plans to replace roughly 70% of this field work (which cost almost $450 million for the 2010 census) with in-office canvassing, using data from satellite imagery, the U.S. Postal Service (USPS), federal administrative records, subnational governments, and third-party sources.

EMPHASIS ON PROMPT RESPONSES

The bureau is emphasizing prompt responses in the initial phase of the census, to limit the need for later follow-up by personal visits. NRFU long has been the most costly part of the census (about $2 billion in 2010). The public outreach strategy for 2020 includes paid advertising in print and on television, radio, and social media; and partnering with outside organizations, especially those trusted by harder-to-count population groups. The census also will feature a new internet response option, to make answering easier and replace as much of the more expensive mail-out, mail-back census operation as possible. Those not able or willing to respond online can provide their answers by calling questionnaire assistance centers or can fill out paper forms.

Administrative Records to Limit NRFU Before NRFU begins, the bureau will use governmental administrative records—for example, "Undeliverable-as-Addressed" information from USPS—to identify and remove the addresses of vacant housing units from the NRFU workload. In addition, the bureau may use records— such as those from the Internal Revenue Service, the Centers for Medicare and Medicaid Services, the Indian Health Service, and the Social Security Administration, plus information the bureau already has and commercial data—if feasible, to enumerate some occupied nonresponding households.

TECHNOLOGY TO STREAMLINE FIELDWORK

The bureau expects that address canvassers and NRFU field staff will work remotely, using mobile devices for most administrative tasks and data collection. Supervisors, too, will use the devices for working and communicating with staff remotely. This technology, according to the bureau, will greatly reduce the physical space and staff needed for fieldwork, from 12 regional centers and almost 500 area offices for the 2010 census to six regional centers and just under 250 administrative support centers for 2020.

ISSUES FOR 2020

Funding Challenges

Heightened preparations for any census generally require corresponding increases in appropriations. During the earlier "ramp up" to 2020, enacted funding was less than requested and was delayed. The FY2016 budget request for the census was $662.6 million; the enacted amount was $598.9 million. The FY2017 request was $778.3 million; the Census Bureau's approved spend plan allocated $767.3 million to the census. In contrast, the FY2018 request for the census was $800.2 million; the spend plan approved $2,094.9 million. The amount for Periodic Censuses and Programs (PCP), the account that includes the census, was $2,545.4 million, available until September 30, 2020. For FY2019, the census request was $3,015.1 million. H.J.Res. 31, P.L. 116-6, the Consolidated Appropriations Act, 2019, Division C, funds PCP at $3,551.4 million, with a transfer of $3.6 million from PCP to the DOC Office of Inspector General (OIG) for ongoing bureau oversight. The proposed amount for the census in FY2020 includes $5,297.0 million in new budget authority, $1,020.0 million in prior-year funds, and about $100.0 million from the Enterprise Data Collection and Dissemination System, totaling about $6,400.0 million. Of the $5,885.4 million requested for PCP, $3.6 million is to be transferred to the DOC OIG for continuing bureau oversight.

Reduced Testing

Throughout each decade, the Census Bureau tests parts of census operations and procedures to determine whether they will work as intended. Testing is considered essential for a successful enumeration; however, funding delays and shortfalls have truncated some 2020 census tests. In 2017, for example, the bureau tested new internet systems on a nationwide sample of about 80,000 housing units. The test was to have included field operations in Puerto Rico, the Standing Rock Indian Reservation in North and South Dakota, and the Colville Indian Reservation and off-reservation trust land in Washington. In late 2016, the bureau announced that it would not include these areas, due to uncertain FY2017 funding. Similarly, the 2018 census test of all major 2020 census components—the bureau's last chance to identify and correct problems ahead of the census—was to have covered more than 700,000 housing units in Pierce County, Washington; Providence County, Rhode Island; and nine West Virginia counties. Inadequate funding caused the bureau to test only address canvassing in all these areas; the full test, which concluded on March 29, 2019, was limited to Providence County.

Citizenship Question

The 1950 census was the last one to date that collected citizenship information from the whole U.S. resident population. The 1960 census had no citizenship question per se but queried a sample of respondents about birthplace. From 1970 on, the Census Bureau asked a population sample about citizenship or naturalization status, first as part of the census, then in the American Community Survey (ACS). Secretary of Commerce Wilbur Ross and his staff reportedly asked the U.S. Department of Justice (DOJ) if it would request the Census Bureau to collect citizenship data in the 2020 census. DOJ made the request on December 12, 2017. Secretary Ross announced on March 26, 2018, that the 2020 census will ask the ACS question "Is this person a citizen of the United States?" The choice of ACS answers is "Yes, born in the United States"; "Yes, born in Puerto Rico, Guam, the U.S. Virgin Islands, or Northern Marianas"; "Yes, born abroad of U.S. citizen parent or parents"; "Yes, U.S. citizen by naturalization—Print year of naturalization"; or "No, not a U.S. citizen." DOJ stated that the census, not a survey with associated sampling error, "is the most appropriate vehicle for collecting" citizenship data "critical to the Department's enforcement of Section 2 of the Voting Rights Act" and its "protections against racial discrimination in voting."

Opponents of the citizenship question have expressed concern that it may depress immigrants' census response rates or cause them to falsify data, especially if their status in the United States, or that of their friends or families, is illegal. Census Bureau fieldworkers in 2017 noted heightened anxiety about data confidentiality among certain foreign-born respondents and reluctance to answer questions, particularly about citizenship status. Six former bureau directors, from both Republican and Democratic administrations, signed a January 26, 2018, letter to Secretary Ross, opposing the late-date introduction of an untested citizenship question. Multiple lawsuits were filed to block the question; Judge Jesse Furman, U.S. District Court for the Southern District of New York, ruled on July 26, 2018, that the consolidated suit *State of New York et al. vs. U.S. Department of Commerce et al.* could proceed. The U.S. Supreme Court will hear the case on April 23, 2019.

Technology Challenges

According to GAO, the Census Bureau planned heavy reliance on new and existing IT systems and infrastructure to support operations, first in the 2018 test, then in the actual census. During the test, the bureau was to deploy 44 systems to support address canvassing; responses by internet, on paper, and by phone; field enumeration; and data tabulation and dissemination. By June 2018, 36 of the 44 systems for the test had been developed; development of the remaining 8 was progressing. As of August 2018, 11 of the systems were being developed or adapted as part of the bureau's new Census Enterprise Data Collection and Processing (CEDCaP) "system of systems." CEDCaP will provide, in the bureau's words, "shared data collection and processing across all censuses and surveys." GAO's February 2015 and February 2017 reports on "high-risk" programs, however, called CEDCaP "an IT investment in need of attention." The 2017 report added the 2020 census itself to the high-risk list, where it remained in March 2019, partly because of the bureau's continuing problems and delays in developing, testing, correcting, securing, and managing IT systems. The March 2019 report, for example, stated that by December 2018, the bureau "had identified nearly 1,100 system security weaknesses" requiring attention. The report noted the short time available for "the remaining system testing and security assessments," with potentially increased "risk that deployed systems will either not function as intended, have security vulnerabilities, or both."

Temporary Workforce

An additional challenge facing the Census Bureau as 2020 approaches is the need for a large, diverse applicant pool from which to hire qualified temporary workers, such as address canvassers and NRFU enumerators. The bureau is competing for talent in a tighter labor market than that before and during the 2010 census. The unemployment rate was 3.8% in March 2019, compared with 10.0% in October 2009 and 9.3% to 9.8% throughout 2010, when the bureau recruited about 3.9 million applicants. Especially for NRFU, the bureau needs workers proficient in English and other languages. Enumerators ideally will approximate the demographic makeup of the communities where they are assigned, so that they can win respondents' trust.

In: A Closer Look at the 2020 Census
Editor: Sille M. Schou

ISBN: 978-1-53616-508-1
© 2019 Nova Science Publishers, Inc.

Chapter 3

COMMERCE DEPARTMENT ANNOUNCES CITIZENSHIP QUESTION ON 2020 CENSUS AND LAWSUITS FILED[*]

L. Paige Whitaker

On March 26, 2018, the Commerce Department, which houses the U.S. Census Bureau, announced that the 2020 decennial census questionnaire will include a citizenship question. Thereafter, the State of California and a coalition of states and cities led by the State of New York filed lawsuits to stop Commerce from including the question, generally arguing that including a citizenship question would suppress the census response rate and result in undercounts that would violate the U.S. Constitution's mandate to count every resident. Commerce maintains, among other things, that inclusion of the citizenship question in the census questionnaire to the entire U.S. population will produce census block level data on "citizenship voting age population" (CVAP) that is more accurate and complete than current data, thereby outweighing concerns of a lower response rate, and that such data will assist the Department of Justice in

---
[*] This is an edited, reformatted and augmented version of Congressional Research Service Publication No. LSB10114, dated April 6, 2018.

enforcing the Voting Rights Act. This sidebar provides an overview of the Commerce Department's announcement; relevant constitutional and statutory provisions; how census data is used in redistricting and ensuring compliance with the Voting Rights Act; and pending legal challenges.

BACKGROUND AND COMMERCE ANNOUNCEMENT

In the memorandum announcing the decision to include a question on citizenship in the 2020 census, Commerce Secretary Wilbur Ross references a December 12, 2017 request from the Department of Justice (DOJ) that the Census Bureau "reinstate a citizenship question on the decennial census to provide census block level citizenship voting age population ('CVAP') data that are not currently available from government survey data" for use by the courts and DOJ "for determining violations of Section 2 of the Voting Rights Act ('VRA')." Further, the memorandum states that "having these data at the census block level will permit more effective enforcement of the Act."

Most decennial censuses through 1950 included a citizenship question. In addition, as the memorandum explains, the 2000 decennial census "long form" survey, which was distributed to one in six people in the U.S., included a question on citizenship. Subsequently, the "long form" survey was replaced by the American Community Survey (ACS), which has included a citizenship question since 2005. The ACS gathers social, economic, demographic, and housing data monthly from a sample of the population and aggregates the data over time to produce yearly estimates for areas with at least 65,000 people and five-year estimates for less populous areas.

According to Secretary Ross' memorandum, "DOJ seeks to obtain CVAP data for census blocks, block groups, counties, towns, and other locations where potential Section 2 violations are alleged or suspected, and DOJ states that the current data collected under the ACS are insufficient in scope, detail, and certainty to meet its purpose under the VRA." Further, the memorandum states that "the census-block-level citizenship data requested by DOJ are not available using the annual ACS, which . . . does ask a citizenship question and is the present method used to provide DOJ and the courts with data used to enforce Section 2 of the VRA."

Key Constitutional and Statutory Provisions

Every 10 years, the U.S. Constitution requires a population census or "actual Enumeration" for the apportionment of seats in the House of Representatives. Specifically, Article I, Section 2, clause 3, as amended by Section 2 of the Fourteenth Amendment, provides that the House of Representatives is to be apportioned—or divided —among the 50 states, based on each decennial census that is conducted "in such Manner" as Congress "shall by Law direct."

Accordingly, federal law addresses how the questions to be included on the census questionnaire are determined. Specifically, 13 U.S.C. §5 provides that "[t]he Secretary [of Commerce] shall prepare questionnaires, and shall determine the inquiries, and the number, form, and subdivisions thereof, for the statistics, surveys, and censuses provided for in this title."

Census Data, Redistricting, and the Voting Rights Act

When congressional and state legislative redistricting maps are drawn, census data is integral for ensuring population equality among districts and compliance with the Voting Rights Act. The Supreme Court has interpreted Article I, Section 2, clause 1 of the Constitution to require that each electoral district within a state contain approximately the same population. This requirement is known as the "equality standard" or the principle of "one person, one vote." Ideal or precise equality is the average population that each district would contain if a state population were evenly distributed across all districts. According to the Court, congressional districts are required to have less deviation from precise equality than is permissible for state legislative districts. While the Court has issued several decisions since 1964 on the extent to which precise mathematical equality among districts is constitutionally required, the Court has not specifically addressed the question of *who* should be counted (i.e., total population, voting age population (VAP), CVAP, or some other measure of eligible voters or population) within districts in order to achieve such equality. In in a 2016 ruling, *Evenwel v. Abbott*, against a Fourteenth Amendment equal protection claim, the Court held that states are permitted to use total population to draw electoral districts; however, the Court did not rule specifically on the constitutionality of a state drawing district lines based on some other measure of population, such as eligible, CVAP, or registered voters. Therefore, that question could come before the Court in a future case.

In addition, census data is relevant in ascertaining whether congressional and state legislative district boundaries comply with Section 2 of the VRA. Section 2 authorizes the federal government and private citizens to challenge discriminatory voting practices or procedures, including minority vote dilution, (that is, the diminishing or weakening of minority voting power). Specifically, Section 2 prohibits any voting qualification or practice applied or imposed by any state or political subdivision that results in the denial or abridgement of the right to vote based on race, color, or membership in a language minority. Section 2 further provides that a violation is established if, based on the totality of circumstances, electoral processes are not equally open to participation by members of a racial or language minority group in that the group's members have less opportunity than other members of the electorate to elect representatives of their choice. Accordingly, in certain circumstances, Section 2 requires the creation of one or more "majority-minority" districts in a redistricting plan. A majority-minority district is one in which a racial or language minority group comprises a voting majority. The creation of such districts can avoid racial vote dilution by preventing the submergence of minority voters into the majority, and the denial of an equal opportunity to elect candidates of choice. In ascertaining whether a violation of Section 2 has occurred, the Supreme Court has utilized both the CVAP and the VAP as the measure of population.

Legal Challenges

Both the State of California and a coalition of states and cities led by the State of New York have recently filed lawsuits in federal district courts seeking to stop the Commerce Department from including a question about citizenship on the 2020 census. In both lawsuits, the parties argue, among other things, that including a citizenship question in the census questionnaire will suppress the census response rate and result in undercounts of their population in violation of the Constitution's mandate to conduct an "actual Enumeration." The parties further argue that the inclusion of the citizenship question in the census is agency action subject to the Administrative Procedure Act, and that it violates that Act's prohibition against arbitrary and capricious agency action and action that is not in accordance with the law, contrary to constitutional right, and beyond statutory authority. The parties in both lawsuits allege harms from inclusion of a citizenship question, including that an undercount will negatively impact their apportionment of congressional seats, Electoral College electors, and federal funding.

In: A Closer Look at the 2020 Census ISBN: 978-1-53616-508-1
Editor: Sille M. Schou © 2019 Nova Science Publishers, Inc.

Chapter 4

THE SUPREME COURT TEMPORARILY BLOCKS CITIZENSHIP QUESTION ON THE 2020 CENSUS[*]

Mainon A. Schwartz and Benjamin Hayes

Update: After the Supreme Court's June 27 decision, the Department of Justice and the Secretary of Commerce stated that the 2020 census form would not include a citizenship question. However, on July 3, President Trump stated that the Administration would continue its efforts to add a citizenship question to the 2020 census. Subsequently, the Department of Justice told a federal court that the Administration will continue to pursue adding a citizenship question to the 2020 census.

The original post from June 28, 2019, is below.

On June 27, 2019, the Supreme Court issued its decision in Department of Commerce v. New York—the case involving several challenges to the decision by the Secretary of the Department of Commerce (Commerce), Wilbur Ross, to add a citizenship question to the 2020 census. Chief Justice Roberts authored the opinion for a majority of

---

[*] This is an edited, reformatted and augmented version of Congressional Research Service Publication No. LSB10319, Updated July 5, 2019.

the Court, though different combinations of Justices comprised the majority for different parts of the opinion. In that opinion, the Supreme Court held that the Secretary's decision did not violate the Enumeration Clause of the U.S. Constitution or the Census Act, and that the Secretary's decision was supported by evidence before the agency. However, the Chief Justice—joined by Justices Ginsburg, Breyer, Sotomayor, and Kagan—concluded that the Secretary's decision was unlawful because the reason he gave for adding the citizenship question was not the actual reason for his decision. The Court thus instructed that the case be sent back to Commerce to allow the Secretary to provide a nonpretextual justification for his decision. But the window for the agency to provide that justification is closing: the United States has represented that the deadline for finalizing the 2020 census questionnaire is the end of June 2019 while the plaintiffs have suggested that the deadline is the end of October 2019. Moreover, at least one ongoing lawsuit challenging the Secretary's decision involves a legal argument not addressed by the Supreme Court's decision, thus presenting another possible barrier to the addition of a citizenship question to the 2020 census.

This Sidebar provides an overview of the legal framework governing the census and the legal challenges to Commerce's decision to include a citizenship question on the 2020 census. The Sidebar then discusses the Supreme Court's decision, identifies issues left unresolved by the decision, and addresses potential considerations for Congress.

LEGAL FRAMEWORK FOR THE CENSUS

Article I, section 2 of the U.S. Constitution, as amended by Section 2 of the Fourteenth Amendment, requires that an "actual Enumeration" be taken—that is, that "the whole number of . . . persons" in each State be counted—"every . . . Term of ten Years, in such Manner as [Congress] shall by Law direct." The results of the decennial census are used to determine the number of seats each state will have in the U.S. House of

Representatives for the next decade and to allocate certain federal funds among the states.

In line with the Constitution's directive, Congress, through the Census Act, has required the Secretary of Commerce to "take a decennial census of population" and grants the Secretary discretion to do so "in such form and content as he may determine" and to "obtain such other census information as necessary." The discretion conferred by the Census Act, however, is not unlimited. Though the Secretary has authority to "prepare questionnaires" to obtain information by means of "direct inquir[y]," Section 6(c) of the Act instructs the Secretary to first attempt to obtain such information from federal, state, or local government administrative sources "[t]o the maximum extent possible" and "consistent with the kind, timeliness, quality and scope" of the information needed. Moreover, to facilitate congressional oversight, Section 141(f) of the Act directs the Secretary to "submit [reports] to the [appropriate] committees of Congress" identifying

1. the "subjects proposed to be included [on the census questionnaire], and the types of information to be compiled";
2. "the questions proposed to be included in [the] census"; and
3. if "new circumstances exist" that require the "subjects, types of information, or questions" to be modified, a report containing those modifications.

To help ensure accurate census data, federal law requires individuals to respond to the census questionnaire. Those who refuse, willfully neglect to respond, or willfully give false answers, may be subject to monetary penalties. And to protect personal privacy, federal law prohibits Commerce employees (which includes Census Bureau employees) from using, publishing, or allowing others to "examine" census information (except in narrowly defined circumstances). Violators may face monetary penalties and imprisonment.

Legal Challenges

Many prior decennial censuses have included a question related to national origin or citizenship. With one exception, a question about citizenship was asked of at least some of the population as part of every census from 1820 through 1950, though that question was removed from the general census questionnaire after the 1950 census. From 1970 through 2000, a citizenship question was included in a longer version of the decennial census form sent to a fraction of the population. This "long form survey" was later replaced by the American Community Survey—an annual survey sent to only a portion of the population—which has included a citizenship question since 2005.

On March 26, 2018, Secretary Ross issued a memorandum stating that the Census Bureau would add a citizenship question to the 2020 decennial census form that would be distributed to every household. As the sole basis for the inclusion of this question, Secretary Ross explained that he made this decision because the Department of Justice (DOJ) had requested the inclusion of a citizenship question to facilitate enforcement of Section 2 of the Voting Rights Act (VRA). Section 2 of the VRA prohibits voting practices that dilute minority voting power and a plaintiff making a "vote dilution" claim must show (among other things) that the "eligible voters" of a minority group—who usually must be citizens—are "a majority in a single-member district" capable of electing their candidate of choice.

After the memorandum was released, several plaintiff groups filed lawsuits in federal district court in California, Maryland, and New York, challenging the Secretary's decision. They argued, among other things, that the decision violated (1) the Enumeration Clause, (2) the equal protection component of the Fifth Amendment's Due Process Clause, (3) Sections 6(c) and 141(f) of the Census Act, and (4) the Administrative Procedure Act (APA).

On January 15, 2019, the U.S. District Court for the Southern District of New York issued a 277-page opinion concluding that Secretary Ross's decision to add a citizenship question to the 2020 census was unlawful.

First, the court ruled that the Secretary's decision violated Section 6(c)'s requirement that Commerce rely "[t]o the maximum extent possible" on state and federal administrative records to obtain desired information. Second, the court held that the Secretary violated Section 141(f) by failing to timely report to Congress that citizenship would be a "subject" addressed on the census questionnaire. Finally, the court concluded that Secretary Ross's decision was arbitrary and capricious, reasoning that his reliance on the DOJ's request was pretextual because he "made the decision to add the citizenship question well before DOJ requested its addition in December 2017." The court further held that Secretary Ross unjustifiably departed from certain administrative procedures and failed to fully consider possible alternatives in light of the evidence before him. To reach these conclusions, the district court relied on evidence outside the administrative record that the plaintiffs had obtained through discovery— an action it justified (in part) by concluding that the Secretary had likely acted in bad faith by not disclosing the true basis for his decision. Finally, the court concluded the plaintiffs had not produced sufficient evidence to support their equal protection claim. In so doing, the court dispensed with the last of the plaintiffs' constitutional claims, having dismissed their Enumeration Clause claim in a prior order.

Though district court decisions are normally appealed to a federal court of appeals, the United States asked the Supreme Court to directly review the Southern District of New York's decision, based on its representation that the census questionnaire must be finalized by the end of June 2019. The Supreme Court agreed. After federal district courts in California and Maryland concluded that the addition of a citizenship question would violate the Enumeration Clause, the Supreme Court expanded the scope of its review to include that issue. However, though the Maryland district court (like the Southern District of New York) had also rejected the plaintiffs' equal protection claim, the Supreme Court did not review that issue.

The Supreme Court's Decision

On June 27, 2019, the Supreme Court issued its decision in *Department of Commerce v. New York*. Chief Justice Roberts's opinion garnered a majority of the Court, though the Justices comprising the majority for each issue varied. The Court rejected the plaintiffs' Enumeration Clause and Census Act claims, while also concluding that the Secretary's decision to reinstate a citizenship question could be supported by the evidence before him. However, the Court also recognized that agencies are required to disclose the reasons for their decisions in order to facilitate meaningful judicial review. Upon reviewing the evidence, the Court determined that the Secretary's stated reason for reinstating the citizenship question—to provide DOJ with citizenship information for VRA enforcement—was not the actual reason for his decision. On that basis, the Court ruled that the Secretary's decision was unlawful.

The Majority Opinion

On the merits, the Chief Justice—joined by Justices Thomas, Alito, Gorsuch, and Kavanaugh—first concluded that the Secretary's decision to reinstate a citizenship question did not violate the Enumeration Clause. In particular, the Court observed that "demographic questions have been asked in *every* census since 1790" and that "questions about citizenship in particular have been asked for nearly as long." Based on this "consistent historical practice"—combined with the "'virtually unlimited discretion'" given Congress to conduct the census—the Court determined that the Enumeration Clause does not prohibit the Secretary of Commerce from inquiring about citizenship on the census questionnaire.

Next, these Justices disagreed with the district court's determination that the Secretary's decision was contrary to the evidence. The Court concluded that the Secretary's decision to rely on both administrative records and a citizenship question to obtain accurate citizenship data—rather than relying *solely* on administrative records—was a reasonable exercise of the Secretary's discretion in light of the available evidence. Either option, the Court concluded, "entailed tradeoffs between accuracy and completeness," and, where the "choice [is] between reasonable policy alternatives," the Secretary has authority to choose. The Court also decided that the Secretary had reasonably weighed the costs and benefits of reinstating the citizenship question. The Court noted that the Secretary had explained why the "risk[s] w[ere] difficult to assess," and concluded that he had reasonably "[w]eigh[ed] that uncertainty against the value of obtaining more complete and accurate citizenship data." In the end, the Court was unwilling to second-guess the Secretary's conclusion, particularly as "the evidence before [him] hardly led ineluctably to just one reasonable course of action."

The same Justices also ruled that the Secretary's decision did not violate the Census Act. With respect to Section 6(c), the Court determined that the Secretary reasonably concluded that exclusive reliance on administrative records to obtain citizenship data "would not . . . provide the more complete and accurate data that DOJ sought." Thus, because administrative records alone would not supply the "kind and quality" of "'statistics required,'" the Court ruled that the Secretary had complied with Section 6(c)'s requirement to rely "to the maximum extent possible" on administrative records. The Court also determined that the Secretary complied with Section 141(f) of the Census Act. Though the Secretary had not included "citizenship" as a "subject" in his initial report to Congress, the Court concluded that by listing "citizenship" as a "question" in a later report, the Secretary had complied with the Census Act's procedures for modifying an earlier report. Regardless, the Court reasoned that any violation "would surely be harmless" as "the Secretary nonetheless fully informed Congress of, and explained, his decision."

Lastly, the Chief Justice—joined now by Justices Ginsburg, Breyer, Sotomayor, and Kagan—held that the Secretary's sole stated reason for adding the citizenship question to the census (*i.e.*, providing the DOJ with citizenship data for VRA enforcement) was not the real reason for his decision. The Court began by reaffirming that agencies are required to disclose the actual reasons for their decisions in order to facilitate effective judicial review. And, while courts normally accept as true an agency's stated reason for its action, courts may review evidence outside the agency record to probe the justifications for an agency action if there has been a strong showing of bad faith or improper behavior by the agency.

Based on these principles, the Court first determined that evidence outside the agency record was properly considered in evaluating the lawfulness of the Secretary's action because some of the evidence suggested that the Secretary's stated reason for adding a citizenship question was pretextual. The Court then conducted its own review of the evidence, and noted that while the Secretary "began taking steps to reinstate a citizenship question about a week into his tenure," there was "no hint that he was considering VRA enforcement" at that time. In addition, the Court observed that Commerce had itself gone "to great lengths to elicit the request [to add a citizenship question] from DOJ." In the end, "viewing the evidence as a whole," the Court concluded that "the decision to reinstate a citizenship question [could not] be adequately explained in terms of DOJ's request for improved citizenship data to better enforce the VRA."

Given this "disconnect between the decision made and the explanation given," the Court agreed with the Southern District of New York that the Secretary's decision violated the APA because the Secretary had not disclosed the actual reason for his decision. However, the Court was clear that it was "not hold[ing] that the [Secretary's] decision . . . was substantively invalid," but was instead requiring the Secretary to disclose his reason for that decision. And to give the Secretary this opportunity, the Court directed the district court to send the case back to the Department of Commerce.

Justice Thomas's Dissent

Though various Justices dissented from portions of the Court's opinion, the most immediately consequential portion of the Court's ruling—that the Secretary's stated reason for reinstating the citizenship question was pretextual—prompted a dissent from Justice Thomas that was joined by Justices Gorsuch and Kavanaugh.

Justice Thomas first argued that the Court was wrong to rely on evidence outside the administrative record to assess whether the Secretary's justification was pretextual. Under the APA, Justice Thomas explained, judicial review of an agency decision is normally based on "the agency's contemporaneous explanation" for its decision, and courts may not invalidate the agency's action even if it "ha[d] other, unstated reasons for the decision." And though Justice Thomas acknowledged that review of extra-record materials may be permissible upon a showing of bad faith, in his view this case did not meet that standard. Moreover, Justice Thomas concluded that, even if such review were appropriate, none of the evidence established that the Secretary's stated basis for his decision "did not factor *at all* into [his] decision." In Justice Thomas's view, the evidence showed "at most, that leadership at both the Department of Commerce and the DOJ believed it important—for a variety of reasons—to include a citizenship question on the census." Finally, Justice Thomas criticized the Court's decision as being the "the first time the Court has ever invalidated an agency action as 'pretextual,'" and contended that the Court had "depart[ed] from traditional principles of administrative law" and "opened a Pandora's box of pretext-based challenges in administrative law."

Post-Supreme Court Issues and Claims

Though the Supreme Court's decision resolved most of the plaintiffs' claims, it still left some issues unresolved. To begin, the Court's decision appears to leave open the possibility that the citizenship question could still be added to the census. The Court made clear that it had not deemed the Secretary's decision "substantively" unlawful, and so the Secretary may be able to reinstate the citizenship question if he provides a non-pretextual explanation for doing so. In the event the Secretary again decides to add a citizenship question to the 2020 census, that decision (like his first) could be challenged in federal district court. If it is, the losing party could still appeal that decision to the court of appeals or seek expedited review in the Supreme Court.

In addition, although the Supreme Court rejected the plaintiffs' Enumeration Clause claim, it did not address the lower court's rulings that the plaintiffs failed to establish a violation of the equal protection component of the Due Process Clause. In the Maryland case, the plaintiffs had appealed the dismissal of their equal protection claim to the U.S. Court of Appeals for the Fourth Circuit, but they later sought to have that claim reevaluated by the district court in light of new evidence allegedly indicating that Secretary Ross had a discriminatory motive for reinstating the citizenship question. The Fourth Circuit recently granted this request so the district court could conduct further proceedings. Once the district court issues a ruling on this claim, the non-prevailing party may seek review in the Fourth Circuit or the Supreme Court. In the meantime, the plaintiffs in the Maryland case have requested that the district court enter an order preventing the United States from adding a citizenship question to the census while their equal protection claim is being adjudicated.

These ongoing proceedings could pose practical challenges for the inclusion of the citizenship question on the 2020 census. The United States has represented that the census questionnaire must be finalized by June 30 of this year, though some of the plaintiffs have contended that October 31 is the actual deadline. Whether the Department of Commerce will be able to add a citizenship question to the 2020 census could depend on which of these deadlines holds true. However, even if the October 2019 date applies, the parties may have difficulty obtaining full judicial review—from a court of appeals and/or the Supreme Court—of any rulings from the district courts before that deadline.

Considerations for Congress

Though Congress has delegated significant responsibility for the census to the Secretary of Commerce, the Constitution makes clear that Congress has ultimate authority over how it is conducted. Congress thus has the authority to pass legislation, subject to presidential veto, that would either require or prohibit the inclusion of a citizenship question or other demographic questions in the future or impose additional restraints on the Secretary's existing authority to add questions to the decennial census.

Alternatively, Congress could include language in the appropriations bill for the Department of Commerce regulating the manner in which funds may be used to implement a citizenship question on the 2020 census.

Congress could also enact more general guidance. For example, bills introduced in the 116th Congress would mandate a certain amount of research, study, and testing for any new questions or design features, and also require the Secretary to submit detailed statements on such testing to Congress and the general public. Though such requirements would not necessarily prevent the inclusion of a citizenship question on future census forms, they could require more extensive analysis before any question may be added to the census, thus providing Congress with more complete information about the consequences of doing so.

In: A Closer Look at the 2020 Census
Editor: Sille M. Schou

ISBN: 978-1-53616-508-1
© 2019 Nova Science Publishers, Inc.

Chapter 5

DEPARTMENT OF COMMERCE – MEMORANDUM REGARDING A CITIZENSHIP QUESTION ON THE 2020 DECENNIAL CENSUS QUESTIONNAIRE[*]

United States Government Accountability Office

The Honorable Brian Schatz
United States Senate

Dear Senator Schatz:

This is in response to your request for our opinion on whether a memorandum issued by the Secretary of Commerce on March 26, 2018, regarding a citizenship question on the 2020 decennial census questionnaire, is a rule for purposes of the Congressional Review Act (CRA). The memorandum, issued to the Commerce Under Secretary for Economic Affairs who oversees the U.S. Census Bureau, provides the Secretary's rationale for including a citizenship question and directs the Under Secretary to do so. We conclude the memorandum is not a rule

---

[*] This is an edited, reformatted and augmented version of the United States Government Accountability Office Publication No. B-330288, dated February 7, 2019.

because it was direction from a supervisor to a subordinate in conjunction with the statutory process whereby the Secretary informs Congress of the questions that will be on the census. 13 U.S.C. § 141(f)(2). As such, the memorandum does not meet CRA's definition of a rule because it was not designed to implement, interpret, or prescribe law or policy. By releasing the memorandum, the agency was exercising its inherent authority to inform the public about agency activities and the policy views that underlie those activities.

In accordance with our regular practice, we contacted the Department of Commerce (Commerce) to seek factual information and its legal views on this matter. Letter from Assistant General Counsel, GAO, to General Counsel, Commerce (Aug. 15, 2018). In its response, Commerce provided its explanation of the pertinent facts and its view that the memorandum is not a rule. Letter from Chief Counsel for Regulation, Commerce, to Assistant General Counsel, GAO (Sept. 10, 2018) (Response Letter).

BACKGROUND

The American decennial census is mandated by the Constitution of the United States. U.S. Const., art. I, § 2, cl. 3. The Constitution requires that the census be conducted in such a manner as Congress, by law, directs. Id. Congress laid out the process for conducting the census in title 13 of the United States Code and delegated the duty of conducting the census to the Secretary of Commerce. 13 U.S.C. § 141(a). No later than two years before the date of the census, the Secretary is required to submit a report to Congress that contains the Secretary's determination of the questions that are proposed to be included on the census. Id. § 141(f)(2).

In March of 2018, the Secretary of Commerce issued a memorandum to Commerce's Under Secretary for Economic Affairs, who oversees the United States Census Bureau. Secretary of Commerce Memorandum to Under Secretary for Economic Affairs, Reinstatement of a Citizenship Question on the 2020 Decennial Census Questionnaire (Mar. 26, 2018). The memorandum described a December 12, 2017 request from the

Department of Justice (DOJ) that the Census Bureau include a citizenship question on the 2020 census.

In the memorandum, the Secretary granted DOJ's request and provided his rationale for doing so. The memorandum noted that, by law, the list of questions to be included on the census had to be submitted to Congress by March 31, 2018. Id. at 2. The memorandum then directed the Under Secretary to include a citizenship question. Id. Accordingly, in satisfaction of the requirements of section 141(f)(2) of title 13 and the direction contained in the memorandum, the Census Bureau delivered a report to Congress that contained its planned questions for the 2020 decennial census. The report, entitled Questions Planned for the 2020 Census and the American Community Survey, included a citizenship question. The memorandum was not submitted to Congress or to GAO as a rule under CRA.

CRA was enacted in 1996 to strengthen congressional oversight of agency rulemaking. Pub. L. No. 104-121, title II, subtitle E, 110 Stat. 857, 868 (Mar. 28, 1996), codified at 5 U.S.C. §§ 801–808. The statute requires all federal agencies to submit a report on each new rule to both Houses of Congress and to the Comptroller General before it can take effect. 5 U.S.C. § 801(a)(1)(A). The agency must submit to the Comptroller General a complete copy of the cost-benefit analysis of the rule, if any, and information concerning the agency's actions relevant to specific procedural rulemaking requirements set forth in various statutes and executive orders governing the regulatory process. Id. § 801(a)(1)(B). CRA also provides for expedited procedures under which Congress may pass a joint resolution of disapproval for a rule subject to CRA, that if enacted into law, overturns the rule. Id. §§ 801(b), 802.

CRA adopts the definition of a rule under section 551 of the Administrative Procedure Act (APA), which states in relevant part that a rule is "the whole or part of any agency statement of general or particular applicability and future effect designed to implement, interpret, or prescribe law or policy or describing the organizations, procedure or practice requirements of an agency." Id. § 804(3). CRA excludes three categories of rules from coverage: (a) rules of "particular applicability"; (b) rules "relating to agency management or personnel"; and (c) rules of "agency organization, procedure, or practice that do not substantially affect the rights or obligations of non-agency parties." *Id.*

ANALYSIS

At issue here is whether the March 26, 2018 memorandum issued by the Secretary of Commerce is a rule subject to CRA. We first address whether it meets APA's definition of a rule upon which CRA relies, and then, if it does, whether any of the CRA exceptions apply. As explained below, we conclude that the memorandum does not meet APA's definition of a rule and thus is not subject to the CRA process.

Not all agency actions constitute agency rulemaking and not all agency statements meet APA's definition of a rule. *See Golden & Zimmerman, LLC v. Domenech*, 599 F.3d 426, 431-432 (4th Cir. 2010). At issue in the *Golden* case was Bureau of Alcohol, Tobacco, Firearms and Explosives (ATF) Frequently Asked Question (FAQ) F13 featured in the *Federal Firearms Regulations Reference Guide,* an ATF publication. On appeal, the 4th Circuit Court addressed whether FAQ F13 was designed to "implement, interpret, or prescribe law" and, therefore, constituted a rule under APA. Finding that the questions and answers were not themselves designed to be enforceable rules but simply informational, the court concluded that FAQ F13 did not implement, interpret, or prescribe law or policy.

Similarly, the March 26, 2018 memorandum did not implement, interpret, or prescribe law or policy. We conclude here that the March 26, 2018 memorandum was direction from a supervisor to a subordinate to take action in conjunction with the statutory process whereby the Secretary informs Congress of the questions that will be on the census. 13 U.S.C. § 141 (f)(2). As such, the memorandum did not implement, interpret, or prescribe law or policy. Rather, the memorandum explained to the Under Secretary the Secretary's rationale for a decision with regard to the census questions and contained the Secretary's instructions to the Under Secretary to include a citizenship question in the required report to Congress.

Our conclusion is also consistent with our prior CRA opinions, which have addressed circumstances whereby the release to the public of an agency memorandum, plan, or policy statement was designed to implement, interpret, or prescribe law or policy. In those circumstances, unlike the memorandum at issue here, the agency was seeking to directly establish or implement administrative criteria or policies for nonagency parties.

For example, we examined whether a 2016 amendment to the Tongass Land and Resource Management Plan was a rule under CRA. B-238859, Oct. 23, 2017. There, the Forest Service made several changes to the plan, including changes affecting the sale of timber to nonagency parties, and established criteria for doing so. *Id.* at 5. We found that the purpose of the amendment was to implement the National Forest Management Act of 1976 which requires the Forest Service to "develop, maintain, and, as appropriate, revise land and resource management plans for units of the National Forest systems." *Id.* at 9. We also examined whether a 2013 bulletin issued by the Consumer Financial Protection Bureau (CFPB) was a rule for purposes of CRA. *See* B-329129, Dec. 5, 2017. The bulletin, intended for the use of nonagency parties, directed certain lenders to take steps to ensure they were in compliance with identified laws and regulations and provided a variety of steps and tools for that purpose. *Id.* at 3. We concluded that the bulletin was a general statement of policy for nonagency parties regarding compliance with law and regulation, and as such, was a rule subject to the requirements of CRA. *Id.* at 7.

By making the memorandum public, the agency was not engaging in any rulemaking, rather it was informing the public about both agency activities and the policy views that underlie those activities. We have previously held that agencies have inherent authority to inform the public about both agency activities and the policy views that underlie those activities. *See* B-329199, Sept. 25, 2018, B-329504, Aug. 22, 2018; B-319834, Sept. 9, 2010; B-319075, Apr. 23, 2010. We have noted that agencies have a general responsibility, even in the absence of specific direction, to inform the public of the agency's policies. B-319834, Sept. 9, 2010. For example, we concluded that appropriations for the U.S. Department of Health and Human Services (HHS) were available for HHS to disseminate information about its activities and policy views related to the Patient Protection and Affordable Care Act. B-329199.

We requested Commerce's views on whether the memorandum is a rule for purposes of CRA. Commerce shared its view that the memorandum was not a rule and merely provided an explanation of the Secretary's decision to include the question on the census. Letter from Chief Counsel for Regulation, Commerce, to Assistant General Counsel, GAO (Sept. 10, 2018).

CONCLUSION

The Secretary of Commerce's March 26, 2018 memorandum does not meet CRA's definition of a rule and is not subject to the CRA process. The memorandum was issued in conjunction with the statutory process for informing Congress of the questions that the Secretary intended to include on the 2020 decennial census. The memorandum provided direction from a supervisor to a subordinate in conjunction with that process and as such, was not designed to implement, interpret, or prescribe, law or policy.

In a recent decision issued by the United States District Court, Southern District of New York, the court found that the Secretary's decision to add a citizenship question to the 2020 decennial census violated the APA. New York v. U.S. Dept. of Commerce, Docket No. 18-cv-2921, 18-cv-5025 _ F. Supp. 3d. _, (S.D.N.Y. Jan. 15, 2019). While CRA's definition of a rule incorporates APA's definition of a rule, the matters before the district court did not involve whether the agency's actions constituted a rule under APA. Rather, the relevant issues involved allegations that the Secretary's decision violated APA because it was arbitrary and capricious and not in accordance with certain statutory provisions related to the census. We view the matters before the court as

unrelated to whether the memorandum constitutes a rule under CRA and note that it is not our intent here to weigh in on any issue before the court.
Sincerely,

Thomas H. Armstrong
General Counsel

In: A Closer Look at the 2020 Census　　　ISBN: 978-1-53616-508-1
Editor: Sille M. Schou　　　　　　　　　　© 2019 Nova Science Publishers, Inc.

Chapter 6

2020 CENSUS: ADDITIONAL ACTIONS NEEDED TO MANAGE RISK[*]

United States Government Accountability Office

ABBREVIATIONS

Bureau	Census Bureau
CIO	Chief Information Officer
Commerce	Department of Commerce
DHS	Department of Homeland Security
ERM	Enterprise Risk Management
IT	Information Technology
OIG	Office of Inspector General
OMB	Office of Management and Budget
SRQA	Self-Response Quality Assurance

---

[*] This is an edited, reformatted and augmented version of United States Government Accountability Office; Report to Congressional Requesters, Publication No. GAO-19-399, dated May 2019.

Standards for   Standards for Internal Control in the
Internal Control   Federal Government

WHY GAO DID THIS STUDY

With less than 1 year until Census Day, many risks remain. For example, the Bureau has had challenges developing critical information technology systems, and new innovations—such as the ability to respond via the internet—have raised questions about potential security and fraud risks. Fundamental to risk management is the development of risk mitigation and contingency plans to reduce the likelihood of risks and their impacts, should they occur.

GAO was asked to review the Bureau's management of risks to the 2020 Census. This chapter examines (1) what risks the Bureau has identified, (2) the risks for which the Bureau has mitigation and contingency plans, (3) the extent to which the plans included information needed to manage risk, and (4) the extent to which the Bureau's fraud risk approach aligns with leading practices in GAO's Fraud Risk Framework. GAO interviewed officials, assessed selected mitigation and contingency plans against key attributes, and assessed the Bureau's approach to managing fraud risk against GAO's Fraud Risk Framework.

WHAT GAO RECOMMENDS

GAO is making seven recommendations, including that the Bureau set clear time frames for developing mitigation and contingency plans, require that mitigation and contingency plans include all key attributes, hold risk owners accountable for carrying out their risk management responsibilities, and update its antifraud strategy to include a fraud risk tolerance and OIG referral plan. The Department of Commerce agreed with GAO's recommendations.

WHAT GAO FOUND

As of December 2018, the Census Bureau (Bureau) had identified 360 active risks to the 2020 Census. Of these, 242 required a mitigation plan and 232 had one; 146 required a contingency plan and 102 had one (see table). Mitigation plans detail how an agency will reduce the likelihood of a risk event and its impacts, if it occurs. Contingency plans identify how an agency will reduce or recover from the impact of a risk after it has been realized. Bureau guidance states that these plans should be developed as soon as possible after a risk is added to the risk register, but it does not establish clear time frames for doing so. Consequently, some risks may go without required plans for extended periods.

2020 Census Risks with Required Mitigation and Contingency Plans

Plan	Risks requiring plan	Risks with plan
Mitigation	242	232 (96%)
Contingency	146	102 (70%)

Source: GAO analysis of U.S. Census Bureau 2020 Census risk registers as of December 2018. | GAO-19-399

GAO reviewed the mitigation and contingency plans in detail for six risks which the Bureau identified as among the major concerns that could affect the 2020 Census. These included cybersecurity incidents and integration of the 52 systems and 35 operations supporting the census. GAO found that the plans did not consistently include key information needed to manage the risk. For example, three of the mitigation plans and five of the contingency plans did not include all key activities. Among these was the Bureau's cybersecurity mitigation plan. During an August 2018 public meeting, the Bureau's Chief Information Officer discussed key strategies for mitigating cybersecurity risks to the census— such as reliance on other federal agencies to help resolve threats—not all of which were included in the mitigation plan.

GAO found that gaps stemmed from either requirements missing from the Bureau's decennial risk management plan, or that risk owners were not fulfilling all of their risk management responsibilities. Bureau officials said that risk owners are aware of these responsibilities but do not always fulfill them given competing demands. Bureau officials also said that they are managing risks to the census, even if not always reflected in their mitigation and contingency plans. However, if such actions are reflected in disparate documents or are not documented at all, then decision makers are left without an integrated and comprehensive picture of how the Bureau is managing risks to the census.

The Bureau has designed an approach for managing fraud risk to the 2020 Census that generally aligns with leading practices in the commit, assess, and design and implement components of GAO's Fraud Risk Framework. However, the Bureau has not yet determined the program's fraud risk tolerance or outlined plans for referring potential fraud to the Department of Commerce Office of Inspector General (OIG) to investigate. Bureau officials described plans to take these actions later this year, but not for updating the antifraud strategy. Updating this strategy to include the Bureau's fraud risk tolerance and OIG referral plan will help ensure the strategy is current, complete, and conforms to leading practices.

May 31, 2019
Congressional Requesters

The federal government is constitutionally mandated to count the U.S. population every 10 years.[1] However, achieving a complete count is complex and costly. For example, the U.S. Census Bureau (Bureau) must meet certain immutable deadlines, including counting the population as of April 1, 2020 (Census Day); delivering state apportionment counts to the President by December 31, 2020; and providing redistricting data to the states by April 1, 2021. To meet these deadlines, the Bureau—an agency within the Department of Commerce—carries out thousands of interrelated activities which, for 2020, the Bureau estimates will cost $15.6 billion after adjusting for inflation to the current 2020 Census time frame (fiscal years 2012 to 2023), which would be the most expensive decennial census to

---

[1] U.S. Const., art. I, § 2, cl. 3.

date. In February 2017, we added the 2020 Census to our High-Risk List because operational and other issues were threatening the Bureau's ability to deliver a cost-effective enumeration, and the census remains on our 2019 High-Risk List as these issues have persisted.[2]

With less than 1 year remaining until Census Day, many risks remain. For example, as discussed in our high-risk reports, the Bureau decided to scale back census field testing in 2017 and 2018 citing budget uncertainty, and the Bureau has had challenges developing critical information technology systems. Moreover, new innovations—such as an option for the public to respond to the census using the internet—have raised questions about potential security and fraud risks. Adequately addressing risks is critical not just for individual operations but also for ensuring a cost-effective and high-quality census. In our prior work, we noted that problems with one operation can have a cascading effect and affect subsequent activities and thus the entire enumeration.[3]

You asked us to review the Bureau's efforts to manage risks to the 2020 Census. This chapter (1) describes the risks to the 2020 Census that the Bureau has identified, (2) identifies the risks for which the Bureau has mitigation and contingency plans, (3) assesses the extent to which the Bureau's mitigation and contingency plans included information needed to manage risk, and (4) assesses the extent to which the Bureau's approach to managing fraud risks to the 2020 Census aligns with leading practices outlined in our Fraud Risk Framework.[4]

To answer our first three objectives, we reviewed Bureau documentation of its approach to managing risks facing the 2020 Census—including its decennial risk management plan; operational plan; governance management plan; guidance and training documents; and meeting minutes and agendas from the Bureau's 2020 Census Risk Review Board, which is responsible for identifying, assessing, managing,

---

[2] GAO, *High-Risk Series: Substantial Efforts Needed to Achieve Greater Progress on High-Risk Areas*, GAO-19-157SP (Washington, D.C.: Mar. 6, 2019).

[3] GAO, *2010 Census: The Bureau's Plans for Reducing the Undercount Show Promise, but Key Uncertainties Remain*, GAO-08-1167T (Washington, D.C.: Sept. 23, 2008).

[4] GAO, *A Framework for Managing Fraud Risks in Federal Programs*, GAO-15-593SP (Washington, D.C.: July 28, 2015).

monitoring, and reporting risks to the 2020 Census. In addition, we interviewed Bureau officials responsible for overseeing risk management for the 2020 Census.

To describe what risks to the 2020 Census the Bureau has identified and the risks for which the Bureau has mitigation and contingency plans, we also reviewed the Bureau's portfolio- and program-level decennial risk registers. These registers catalogue information regarding all risks to the 2020 Census that the Bureau has identified, including risk descriptions and mitigation and contingency plans.

To assess the extent to which the Bureau's mitigation and contingency plans included information needed to manage risk, we selected a nongeneralizable sample of six risks from the Bureau's risk registers based on factors such as likelihood of occurrence and potential impact. For each selected risk, we reviewed relevant Bureau documentation— including risk mitigation and contingency plans—and we conducted semistructured interviews with the Bureau officials responsible for managing the risk. In addition, drawing principally from our Enterprise Risk Management (ERM) framework as well as secondary sources, we identified seven key attributes for risk mitigation and contingency plans to help ensure they contain the information needed to manage risks.[5] We assessed the risk mitigation and contingency plans entered in the Bureau's risk registers as of December 2018—as well as the separate mitigation and contingency plans for the six selected risks—against the seven key attributes.

To evaluate the extent to which the Bureau's approach to managing fraud risks to the 2020 Census aligns with leading practices outlined in our Fraud Risk Framework, we reviewed Bureau documentation related to the 2020 Census antifraud strategy.[6] This strategy includes a fraud risk assessment that identifies and evaluates scenarios in which fraudulent activity could impact the 2020 Census results. It also includes a risk

---

[5] GAO, *Enterprise Risk Management: Selected Agencies' Experiences Illustrate Good Practices in Managing Risk*, GAO-17-63 (Washington, D.C.: Dec. 1, 2016). To determine key attributes for mitigation and contingency plans, we also reviewed risk management publications from sources including the Office of Management and Budget, the Project Management Institute, and the Chief Financial Officers Council and Performance Improvement Council.

[6] GAO-15-593SP.

response plan that uses the fraud risk assessment to develop risk responses and its fraud detection systems. In addition, we interviewed Bureau officials responsible for antifraud efforts for the 2020 Census. We evaluated the information gathered based on selected components of our Fraud Risk Framework.

Our assessment was limited to a review of the presence or absence of leading practices from the framework, not whether they were sufficient. We also did not assess the Bureau's approach against leading practices in the "evaluate and adapt" component of the framework because the Bureau will not be able to implement practices in this component until the 2020 Census begins. Appendix I presents a more detailed description of our scope and methodology.

We conducted this performance audit from May 2018 to May 2019 in accordance with generally accepted government auditing standards. Those standards require that we plan and perform the audit to obtain sufficient, appropriate evidence to provide a reasonable basis for our findings and conclusions based on our audit objectives. We believe that the evidence obtained provides a reasonable basis for our findings and conclusions based on our audit objectives.

BACKGROUND

The decennial census produces data vital to the nation. The data are used to apportion the seats of the U.S. House of Representatives; realign the boundaries of the legislative districts of each state; allocate billions of dollars each year in federal financial assistance; and provide a social, demographic, and economic profile of the nation's people to guide policy decisions at each level of government. Furthermore, businesses, nonprofit organizations, universities, and others regularly rely on census data to support their work.

Given the importance of the decennial census to the nation, it is important for the Bureau to manage risks that could jeopardize a complete, accurate, and cost-effective enumeration. To assist federal government leaders in managing such complex and inherently risky missions across their organizations, in prior work we developed an ERM framework that, among other things, identifies essential elements for federal ERM and good practices that illustrate those essential elements.[7] Notably, these elements and practices apply at all levels of an organization and across all functions—such as those related to managing risks to the 2020 Census. Furthermore, Office of Management and Budget (OMB) Circulars No. A-11 and A-123 require federal agencies to implement ERM to ensure their managers are effectively managing risks that could affect the achievement of agency strategic objectives.[8] As discussed in our ERM Framework, ERM is a decision-making tool that allows leadership to view risks as an interrelated portfolio rather than addressing risks only within silos.

Fundamental to ERM is the development of risk mitigation and contingency plans. Mitigation plans detail how an agency will reduce the likelihood of a risk event and its impacts, should it occur. Contingency plans identify how an agency will reduce or recover from the impact of a risk after it has been realized. Among other things, these plans provide the roadmap for implementing the agency's selected risk response and the vehicle for monitoring, communicating, and reporting on the success of that response. In developing these plans, it is important that agencies keep in mind the interaction of risks and risk responses, as the response to one risk may affect the response to another or create a new risk entirely.

We also developed a Fraud Risk Framework to provide a comprehensive set of leading practices that serves as a guide for agency managers developing and enhancing efforts to combat fraud in a strategic, risk- based manner.[9] The framework is designed to focus on preventive activities, which generally offer the most cost-efficient use of resources

---

[7] See GAO-17-63.
[8] OMB, *Preparation, Submission, and Execution of the Budget*, Circular No. A-11 (June 2018); and *Management's Responsibility for Enterprise Risk Management and Internal Control*, Circular No. A-123 (July 15, 2016).
[9] GAO-15-593SP.

since they enable managers to avoid a costly and inefficient pay-and-chase model of recovering funds from fraudulent transactions after payments have been made.

THE BUREAU IDENTIFIED 360 ACTIVE RISKS TO THE 2020 CENSUS

Consistent with our ERM framework, the Bureau developed a decennial risk management plan which, among other things, requires that it identify risks to the 2020 Census at the portfolio and program levels.[10] Portfolio risks are those that could jeopardize the success of the 2020 Census as a whole, and they typically span several years with many potential risk events over the period. Program risks are narrower—they could jeopardize the success of an individual program, including the 35 operations that support the 2020 Census as well as the 2018 End-to-End Test.[11]

As of December 2018, the Bureau had identified 360 active risks to the 2020 Census—meaning the risk event could still occur and adversely impact the census.[12] Of these, 30 were at the portfolio level and 330 were at the program level. As shown in Figure 1, the greatest number of active program risks was to the Systems Engineering and Integration operation which manages the Bureau's delivery of an IT "System of Systems" to meet 2020 Census business and capability requirements. For example, the Bureau's description of one of the risks to this operation indicated that if certain key system test plans and schedules are not clearly communicated among and collaborated on by relevant Bureau teams, then the 2020 Census systems are at risk of not meeting performance, cost, and schedule goals and objectives.

---

[10] Our ERM framework identifies six essential elements for federal ERM, the second of which is risk identification. See GAO-17-63. In April 2018, the Bureau updated its decennial risk management plan and, in doing so, changed its terminology for the two risk levels from program and project to portfolio and program.

[11] See appendix II for an overview of the 35 operations.

[12] Throughout this chapter, when referring to risks we are referring to both portfolio and program risks, unless otherwise indicated.

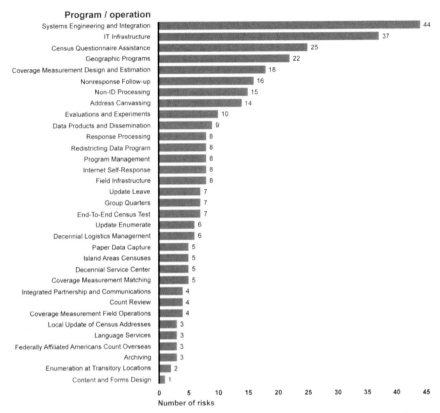

Source: GAO analysis of U.S. Census Bureau 2020 Census risk registers. | GAO-19-399

Figure 1. The Bureau Identified 330 Active Program Risks to the 2020 Census as of December 2018.

The Bureau Classified 21 Percent of Active Risks as High Priority

The Bureau's decennial risk management plan requires that it classify risks by priority level. These classifications are intended to highlight the most critical risks and identify where to allocate additional resources. Figure 2 shows how the Bureau had classified the 360 active risks as of December 2018.

2020 Census: Additional Actions Needed to Manage Risk 79

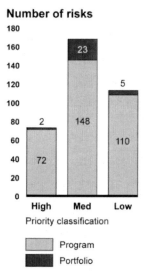

Source: GAO analysis of U.S. Census Bureau 2020 Census risk registers. | GAO-19-399

Figure 2. Active Risks to the 2020 Census as of December 2018, by Priority Classification.

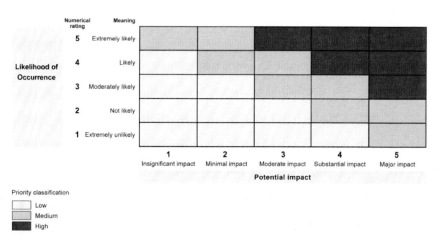

Source: GAO analysis of U.S. Census Bureau decennial risk management plan. | GAO-19-399

Figure 3. 2020 Census Risk Priority Calculation.

To determine risk priority, the Bureau's decennial risk management plan requires that it assign each risk numerical ratings for likelihood of occurrence and potential impact. When multiplied, the result is a numerical priority rating, which the Bureau divides into three classifications for high priority, medium priority, and low priority (see Figure 3).

The Bureau Determined That It Should Mitigate 67 Percent of Active Risks

According to the Bureau's decennial risk management plan, all portfolio-level risks must be mitigated to reduce the likelihood of the risk event and its impacts, should it occur. In contrast, when a program-level risk is identified, risk owners—the individuals assigned to manage each risk—are to select from the following risk responses.

- Mitigate. This may be an appropriate response where there are actions or techniques that will reduce the likelihood of the risk event and its impact, should it occur.
- Watch. This may be an appropriate response where a trigger event can be identified far enough in advance so that mitigation activities can be delayed until then.
- Accept. This may be an appropriate response where the probability and potential impact of the risk is so low that mitigation actions do not appear necessary or the impact can be absorbed if the risk occurs.

As of December 2018, the Bureau planned to mitigate 67 percent of the active risks it had identified (see Table 1). Notably, this signifies that the Bureau determined there were actions it could take or techniques it could employ to reduce the likelihood of the majority of risks to the enumeration or their impact, should they occur.[13]

THE BUREAU HAD MITIGATION AND CONTINGENCY PLANS FOR MOST RISKS, BUT NOT CLEAR TIME FRAMES FOR PLAN DEVELOPMENT AND APPROVAL OR A CLEAR STATUS FOR MITIGATION PLANS

The Bureau had Mitigation and Contingency Plans for Most Risks that Required Them

The Bureau's decennial risk management plan sets out the following requirements for developing mitigation and contingency plans:

- Mitigation plans are required for all active portfolio risks and for all active program risks with a mitigate risk response.[14]
- Contingency plans are required for all active portfolio risks with a high- or medium-priority rating, and a moderate or higher likelihood of occurrence.

Table 1. Active Risks to the 2020 Census as of December 2018, by Risk Response

Risk level	Risk response Mitigate	Risk response Watch	Risk response Accept	Total
Portfolio	30	0	0	30
Program	212	42	76	330
Total	242	42	76	360

Source: GAO analysis of U.S. Census Bureau 2020 Census risk registers. | GAO-19-399

---

[13] According to the Bureau's decennial risk management plan, there may be situations where actions or techniques exist to reduce the likelihood of a risk, but the associated cost or resources required are prohibitive and hence mitigation is not selected as the risk response.

[14] As previously discussed, the Bureau's decennial risk management plan requires risk owners to mitigate all portfolio-level risks and to mitigate, watch, or accept program-level risks.

- Contingency plans are also required for active program risks with a high- or medium-priority rating, a moderate or higher likelihood of occurrence, and a risk response of mitigate or accept.

Of the 360 active risks to the census as of December 2018, 242 (67 percent) met the Bureau's criteria for requiring a mitigation plan (see Table 2). According to the Bureau's risk registers, 232 of these risks (96 percent) had a mitigation plan. In addition, 146 of the active risks (41 percent) met the Bureau's criteria for requiring a contingency plan. According to the Bureau's risk registers, 102 of these risks (70 percent) had a contingency plan.

Our prior reporting similarly found that earlier in the decennial cycle, the Bureau did not have mitigation and contingency plans for all risks that required them. In November 2012, we found that the Bureau had mitigation and contingency plans for each of the portfolio risks it had identified at the time, but none for the program risks.[15] We reported that such plans were needed to help the Bureau fully manage associated risks, and we recommended that the Bureau develop risk mitigation and contingency plans for all program risks. In April 2014, the Bureau provided us with program-level risk registers that contained both risk mitigation and contingency plans where appropriate, and we closed the recommendation as implemented. However, as of December 2018, the Bureau is missing required mitigation and contingency plan for both portfolio and program risks.

The Bureau has not Set a Clear Time Frame for Developing Mitigation and Contingency Plans

Some of the risks that were missing required plans had been added to the risk registers in recent months, but others had been added more than 3 years earlier. Specifically, the 10 risks without mitigation plans were added

---

[15] GAO, *2020 Census: Initial Research Milestones Generally Met but Plans Needed to Mitigate Highest Risks*, GAO-13-53 (Washington, D.C.: Nov. 7, 2012).

from June to December 2018, and the 44 risks without contingency plans were added from June 2015 to December 2018. The one portfolio risk without a required mitigation plan was added in December 2018, and the five portfolio risks without required contingency plans were added in July 2015, July 2016, October 2017, August 2018, and December 2018, respectively. In some instances, a risk may not meet the Bureau's criteria for requiring a mitigation or contingency plan when first added to the risk register. However, we found that all 10 risks without required mitigation plans and 37 of the 44 risks without required contingency plans met the Bureau's criteria for requiring such plans within a month of being added to the register (of the 37 risks without a required contingency plan, five were at the portfolio level and 32 were at the program level).

Table 2. Risks to the 2020 Census with Required Mitigation and Contingency Plans, as of December 2018

Risk level	Mitigation plan		Contingency plan	
	Risks requiring plan	**Risks with plan**	**Risks requiring plan**	**Risks with plan**
Portfolio	30	29 (97%)	12	7 (58%)
Program	212	203 (96%)	134	95 (71%)
Total	242	232 (96%)	146	102 (70%)

Source: GAO analysis of U.S. Census Bureau 2020 Census risk registers. | GAO-19-399

The Bureau's decennial risk management plan states that mitigation and contingency plans should be developed as soon as possible after risks requiring such plans are added to the risk registers, but it does not include a clear time frame for doing so. According to the Bureau's 2020 Census Portfolio Risk and Issue Process Manager—responsible for developing, maintaining, and administering the risk management process for both portfolio and program risks to the 2020 Census—no time frame is included because risk owners are aware of their responsibility and a specific time frame would not speed up the process given competing demands on their time.

> **Example of 2020 Census Risk without Required Contingency Plan**
>
> In July 2016, the Bureau added a risk titled, Major Disasters, to its portfolio risk register. The Bureau's description of the risk stated that if a major disaster—such as an earthquake—occurs during final preparations for or implementation of the 2020 Census, then census operations may not be executed as planned, leading to increased costs, schedule delays, or lower quality data.
>
> Leading up to the 2010 Census, Hurricane Katrina devastated the coastal communities of Louisiana, Mississippi, and Alabama; a few weeks later, Hurricane Rita cut across Texas and Louisiana. Damage was widespread. Among other things, in the aftermath of Katrina, the Red Cross estimated that nearly 525,000 people were displaced and their homes were declared uninhabitable.
>
> If a major disaster, such as a hurricane, occurs leading up to or during the 2020 Census, having a contingency plan would help ensure that housing units and their residents are accurately counted, particularly when hundreds of thousands of people— temporarily or permanently—may migrate to other areas of the country. As of December 2018, however, the Bureau had neither a draft nor approved contingency plan for this risk, although it required one since first added to the risk register nearly 2.5 years earlier.
>
> According to the Bureau, though not documented in a contingency plan, it is taking actions to respond if this risk is realized. However, if such actions are reflected in disparate documents or no documents at all, then decision makers are left without a comprehensive picture of how the Bureau is managing this risk to the 2020 Census.
>
> Source: GAO analysis of U.S. Census Bureau 2020 Census risk registers and prior work. | GAO-19-399

However, the official said the Bureau would consider adding a specific time frame when it updates the decennial risk management plan in 2019. *Standards for Internal Control in the Federal Government* (*Standards for Internal Control*) states that management should define objectives in specific terms—including the time frames for achievement—so that they are understood at all levels of the entity.[16] In addition, OMB Circular No. A-123 states that effective risk management is systematic, structured, and timely. Without setting a clear time frame for developing mitigation and contingency plans, some risks may go without them for extended periods, potentially leaving the 2020 Census open to the impact of unmanaged risks.

The Bureau's Risk Registers Clearly Indicated the Status of Contingency but not Mitigation Plans

The Bureau's decennial risk management plan requires that both portfolio and program risk registers include the word "draft" or "approved" alongside each contingency plan. As of December 2018, this status showed that 41 percent of contingency plans in the Bureau's risk registers were still in draft form and had not been approved by management (29 percent at the portfolio level and 42 percent at the program level). Specifically, management had approved 60 of the 102 contingency plans (five at the portfolio level and 55 at the program level) but not the remaining 42 (two at the portfolio level and 40 at the program level).

On the other hand, the Bureau's decennial risk management plan includes no requirements for indicating the status of either portfolio or program risk mitigation plans in the risk registers. Our review of the risk registers found that some of the portfolio risk mitigation plans included the word "draft" alongside the plan, but none included any indication of whether the plan had been approved by management. In addition, none of the program risk mitigation plans indicated whether the plan was in draft or had been approved by management, but we found that at least some appeared to be in draft. For example, one program risk mitigation plan stated that the Risk Review Board had recommended contacting three individuals for next steps; however, the plan did not appear finalized

---

[16] GAO, *Standards for Internal Control in the Federal Government*, GAO-14-704G (Washington, D.C.: Sept. 10, 2014).

because it did not discuss any next steps and it is not clear that further action had been taken.

Although the Bureau had mitigation plans in place for 96 percent of risks that required them, without a clear indication of the status of these plans in the risk registers, we were unable to determine how many had been approved by management. According to Bureau officials, the risk registers are Bureau management's primary source of information regarding risks to the census. *Standards for Internal Control* states that management should use quality information from reliable sources and clearly document internal controls to achieve the entity's objectives and respond to risks.[17] Including a clear indication of the status of both mitigation and contingency plans in the risk registers would help to support Bureau officials' management of risks to the census; in addition, it would help to ensure that those plans are finalized and that the census is not left open to unmanaged risks.

The Bureau Does Not Have a Clear Time Frame for Obtaining Management Approval of Mitigation and Contingency Plans

Of the 42 contingency plans awaiting approval, many had been added to the risk registers in recent months, but others had been added more than 4 years earlier. Specifically, the two portfolio risks were added in September 2014 and August 2017, and the 40 program risks were added from October 2015 to December 2018. Moreover, we found that both of the portfolio risks and 34 of the 40 program risks without finalized contingency plans met the Bureau's criteria for requiring such a plan within a month of being added to the register.

The Bureau's decennial risk management plan requires risk owners to present mitigation and contingency plans to management for approval as soon as possible after risks requiring such plans are added to the risk registers. However, as with development of the mitigation and contingency plans, the Bureau's decennial risk management plan does not include a

---

[17] GAO-14-704G

clear time frame for doing so because, according to the Bureau's 2020 Census Portfolio Risk and Issue Process Manager, a specific time frame would not speed up the process given competing demands on risk owners' time. As previously noted, *Standards for Internal Control* states that management should define objectives in specific terms—including the time frames for achievement—so that they are understood at all levels of the entity.[18] In addition, OMB Circular No. A-123 states that effective risk management is systematic, structured, and timely. Without setting a clear time frame for approving draft mitigation and contingency plans, some risks may not be finalized.

THE BUREAU DID NOT CONSISTENTLY INCLUDE KEY INFORMATION FOR MANAGING RISKS IN THE MITIGATION AND CONTINGENCY PLANS WE REVIEWED

Mitigation and contingency plans assist agencies in managing and communicating to agency stakeholders the status of risks. We reviewed the mitigation and contingency plans for six portfolio-level risks to the 2020 Census which the Bureau identified as among the "major concern that could affect the design or successful implementation of the 2020 Census" (see Table 3).[19] We found that the Bureau's mitigation and contingency plans for these risks did not consistently include key information needed to manage them. These six risks, if not properly managed, could adversely affect the cost and quality of the 2020 Census.

According to the Bureau's decennial risk management plan, for each portfolio-level risk the risk owner must develop mitigation and

---

[18] GAO-14-704G.
[19] To select these risks, we began with the 12 risks identified by the Bureau in its 2020 Census Operational Plan as the "major concerns that could affect the design or successful implementation of the 2020 Census." Next, we sorted the risks by numerical priority rating as of June 2018, a Bureau-assigned figure calculated by multiplying numerical scores for likelihood of occurrence and potential impact. We then selected the six risks with the highest priority ratings.

contingency plans using the Bureau's mitigation and contingency plan templates (see appendixes III and IV for the Bureau's templates).

Table 3. Selected Risks to the 2020 Census GAO Reviewed

Risk	Description
Administrative records and third-party data—external factors	The Bureau plans to use administrative records and third-party data for various purposes, such as reducing the need to follow up with nonrespondents through identification of vacant housing units. However, external factors or policies—such as congressional action—could prevent the Bureau from using the records and data as planned, in which case the Bureau may be unable to meet its cost goals for the census, among other impacts.
Cybersecurity incidents	The Bureau plans to put in place information technology (IT) security controls to protect the confidentiality, integrity, and availability of its IT systems and data for the 2020 Census. However, if a cybersecurity incident occurs, additional technological efforts may be required to repair or replace the systems affected to maintain secure services and data.
Insufficient levels of staff with subject-matter skillsets	Due to factors including hiring freezes, budgetary constraints, and staff eligible for retirement before 2020, the Bureau may be unable to hire and retain staff with the appropriate skillsets at sufficient levels. As a result, it may be difficult to achieve the goals and objectives of the 2020 Census.
Late operational design changes	After key planning and development milestones for the 2020 Census are completed, stakeholders may disagree with the planned innovations behind the 2020 Census and decide to modify the design, resulting in late operational design changes. In this event, costly design changes may have to be implemented, increasing the risk for a timely and complete 2020 Census.
Operations and systems integration	The Bureau plans to use 52 different IT systems to carry out 35 operations supporting the 2020 Census. If the various operations and systems are not properly integrated prior to implementation, then the strategic goals and objectives of the 2020 Census may not be met.
Public perception of ability to safeguard response data	If a substantial segment of the public is not convinced that the Bureau can safeguard its data against data breaches and unauthorized use, then response rates may be lower than projected, leading to increased cases for follow-up and greater cost.

Source: GAO analysis of U.S. Census Bureau 2020 Census risk registers. | GAO-19-399

Those templates require, among other things, that the Bureau specify key activities for reducing the likelihood of the risk and its impacts. We found that the Bureau's decennial risk management plan generally aligns with our ERM framework which is designed to help agencies, among other actions, identify, assess, monitor, and communicate risks.[20] However, we also found some instances where the Bureau's risk management plan did not require mitigation and contingency plans to include certain key attributes we identified, which we discuss below.[21] See Figure 4 for a list of key attributes that we used when reviewing mitigation and contingency plans. As indicated in the attribute descriptions, six of the seven attributes are applicable to mitigation plans. Clearly defined trigger events do not apply to mitigation plans because they signal when a risk has been realized and contingency activities must begin. Each of the seven attributes are applicable to contingency plans, although two attributes—activity start and completion dates and activity implementation status—are only applicable if the risk has been realized.

As of December 2018, the results of our review of the Bureau's mitigation and contingency plans for the six portfolio-level risks we selected were in most cases mixed: some mitigation and contingency plans aligned with a particular key attribute, while others did not (see Table 4). For two attributes—activity start and completion dates and activity implementation status—we found the Bureau generally included the relevant information across the six selected mitigation plans, which should help ensure that activities are carried out in a timely manner and that agency officials and stakeholders are informed and assured that the risks are being effectively managed.[22] On the other hand, none of the mitigation or contingency plans included a monitoring plan, which would help the Bureau to track whether plans are working as intended.

---

[20] GAO-17-63.

[21] As previously discussed, to determine key attributes for mitigation and contingency plans, we drew principally from our ERM framework, as well as risk management publications from sources including OMB, the Project Management Institute, and the Chief Financial Officers Council and Performance Improvement Council.

[22] In all the selected mitigation plans, each activity was accompanied by an indicator of its implementation status, although one plan included an incorrect implementation status for two activities. In addition, the Bureau included activity start and completion dates in all the selected mitigation plans, with the exception of two plans that each had no start date for two activities. One plan also had incorrect start and completion dates for two activities.

Attribute	Description
	Up to date Mitigation and contingency plans should be kept up to date to help ensure that they remain relevant and useful.
	All key activities Mitigation and contingency plans should include all key activities to help ensure that agency stakeholders can make well-informed decisions regarding the activities employed.
	Monitoring plan Each mitigation and contingency plan should include a description of how the agency will monitor the risk response—including performance measures and milestones, where appropriate—to help track whether the plan is working as intended.
	Activity start and completion dates Each mitigation activity—and each contingency activity for realized risks—should be assigned a clear start and completion date to help ensure that activities are carried out in a timely manner.
	Activity implementation status Each mitigation activity—and each contingency activity for realized risks—should be accompanied by an indicator of its implementation status to help inform agency stakeholders and assure them that the risk is being effectively managed.
	Individual responsible for activity completion Each mitigation and contingency plan activity should be assigned to an individual responsible for the activity's completion to help ensure accountability for successful execution.
	Clearly defined trigger events Contingency plans should include clearly defined trigger events to signal when the risk has been realized and when contingency activities should begin.

Source: GAO analysis of risk management publications from GAO and others. | GAO-19-399

Note: To determine key attributes for mitigation and contingency plans we drew principally from our ERM framework, as well as risk management publications from sources including the Office of Management and Budget, the Project Management Institute, and the Chief Financial Officers Council and Performance Improvement Council.

Figure 4. Key Attributes for Risk Mitigation and Contingency Plans.

We found that where attributes are required but not consistently implemented, the gap stems from the Bureau not always holding risk owners accountable for fulfilling all of their risk management responsibilities, such as keeping plans up to date. Bureau officials responsible for overseeing risk management for the 2020 Census stated that they encourage risk owners to complete all of their risk management responsibilities; however, risk owners do not always do so because they have competing demands on their time. Therefore, the officials said they are generally satisfied if the risk owners have completed at least some of their risk management responsibilities. However, they also agreed that risk management should be among the Bureau's top priorities and that risk owners should fulfill all of their risk management responsibilities.

Bureau officials also stated that the Bureau is managing risks to the census, even if not always reflected in the mitigation and contingency plans. We acknowledge that the Bureau is taking actions to manage risks to the 2020 Census beyond those reflected in its mitigation and contingency plans. However, if these actions are reflected in disparate documents or are not documented at all, then Bureau officials, program managers, and other decision makers are left without an integrated and comprehensive picture of how the Bureau is managing risks to the 2020 Census. Consequently, the Bureau's risk management efforts are neither clear nor transparent, which may create challenges for decision makers' ability to quickly and accurately identify essential information to set priorities, allocate resources, and restructure their efforts, as needed, to ensure an accurate and cost-effective enumeration. In addition, where mitigation and contingency plans are not clearly documented and only certain individuals know about them, there is potential for the loss of organizational knowledge, particularly as key personnel change roles or leave the agency altogether. Below we provide examples of gaps, by attribute, in the Bureau's mitigation and contingency plans for the six risks we reviewed.

Table 4. Alignment of Key Attributes with Mitigation and Contingency Plans for Selected Risks, as of December 2018

Risk	Plan	Up to date	All key activities	Monitoring plan	Activity start and completion dates	Activity implementation status	Individual responsible for activity completion	Clearly defined trigger events
Administrative records and third-party data—external factors	Mitigation	No	Yes	No	Yes	Yes	Yes	N/A
	Contingency	No	No	No	N/A	N/A	No	No
Cybersecurity incidents	Mitigation	No	No	No	Yes	Yes	No	N/A
	Contingency	No	No	No	N/A	N/A	No	No
Insufficient levels of staff with subject-matter skillsets	Mitigation	No	Yes	No	Yes	Yes	No	N/A
	Contingency	Yes	Yes	No	No	No	No	Yes
Late operational design changes	Mitigation	No	Yes	No	Yes	Yes	No	N/A
	Contingency	No	No	No	N/A	N/A	No	No
Operations and systems integration	Mitigation	No	No	No	◻ Plan did not include dates	◼ Plan included incorrect status	Yes	N/A
	Contingency	No	No	No	N/A	N/A	No	Yes
Public perception of ability to safeguard response data	Mitigation	No	No	No	◻	Yes	No	N/A
	Contingency	No	No	No	N/A	N/A	No	No

Legend: N/A = Not applicable
◻ = Plan did not include start dates, or included incorrect dates, for some activities
◼ = Plan included the incorrect implementation status for some activities
Source: GAO analysis of U.S. Census Bureau 2020 Census risk mitigation and contingency plans. | GAO-19-399

Up to Date

Keeping plans up to date helps to ensure that they remain relevant and useful. The Bureau's decennial risk management plan requires that risk mitigation plans, but not contingency plans, be kept up to date. All six mitigation plans and five of the six contingency plans were not up to date, as shown in the following examples.

Administrative Records and Third-Party Data—External Factors

Administrative records are information already provided to the government as it administers other programs, such as Social Security; third-party data are information provided by commercial entities, such as InfoUSA, which provides data from sources including property taxes, voter registrations, and telephone books. The Bureau plans to use these data for various purposes including updating the address file for the nation's housing units. However, external factors or policies could prevent the Bureau from using the records and data as planned. As of December 2018, we found that neither the mitigation nor contingency plan for this risk was up to date. The mitigation plan included 13 activities, but the status column for nine of the activities had not been updated since December 2015, one since August 2016, and three since March 2017. For example, the three activities last updated in March 2017 pertained to the Bureau's development of a communication plan for outreach to external stakeholders concerning how administrative records would be used for the 2020 Census. According to Bureau officials, they took numerous actions to communicate such use to external stakeholders, including multiple public briefings and updates to their operational plan for the 2020 Census.

However, the mitigation plan indicated that the communication plan had been drafted, but there was no indication when, or if, it had been finalized or implemented. In August 2018, the Bureau provided us a copy of the communication plan, dated April 2017. It was still in draft form. The use of administrative records and third-party data is one of four innovation areas the Bureau is implementing to reduce costs and increase accuracy for the 2020 Census.[23] Thus, it is important that the Bureau keep external stakeholders informed about its use of administrative records and third-

---

[23] The Bureau's three other innovation areas for the 2020 Census are (1) making greater use of local data, imagery, and other office procedures to build its address list; (2) improving self-response by encouraging respondents to use the internet and telephone; and (3) re-engineering field operations using technology to reduce manual effort and improve productivity.

party data for the 2020 Census by finalizing and implementing the communication plan.

Regarding the contingency plan, when we spoke to Bureau officials in August 2018 about the risk, there was no contingency plan in place. In December 2018, the Bureau provided us with a draft contingency plan for the risk, which indicated that the Bureau planned to use a rapid response approach. According to the Bureau's decennial risk management plan, this approach does not require the Bureau to specify contingency activities in the event the risk is realized. Bureau officials stated that a rapid-response approach is generally appropriate where specific contingency activities cannot be identified ahead of time. However, Bureau officials responsible for managing this risk told us that the Bureau took steps to build into the census design the ability to recover from this risk, if it is realized. Nevertheless, the Bureau has not documented these steps in its contingency plan, despite the fact that it has considered what the steps need to be.

Public Perception of Ability to Safeguard Response Data

According to the Bureau, if a substantial segment of the public is not convinced that the Bureau can safeguard its data against data breaches and unauthorized use, then response rates may be lower than projected, leading to increased cases for follow-up and greater cost. In addition, the Bureau indicates that security breaches or the mishandling of data at other government agencies or in the private sector could impact the public's perception of the Bureau's ability to safeguard its own response data, especially if a data breach at another agency were to occur close to Census Day. Multiple high-profile data breaches have affected federal agencies in recent years. For example, in 2015 the Office of Personnel Management announced that two separate but related intrusions had affected the personnel records of about 4.2 million individuals, and the systems and files related to background investigations for at least 21.5 million.

A 2017 report by the Pew Research Center found that 28 percent of Americans are not confident at all that the federal government can keep their personal information safe and secure from unauthorized users, while 12 percent have a very high level of confidence that the government can keep their personal information safe and secure. More recently, the Bureau found that roughly a quarter of respondents to a 2018 survey were concerned about the confidentiality of answers to the 2020 Census, and that racial and ethnic minorities were significantly more concerned about confidentiality than non-Hispanic whites.[24] Furthermore, Bureau officials told us they anticipate misinformation efforts similar to those used in the 2016 and 2018 national elections may be used to disrupt the 2020 Census, which could further undermine public perception of the Bureau's ability to safeguard its data.

The Bureau's mitigation plan for this risk called for it to use a Gallup poll to monitor the "public's perception, trust, and willingness to respond to the census." However, in August 2018, Bureau officials told us that Gallup was no longer conducting the relevant poll and that, instead, the Bureau planned to use an internally administered survey—referenced above—to gauge public perception. In addition, the contingency plan for this risk included an activity of creating a website of frequently asked questions on public trust, but Bureau officials stated that the activity had been added to the plan early in the process and was no longer relevant.[25] As of December 2018, neither plan was up to date, leaving Bureau management and stakeholders with inaccurate information about how the public's perception of the Bureau's ability to safeguard data is being managed.

The Bureau's decennial risk management plan requires risk owners to update mitigation plans at least monthly. However, according to officials responsible for overseeing risk management for the 2020 Census, most risk owners do not update plans monthly, instead doing so in advance of required semiannual meetings before the Bureau's 2020 Census Risk Review Board. In addition, the Bureau's decennial risk management plan states that risk owners should monitor and report the progress of contingency plans, but the plan does not specifically require contingency plans to be kept up to date. Bureau officials responsible for overseeing risk

---

[24] U.S. Census Bureau, *2020 Census Barriers, Attitudes, and Motivators Study Survey Report, A New Design for the 21st Century* (Washington, D.C.: Jan. 24, 2019).
[25] Bureau officials acknowledged this was a mitigation activity, not a contingency activity.

management for the 2020 Census acknowledged that keeping mitigation and contingency plans up to date is important and an area in which the Bureau could improve. However, Bureau officials told us that risk owners have many competing demands on their time and limited resources available to carry out their work; consequently, risk management responsibilities are not always a top priority. Keeping plans up to date is important as Census Day draws closer. When plans are not up to date, Bureau officials are left with dated information regarding how risks to the census are being managed, which limits their ability to make timely decisions about strategies to help ensure a cost-effective and complete enumeration.

All Key Activities

Including all key activities in a plan helps to ensure that agency stakeholders can make well-informed decisions regarding the activities employed. Key activities are those that directly link the agency's selected risk response to the risk itself. The Bureau's decennial risk management plan requires that risk mitigation and contingency plans include all key activities. However, three of the six mitigation plans and five of the six contingency plans did not include all key activities, as shown in the following examples.

Cybersecurity Incidents

The Bureau's information technology (IT) systems supporting the 2020 Census—including the internet self-response instrument, applications on mobile devices used for fieldwork, and data processing and storage systems—could face cybersecurity incidents, such as data breaches and denial of service attacks. According to Bureau risk documents, the Bureau planned to put IT security controls in place to protect the confidentiality, integrity, and availability of the IT systems and data. If a cybersecurity incident occurs, Bureau risk documents indicate that additional technological efforts may be required to repair or replace the systems affected to maintain secure services and data.

We have previously identified significant challenges that the Bureau faces in securing IT systems and data for the 2020 Census including ensuring that individuals gain only limited and appropriate access to census data, and making certain that security assessments are completed in a timely manner and that risks are at an acceptable level.[26] To address these and other challenges, federal law requires, among other things, that the Department of Homeland Security (DHS) provide operational and technical assistance to agencies by conducting system threat and vulnerability assessments. In the last 2 years, DHS provided 17 recommendations for the Bureau to strengthen its cybersecurity efforts. Among other things, the recommendations pertained to strengthening incident management capabilities, penetration testing and web application assessments of select systems, and phishing assessments to gain access to sensitive personally identifiable information. As of February 2019, the Bureau had begun taking action to address the 17 recommendations. We have ongoing work evaluating the Bureau's actions and time frames for fully implementing the recommendations. We found that the Bureau did not include all the key activities in its mitigation plan for this risk. For example, during an August 2018 public meeting, the Bureau's Chief Information Officer (CIO) discussed the Bureau's key strategies for mitigating cybersecurity risks to the 2020 Census. However, not all of the strategies the CIO discussed were included in the Bureau's cybersecurity mitigation plan. For example, the CIO noted the Bureau's reliance on other federal agencies to provide services to resolve threats but none of the mitigation plan activities mentioned such reliance. In August 2018, when we spoke to Bureau officials responsible for managing this risk, they agreed that the mitigation strategies should be included in the mitigation plan.

In September 2018, the Bureau updated the mitigation plan to include a new activity involving, among other things, leveraging cyber threat intelligence from other federal agencies. However, cyber threat intelligence

---

[26] GAO, *2020 Census: Continued Management Attention Needed to Address Challenges and Risks with Developing, Testing, and Securing IT Systems*, GAO-18-655 (Washington, D.C.: Aug. 30, 2018).

is just one of several services being performed by outside agencies. If the Bureau's plan for mitigating cybersecurity risks to the census omits such key activities, then the Bureau is limited in its ability to track and assess those activities, and to hold individuals accountable for completing activities that could help manage cybersecurity risks.

Late Operational Design Changes

According to the Bureau, after key planning and development milestones for the 2020 Census are completed, stakeholders may disagree with the planned design and decide to modify it, resulting in late operational design changes. Bureau officials responsible for managing this risk stated that the most likely foreseeable late operational design changes were removal of a citizenship question as a result of litigation or congressional action, inability to use administrative records and third-party data as planned, and a change to the planned approach for address canvassing.[27] The mitigation plan for this activity included all key activities. However, the Bureau's contingency plan for this risk included no activities specific to these scenarios that the Bureau could carry out to lessen their adverse impact on the enumeration, should they occur. In early 2019, the U.S. District Courts for the Southern District of New York and the Northern District of California ordered removal of the citizenship question, and the Department of Justice requested that the Supreme Court rule on the issue by the end of June 2019.[28] In addition, Members of Congress introduced legislation to prevent the question.[29] Nonetheless, the Bureau's contingency plan for this risk did not have contingency activities in place to guide their actions in the event the question must be removed.

When we spoke with Bureau officials regarding these issues, they stated that the Bureau's contingency plan for this risk is a rapid response

---

[27] In March 2018, the Department of Commerce announced that the 2020 Census will ask: "Is this person a citizen of the United States?" Multiple lawsuits were filed to block the inclusion of the question.

[28] *New York v. U.S. Dept. of Commerce*, No. 18-cv-2921, (S.D.N.Y. Jan. 15, 2019); *California v. Ross*, No. 18-cv-01865, (N.D. Cal. Mar. 6, 2019).

[29] 2020 Census Accountability Act, H.R. 5292, 115th Cong. (as introduced March 15, 2018). Ensuring Full Participation in the Census Act of 2019, H.R. 1734, 116th Cong. (as introduced March 13, 2019).

approach, which does not require the Bureau to specify contingency activities in the event the risk is realized. As previously discussed, Bureau officials stated that a rapid response approach is generally appropriate where specific contingency activities cannot be identified ahead of time. However, Bureau officials told us they planned various contingency activities they would take if a late design change occurs. For example, they said they would use their change control process to assess impacts and facilitate decision-making.

In addition, they discussed various steps they would take if they must remove the citizenship question, including flexibility to make changes to the automated instruments for internet self-response, census questionnaire assistance, and nonresponse follow-up. Nevertheless the Bureau has not documented these activities in its contingency plan despite the fact that it has considered what the activities need to be. Without including all key activities in the contingency plan for this risk, the Bureau may not be able to respond as quickly to lessen any adverse impacts should a late design change occur.

Operations and Systems Integration

If the Bureau's various operations and IT systems are not properly integrated prior to implementation, then the strategic goals and objectives of the 2020 Census may not be met. In prior reporting, we have identified challenges that raise serious concerns about the Bureau's ability to manage its system development.[30] For example, the Bureau faced significant challenges in managing its schedule for developing and testing systems for operational tests that occurred in 2017 and 2018. Regarding the latter, the Bureau experienced delays in its schedule for developing systems to support the 2018 End-to- End Test. These delays compressed the time available for system and integration testing, and several systems experienced problems during the test.

As a result of the lessons learned while completing this test, the Bureau updated its system development and testing schedule for the 2020 Census.

---

[30] GAO-18-655; GAO, *2020 Census: Actions Needed to Mitigate Key Risks Jeopardizing a Cost-Effective and Secure Enumeration*, GAO-18-543T (Washington, D.C.: May 8, 2018).

However, as of February 2019, the Bureau reported that development work remained for about 39 of the 52 systems that the Bureau plans to use for the 2020 Census, as well as performance and scalability testing for about 43.

To integrate all of the key systems and infrastructure for the 2020 Census, the Bureau is relying heavily on a technical integration contractor. As we reported in August 2018, the contractor's work was initially to include evaluating the systems and infrastructure, acquiring the infrastructure to meet the Bureau's scalability and performance needs, integrating all of the systems, supporting technical testing activities, and developing plans for ensuring the continuity of operations.[31] Since the contract was awarded, the Bureau modified the scope to also include assisting with operational testing activities, conducting performance testing for two internet self-response systems, and providing technical support for the implementation of the paper data capture system.

According to the Bureau, the contractor is also involved in all mitigation steps for this risk that relate to integration planning or system development metrics, and would be involved in all contingency activities should the risk be realized. However, neither the mitigation nor contingency plans discuss, among their activities, the integral role played by the contractor in managing this risk. We have previously reported that the Bureau faced challenges in managing its significant contractor support for the 2020 Census.[32] By largely omitting the role of the technical integration contractor from the mitigation and contingency plans for this risk, Bureau management is hampered in its ability to manage key contractor support and, therefore, to respond to and manage this risk.

The Bureau's decennial risk management plan requires that risk mitigation and contingency plans include all key activities. Plans did not include all key activities because Bureau officials did not hold risk owners accountable for fulfilling all of their risk management responsibilities. When key activities are not included in risk mitigation and contingency plans, Bureau officials are hampered in their ability to make well-informed

---

[31] GAO-18-655.
[32] GAO-18-655.

decisions regarding the activities employed to manage risks to the 2020 Census, including whether those activities are appropriate or should be changed to better ensure a cost-effective and complete enumeration.

Monitoring Plan

Including a description of how the agency will monitor the risk response— with performance measures and milestones, where appropriate—helps track whether the plan is working as intended. According to our ERM framework, monitoring the risk response with performance measures allows the agency to track results and impact on the mission, and whether the risk response is successful or requires additional actions.[33] However, the Bureau's decennial risk management plan does not require that mitigation or contingency plans include a description of how the Bureau will monitor the risk response. Consequently, none of the mitigation or contingency plans included such a description.

Bureau officials told us that they plan to include a new section in the next update to their decennial risk management plan that will cover how mitigation and contingency plans are monitored once they are approved. Including such a section will be a good step toward providing clarity regarding monitoring activities; however, without risk-specific monitoring plans in its mitigation and contingency plans, the Bureau is limited in its ability to track the effectiveness of the activities in those plans, and to determine if additional actions are required to manage the various risks to the 2020 Census.

Activity Start and Completion Dates

Assigning clear start and completion dates helps ensure that activities are carried out in a timely manner. Thus, each mitigation activity, and each contingency activity for realized risks, should include a start and completion date. In accordance with the Bureau's decennial risk management plan, each of the six mitigation plans generally included this

---

[33] GAO-17-63.

attribute.[34] However, the contingency plan for the one risk that had been realized—Insufficient Levels of Staff with Subject-Matter Skillsets—did not have start or completion dates for any activity.[35] According to the Bureau's mitigation plan for this risk, factors including hiring freezes, budgetary constraints, and retirements could affect the Bureau's ability to hire and retain staff with the appropriate skillsets at sufficient levels.

Bureau officials told us that with a little more than a year until Census Day, they were facing staffing shortages. We previously reported that the Bureau experienced skills gaps in the government program management office overseeing the $886 million IT contract for integrating the IT systems needed to conduct the 2020 Census.[36] As of February 2019, 15 of the 44 positions in this office were vacant, according to Bureau officials. These vacant positions add risk that the office may not be able to provide adequate oversight of contractor cost, schedule, and performance.

The contingency plan for this risk includes seven activities, but it was not clear which ones were underway because the Bureau did not have start and completion dates in the contingency plan. As was the case with other attributes, Bureau officials did not hold risk owners accountable for fulfilling all of their risk management responsibilities. Without clear start and completion dates for contingency activities, the Bureau does not have reasonable assurance that those activities are being carried out in a timely manner.

Activity Implementation Status

Accompanying each activity with an indicator of its implementation status helps to inform agency stakeholders and assure them that the risk is

---

[34] The Bureau included activity start and completion dates in all the selected mitigation plans. However, the mitigation plan for one risk had "TBD" as the start date for two activities; Bureau officials told us the risk owner had recently changed and that the new owner would be assigning start dates soon. In addition, the mitigation plan for another risk did not have start dates for two activities, but both activities had already been completed. This plan also had incorrect start and completion dates for two activities; specifically, the start dates were in 2018 but the completion dates were in 2017.

[35] We reviewed both the contingency plan for the risk and the separate issue treatment strategy, neither of which included activity start and completion dates.

[36] GAO, *2020 Census: Actions Needed to Mitigate Key Risks Jeopardizing a Cost-Effective Enumeration*, GAO-18-215T (Washington, D.C.: Oct. 31, 2017).

being effectively managed. The Bureau's decennial risk management plan requires mitigation plans, but not contingency plans, to include indicators of implementation status for each activity. Each of the six mitigation plans generally included the implementation status for all activities.[37] However, the contingency plan for the one risk that had been realized—Insufficient Levels of Staff with Subject-Matter Skillsets—did not include an implementation status for any of its seven activities.[38] Without such indicators for contingency activities, Bureau officials are left without key information needed to determine the status of activities designed to manage realized risks.

Individual Responsible for Activity Completion

Assigning an individual responsible for completing each activity helps to ensure accountability for successful execution. However, the Bureau's decennial risk management plan contains inconsistent language regarding to whom responsibility for activity completion should be assigned. For example, in one location, the plan states that each mitigation activity should be "assigned to an individual responsible for completing the action." In another location, it states that responsibility can be assigned to an "individual, division, or team." Consequently, we found that four of the six mitigation plans and each of the six contingency plans did not assign individuals responsibility for completing each activity. Bureau officials told us that when they update their decennial risk management plan in late spring 2019, they plan to clarify that responsibility may be assigned to an "individual, division, or team." However, if groups rather than individuals are assigned responsibility for carrying out activities, there is a risk that members of the group will assume someone else is taking responsibility and the activity may not be completed.

---

[37] The Bureau included activity implementation statuses in all the selected mitigation plans. However, the mitigation plan for one risk did so incorrectly in two instances. Specifically, it included one activity with an implementation status indicating it was "on schedule and likely to be completed successfully" but the scheduled completion date had already passed. It included another activity with an implementation status indicating it was "completed and successful" but Bureau officials told us it was due to be completed in fiscal year 2019.

[38] We reviewed both the contingency plan for the risk and the separate issue treatment strategy, neither of which included activity implementation statuses.

Clearly Defined Trigger Events

Including clearly defined trigger events in contingency plans helps to signal when the risk has been realized and when contingency activities should begin. The Bureau's decennial risk management plan includes detailed requirements for contingency triggers. Specifically, it requires risk owners to define the contingency trigger in terms of specific thresholds (such as response rates falling below a minimum expected level), specific events, or specific types of events (such as natural disasters impacting field operations in one or more geographic regions). Furthermore, it notes that each risk may have more than one contingency trigger. For example, it states that a risk related to continued operations of critical infrastructure during disasters may have triggers for delayed access to certain regions or populations, limited access to certain regions or populations, and a displaced population. In addition, it notes that, for the triggers to be useful, they must be defined in such a way that it is possible to monitor the environment for their occurrence. However, we found that four of the six contingency plans did not include clearly defined trigger events, as shown in the following examples.

Public Perception of the Ability to Safeguard Data

In the contingency plan for this risk, the Bureau defines the trigger event as follows: "The public has expressed significant concern and does not trust that the Census Bureau will safeguard their response data." However, the Bureau did not specify in the plan what constitutes "a significant concern" nor did the Bureau indicate whether high levels of distrust among certain segments of the public—such as certain demographic groups—would trigger the risk. Without such specificity, the Bureau may be unaware when public concern regarding its ability to safeguard data has escalated to levels necessitating contingency activities.

We found that the trigger events for the contingency plans were not clearly defined because, as was the case with other attributes, Bureau officials did not hold risk owners accountable for greater specificity. If contingency triggers are poorly defined, the Bureau may not know when it is time to implement contingency activities to reduce the effect on the census.

After we shared the results of our analysis with the Bureau, Bureau officials updated their mitigation and contingency plans for the six risks we reviewed. In doing so, they addressed some but not all of the issues we raised. For example, in February 2019, the Bureau updated its mitigation plan for Public Perception of Ability to Safeguard Response Data by, among other things, removing the reference to a discontinued Gallup poll that they had intended to use to gauge public perception; they replaced it with a reference to an internally administered survey. Also in February 2019, the Bureau updated its contingency plan for Late Operational Design Changes by removing the term "operational" from the title and adding a reference in the risk description to potential data product design changes; however, the contingency plan did not include activities specific to the three most likely foreseeable late operational design changes.

Furthermore, as of February 2019, the Bureau did not have a finalized contingency plan for Administrative Records and Third-Party Data—External Factors, although the risk required such a plan since it was added to the risk register more than 4 years earlier. The updates to these specific risks are a positive step in the Bureau's management of those risks. However, ensuring that the mitigation and contingency plans for all risks to the 2020 Census contain the information needed to manage the risks would better position the Bureau to quickly and effectively respond to any of the risks that may occur.

Risk-Register Entries were Missing Key Information

For each portfolio and program risk mitigation and contingency plan, the Bureau's decennial risk management plan requires risk owners to enter a description of the plan in the relevant risk register. However, our review of risk register entries for both mitigation and contingency plans across all active risks as of December 2018 found they were missing some key attributes, including monitoring plans, activity start and completion dates for most activities, the implementation status for some activities, individuals responsible for activity completion, and clearly defined trigger events. In some instances, the missing attributes were a result of the Bureau not requiring them in the risk register descriptions.[39]

In other instances, where the Bureau's decennial risk management plan does require the attribute in the risk register descriptions, the gap was due to the Bureau not holding risk owners accountable for them. Some of the attributes missing from the registers were included in the separate mitigation and contingency plans.[40] However, at the program level there are no separate mitigation plans, making the risk registers the only source of information for program-level mitigation activities. According to Bureau officials, after the 2020 Census they plan to require separate mitigation plans for program risks as well. At the same time, Bureau officials noted that they primarily rely on the risk registers to monitor risks to the census and usually do not refer to the separate mitigation and contingency plans.

Standards for Internal Control states that management should use quality information from reliable sources that is appropriate, current, complete, accurate, accessible, and provided on a timely basis to achieve the entity's objectives.[41] Similarly, OMB Circular No. A-123 states that effective risk management is based on the best available information. Because the risk registers are Bureau management's primary source of information regarding risks to the census—and currently their only source of information on program-level risk mitigation—including this information in the risk registers would help to support Bureau officials' ability to manage risks to the 2020 Census.

---

[39] In particular, the Bureau's decennial risk management plan does not require that mitigation and contingency plans entered in the risk registers include monitoring plans, activity start and completion dates, implementation status for contingency activities, individuals responsible for activity completion, or clearly defined trigger events. It does, however, require the risk register entries to include all key activities and the implementation status for mitigation activities. In addition, it requires that mitigation but not contingency plans be kept up to date.

[40] Specifically, the Bureau's decennial risk management plan requires the separate plans, but not the risk register descriptions, to include activity start and completion dates and clearly defined trigger events.

[41] GAO-14-704G.

THE BUREAU'S APPROACH TO MANAGING FRAUD RISK FOR THE 2020 CENSUS GENERALLY ALIGNS WITH SELECTED COMPONENTS OF THE FRAUD RISK FRAMEWORK BUT DOES NOT YET INCLUDE A FRAUD RISK TOLERANCE OR FRAUD REFERRAL PLAN

The Bureau has designed an approach for managing fraud risk for responses to the 2020 Census.[42] We found that the approach generally aligns with leading practices in the commit, assess, and design and implement components of the Fraud Risk Framework.[43] Specifically, the Bureau demonstrated commitment to combating fraud by creating a dedicated entity to lead antifraud efforts for the 2020 Census, conducted a fraud risk assessment, and developed a risk response plan, among other actions, consistent with leading practices from the selected components.[44] However, the Bureau has not yet determined the program's fraud risk tolerance or outlined plans for referring potential fraud to the Department of Commerce Office of Inspector General (OIG) to investigate. Bureau officials described plans and milestones to address these steps but not for updating the antifraud strategy to include them. *Standards for Internal Control* states that management should clearly document internal controls to achieve the entity's objectives and respond to risks.[45] In addition, management should use quality information that is current and complete. Updating the antifraud strategy to include the Bureau's fraud risk tolerance and plan for OIG referral will help to ensure that the strategy is current, complete, and conforms to leading practices. Appendix IV presents additional details of our review of applicable leading practices.

---

[42] The Bureau's fraud risk assessment identifies and addresses fraud risks such as those posed by individuals or groups.

[43] We reviewed the Bureau's design for managing fraud risk for the 2020 Census against leading practices in three of four components—commit, assess, and design and implement components. Specifically, we focused on the design for managing fraud risk related to self-responses received via the internet questionnaire, telephone interviews conducted by Census Questionnaire Assistance staff, or paper questionnaires returned to the Census Bureau. Our assessment is limited to a review of the presence or absence of leading practices from our Fraud Risk Framework.

[44] Bureau officials refer to their risk response plan as the Concept of Operations.

[45] GAO-14-704G.

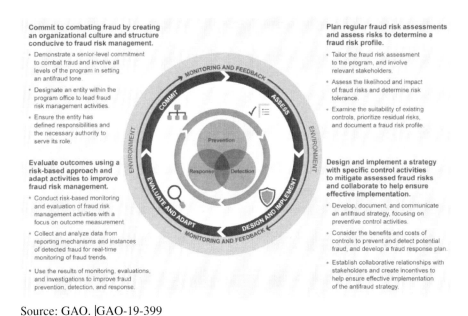

Source: GAO. |GAO-19-399

Figure 5. The Fraud Risk Management Framework and Selected Leading Practices.

Managers of federal programs maintain the primary responsibility for enhancing program integrity and managing fraud risks.[46] Those who are effective at managing their fraud risks collect and analyze data, identify fraud trends, and use the information to improve fraud risk management activities. Implementing effective fraud risk management processes is important to help ensure that federal programs fulfill their intended purpose, funds are spent effectively, and assets are safeguarded. The Fraud Risk Framework provides a comprehensive set of leading practices that serve as a guide for agency managers developing and enhancing efforts to combat fraud in a strategic, risk-based manner. The Fraud Risk Framework

---

[46] Fraud and fraud risk are distinct concepts. Fraud—obtaining something of value through willful misrepresentation—is a determination to be made through the judicial or other adjudicative system, and that determination is beyond management's professional responsibility. Fraud risk exists when individuals have an opportunity to engage in fraudulent activity, have an incentive or are under pressure to commit fraud, or are able to rationalize committing fraud. Although the occurrence of fraud indicates there is a fraud risk, a fraud risk can exist even if actual fraud has not yet been identified or occurred. When fraud risks can be identified and mitigated, agencies may be able to improve fraud prevention, detection, and response.

is also aligned with Principle 8 ("Assess Fraud Risk") of *Standards for Internal Control*.[47] It is designed to focus on preventive activities, which generally offer the most cost-efficient use of resources. The leading practices in the Fraud Risk Framework are organized into four components—commit, assess, design and implement, and evaluate and adapt—as depicted in Figure 5.

The Bureau Designated an Entity to Manage Fraud Risk and Took Steps to Develop an Organizational Culture Conducive to Fraud Risk Management

The commit component of the Fraud Risk Framework calls for an agency to commit to combating fraud by creating an organizational culture and structure conducive to fraud risk management. This component includes demonstrating a senior-level commitment to integrity and combating fraud, and establishing a dedicated entity to lead fraud risk management activities.

The Bureau has taken steps that align with all applicable leading practices in this component, according to our review. Specifically, senior-level commitment to combating fraud helps create an organizational culture to combat fraud. The Bureau showed this commitment by creating an antifraud group, made up of multiple operational divisions within the Bureau—the Decennial Census Management Division, Decennial Information Technology Division, and Decennial Contracts Execution Office—and staff from the Bureau's technical integration contractor.[48] Staff from these divisions make up the Self-Response Quality Assurance (SRQA) group with the primary purpose of identifying and responding to

---

[47] GAO-14-704G.
[48] The Bureau tasked the technical integration contractor with providing the Bureau with Fraud Detection capabilities for the 2020 Census. The technical integration contractor developed the initial drafts of the fraud risk assessment to identify and evaluate scenarios in which fraudulent activity could impact the 2020 Census results, and a risk response plan that uses the fraud risk assessment to develop risk responses and its fraud detection systems. SRQA officials provided final versions of the fraud risk assessment and risk response plan in October 2018.

potentially fraudulent responses received in the 2020 Census.[49] SRQA members were assigned roles and responsibilities to combat fraud in the 2020 Census.

Fraud Risk Framework Component

Commit to combating fraud by creating an organizational culture and structure conducive to fraud risk management

Source: GAO. | GAO-19-399

According to the framework, antifraud entities should understand the program and its operations; have defined responsibilities and the necessary authority across the program; and have a direct reporting line to senior-level managers within the agency. We found that SRQA met these leading practices through our interviews with knowledgeable officials who discussed the Bureau's strategy for managing fraud risk for the 2020 Census, and our review of documentation such as the fraud risk assessment, which listed roles and responsibilities for staff from the divisions in the antifraud group and the technical integration contractor. The group also directly reports to senior-level managers within the agency through weekly status reports that include milestones, activities, and challenges.

According to the Fraud Risk Framework, the antifraud entity, among other things, serves as the repository of knowledge on fraud risks and controls; manages the fraud risk-assessment process; leads or assists with

---

[49] In 2018, the Bureau changed the name of the operation from Fraud Detection to SRQA.

trainings and other fraud-awareness activities; and coordinates antifraud initiatives across the program. The Bureau staffed the antifraud entity with members knowledgeable of the program and tasked them with managing the fraud risk assessment process. Also, the members facilitated communication with management and among stakeholders on fraud-related issues through weekly status reports. According to SRQA officials, issues and concerns are escalated to senior-level managers on an as-needed basis so they can be coordinated across the program.

The Bureau Assessed Fraud Risks and Developed a Risk Profile but Has Not Yet Determined Fraud Risk Tolerances

The assess component of the Fraud Risk Framework calls for federal managers to plan regular fraud risk assessments and to assess risks to determine a fraud risk profile. This includes assessing the likelihood and effect of fraud risks and determining a risk tolerance. Risk tolerance is the acceptable level of variation in performance relative to the achievement of objectives. In the context of fraud risk management, if the objective is to mitigate fraud risks—in general, to have a low level of fraud—the risk tolerance reflects managers' willingness to accept a higher level of fraud risks. Risk tolerance can be either qualitative or quantitative, but regardless of the approach, *Standards for Internal Control* states that managers should consider defining risk tolerances that are specific and measurable.[50]

The first part of the fraud risk assessment process includes leading practices on tailoring the assessment to the program; planning to conduct assessments both at regular intervals and when there are changes to the program or operating environment; identifying specific tools, methods, and sources for gathering information about fraud risks; and involving relevant stakeholders in the assessment process.

---

[50] GAO-14-704G.

> **Fraud Risk Framework Component**
>
> Plan regular fraud risk assessments and assess risks to determine a fraud risk profile
>
>
>
> Source: GAO. | GAO-19-399

The Bureau has met all the leading practices in the first part of the assess component, according to our review. Specifically, the Bureau tailored the fraud risk assessment to the 2020 Census as this is the first time an internet-response option will be available for a decennial census in the United States. To identify specific tools, methods, and sources for gathering information about fraud risks, the Bureau met with relevant stakeholders, along with subject- matter experts, and conducted focus groups to develop various fraud scenarios that became a key part of the assessment. The Bureau also involved relevant stakeholders in the assessment process by outlining their roles and responsibilities for the 2020 Census. For example, the Decennial Census Management Division serves as the fraud lead and oversees managing risks such as operational implementation, methodology, and workload demands with support from the other operational divisions in the antifraud group.

According to the Fraud Risk Framework while the timing can vary, effective antifraud entities plan to conduct fraud risk assessments at regular intervals and when there are changes to the program or operating environment, as fraud risk assessments are iterative and not meant to be onetime exercises. The Bureau's assessment takes this into account by acknowledging that risk assessment is an ongoing process. The assessment also states that the SRQA team will continue to evaluate and develop modeling techniques to train against existing fraud scenarios, and SRQA welcomes input from all stakeholders to ensure the Bureau identifies fraud risks, and works to implement controls and mitigation plans throughout the 2020 Census.

The second part of the fraud risk assessment process includes identifying inherent fraud risks affecting the program; assessing the likelihood and effect of inherent fraud risks; determining a fraud risk tolerance; examining the suitability of existing fraud controls and prioritizing residual fraud risks; and documenting the program's fraud risk profile (see Figure 6).

The Bureau met three out of these five leading practices, including identifying inherent fraud risk; assigning numeric rankings for likelihood and impact of various fraud scenarios; and documenting the 2020 Census fraud risk profile, which outlines the strengths and weaknesses of the program. We concluded that one leading practice, examining the suitability of existing fraud controls and prioritizing residual fraud risks, was not applicable since the fraud detection system is new to the 2020 Census and changes the way the Bureau will detect different fraud scenarios. As a result, all fraud risks for the 2020 Census are residual risks. In reviewing the remaining leading practice in the fraud assessment processes, we found that after identifying inherent fraud risk and assigning numeric rankings for likelihood and impact of various fraud scenarios, the Bureau did not take the next step to determine a fraud risk tolerance.

Some of the steps the Bureau took to develop a risk response plan are similar to steps for developing a fraud risk tolerance. Specifically, the Bureau developed a process that classifies self-responses into risk categories of low, medium, or high. Bureau officials stated that they plan to use the classification to determine appropriate follow-up steps based on risk scores generated by its Fraud Detection Analytics Model that was develop by SRQA for the 2020 Census.[51]

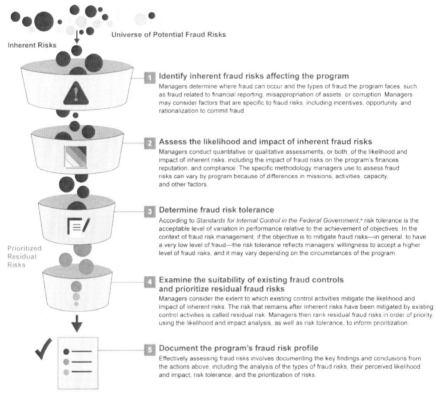

Source: GAO. | GAO-19-399

[a] GAO, *Standards for Internal Control in the Federal Government*, GAO-14-704G (Washington, D.C.: Sept. 10, 2014), 6.08.

Figure 6. Key Elements of the Fraud Risk Assessment Process.

However, the Bureau did not define thresholds for the low-, medium-, and high-risk categories. These thresholds, if defined, would meet the intent of a fraud risk tolerance by indicating the acceptable level of variation in self-responses.

---

[51] The Bureau described its Fraud Detection Analytics Models as a multilayered advanced analytical process that includes both near real-time and batch-job models that detect fraudulent responses.

SRQA officials stated that they are developing these thresholds, and therefore its fraud risk tolerance, and plan to have them completed in August 2019. This includes reviewing available information collected through the 2018 End-to-End Test, running simulations, defining thresholds, and then evaluating the results to make adjustments. Responses will receive a score, but until the Bureau defines fraud risk tolerance thresholds for the low-, medium-, and high-risk categories, it cannot effectively implement its antifraud strategy to allocate responses for follow-up or inclusion. This may also affect the Bureau's ability to evaluate and adapt its antifraud strategy if initial benchmarks are not in place to use for monitoring, with subsequent adjustments potentially requiring additional time and resources. While officials described steps and time frames to develop a fraud risk tolerance, they did not do so for updating the antifraud strategy to include the tolerance. Updating the antifraud strategy to include the Bureau's fraud risk tolerance will help to ensure that the strategy is current, complete, and conforms to leading practices.

The Bureau Designed a Response Plan and Collaborated Internally to Mitigate Fraud Risks but did not Include Plans to Refer Potential Fraud to the Office of Inspector General

The design and implement component of the Fraud Risk Framework calls for federal managers to design and implement a strategy with specific control activities to mitigate assessed fraud risks and collaborate to help ensure effective implementation. This includes determining risk responses and documenting an antifraud strategy; designing and implementing specific control activities; developing a plan outlining how the program will respond to identified instances of fraud; and establishing collaborative relationships and creating incentives to help ensure effective implementation of the antifraud strategy.

Fraud Risk Framework Component
Design and implement a strategy with specific control activities to mitigate assessed fraud risks and collaborate to help ensure effective implementation 
Source: GAO.	GAO-19-399

For determining risk responses and documenting an antifraud strategy, the framework states that managers should (a) use the fraud risk profile to help decide how to allocate resources to respond to residual fraud risks; (b) develop, document, and communicate an antifraud strategy to employees and stakeholders that describes the program's activities for preventing, detecting, and responding to fraud, as well as monitoring and evaluation; (c) establish roles and responsibilities of those involved in fraud risk management activities, such as the antifraud entity and external parties responsible for fraud controls, and communicate the role of the Office of Inspector General (OIG) to investigate potential fraud; (d) create timelines for implementing fraud risk management activities, as appropriate, including monitoring and evaluations; (e) demonstrate links to the highest internal and external residual fraud risks outlined in the fraud risk profile; and (f) link antifraud efforts to other risk management activities, if any.

The Bureau developed and documented an antifraud strategy (the fraud risk assessment and the risk response plan) and communicated it to applicable employees. Bureau officials provided final versions of the antifraud strategy in October 2018 and stated that all stakeholders were provided with excerpts applicable to their area.[52] The antifraud strategy outlines the beginning and end dates for fraud detection operations, and links to the highest residual fraud risks. The risk response includes links to other risk management activities such as a security layer that is designed, created, and maintained by the technical integration contractor security group in coordination with the Office of Information Security and Decennial Information Technology Division. According to the risk response plan, this group protects the fraud detection system and its associated systems from outside attacks such as hacks and distributed denial of service attacks.

However, we found that the Bureau's approach to managing fraud risk did not fully align with two leading practices in this component. First, until the Bureau defines its fraud risk tolerances, such as defining low-, medium-, or high-risk thresholds, it will not be able to effectively allocate resources to respond to residual fraud risks consistent with the Fraud Risk Framework's leading practices. Second, the Bureau did not initially coordinate with the Department of Commerce (Commerce) OIG about its antifraud strategy, which is not consistent with the leading practices. Such lack of coordination could have precluded the OIG from determining if potentially fraudulent activities should be investigated. After discussing the results of our review with the Bureau, the Bureau contacted and met with the Commerce OIG in February 2019. Based on the Bureau's notes from this meeting, the Bureau is on track to addressing the leading practice regarding coordination.

The framework states that to design and implement specific control activities to prevent and detect fraud, managers should (a) focus on fraud prevention over detection; (b) consider the benefits and costs of control activities to address identified residual risks; and (c) design and implement the control activities such as data-analytics to prevent and detect fraud. The 2020 Census antifraud control activities focus on detecting potentially fraudulent responses. The Bureaus plans to use a combination of data

---

[52] The antifraud strategy, which includes the fraud risk assessment and risk response plan, are considered administratively restricted and are only distributed to stakeholders with a need to know. According to Bureau officials, this is because the strategy compiles a list of risk vectors that if obtained by the public could be used to avoid detection.

analytics and follow up to review response data before they are added to the Bureau's overall Census counts. The Bureau's efforts for the 2020 Census also focus on minimizing costs. Specifically, if the Bureau's fraud detection can minimize the amount of cases that require manual investigation or work by field operations staff to collect the information again, it can reduce the cost and workload to the Bureau.

The framework states the antifraud strategy should also ensure that responses to identified instances of fraud are prompt and consistent. In addition, effective managers of fraud risks are to refer instances of potential fraud to the OIG or other appropriate parties, such as law-enforcement entities or the Department of Justice, for further investigation. The Bureau's plan describes its process for scoring responses using its Fraud Detection Analytics Model and then sorting responses into a low-, medium-, or high-risk category. The plan also outlines risk responses that depend on the risk category. For example, medium-risk responses are reviewed internally and could be incorporated into the census count or sent for additional follow up.

However, the Bureau's antifraud strategy does not call for instances of potential fraud to be referred to the Commerce OIG. Specifically, the Bureau's fraud risk assessment and risk response plan do not mention the Commerce OIG. Bureau officials stated that the Commerce OIG did not participate in the development of these documents. In February 2019, after we discussed the results of our review with the Bureau, the Bureau met with the Commerce OIG to discuss potential referrals. As a result, the Bureau agreed to develop and share with the Commerce OIG a plan that outlines a potential referral process by summer 2019.

Managers who effectively manage fraud risks collaborate and communicate with stakeholders to share information on fraud schemes and the lessons learned from fraud control activities. The framework describes collaborative relationships as including other offices within the agency; federal, state, and local agencies; private-sector partners; law- enforcement entities; and entities responsible for control activities.

In addition, managers should collaborate and communicate with the OIG to improve their understanding of fraud risks and align their efforts to address fraud. The Bureau collaborated internally with groups such as the Security Operations Center that maintain the security layer that protects Bureau systems and the nonresponse follow-up groups that visit households to collect information again. The Bureau also provided contractors with guidance by finalizing the antifraud strategy and incentives by entering into an agreement with the technical integrator contractor, which allows the Bureau to exercise an option to continue the contract for another year.[53] However, the Bureau did not begin to collaborate and communicate with the Commerce OIG to improve its understanding of fraud risks and align efforts to address fraud until after we discussed the results of our review with the Bureau.

Bureau officials viewed the primary purpose of the fraud detection system as a way to improve data reliability, according to interviews. As a result, in 2018, the Bureau changed the name of the operation from Fraud Detection to SRQA. According to Bureau officials, the change better reflects the operation's focus on detecting potential falsification in decennial census response data and referring suspected responses to a field resolution operation to collect the data again. Bureau officials initially stated that SRQA would not conduct investigations that lead to the kind of law enforcement activities traditionally associated with fraud detection. As mentioned above, the Bureau met with the Commerce OIG in February 2019 to discuss the potential for referrals and, according to the Bureau, initiate a process for doing so. However, officials did not discuss steps and a time frame for updating the antifraud strategy to include this process. Doing so will help to ensure that the strategy is current, complete, and conforms to leading practices.

---

[53] For creating incentives for employees to manage risks, we concluded that this leading practice was not applicable. Specifically, this leading practice may be more relevant at the Bureau level that covers multiple programs than just the 2020 Census that has fraud detection group specifically tasked with reviewing all self-responses submitted for the 2020 Census and identifying potential fraud.

CONCLUSION

Adequately addressing risks to the census is critical for ensuring a cost- effective and high-quality enumeration. The Bureau has taken important steps to address risks to the 2020 Census, but with less than a year until Census Day, the Bureau has not developed mitigation and contingency plans for all risks that require them. In addition, the Bureau does not have clear time frames for developing and obtaining management approval of mitigation and contingency plans, and some risks have gone without required plans for months and years. Moreover, the status of some plans is unclear and not all plans have received management approval. Some of the plans the Bureau has developed are missing key attributes we identified for helping to ensure the plans contain the information needed to manage risks. For example, none of the Bureau's plans described how the Bureau will monitor the risk response, so the Bureau may not be able to track whether the plans are working as intended. These issues have arisen in some instances because the Bureau's decennial risk management plan does not require mitigation and contingency plans to have each of the seven key attributes we identified; in other instances, the issues have arisen because Bureau officials do not always hold risk owners accountable for fulfilling all their risk management responsibilities. Consistently documenting risk management activities would support management's ability to more quickly make informed decisions in response to risks confronting the 2020 Census. It would also help protect the Bureau from losing institutional knowledge in the event risk owners change roles or leave the agency.

The Bureau's fraud risk strategy generally aligned with our Fraud Risk Framework, including developing response plans and collaborating internally to address risks. However, the Bureau has not yet determined the program's fraud risk tolerance or outlined a plan for referring potential fraud to the Commerce OIG to investigate, but plans to do so later this year. Setting a tolerance would help the Bureau monitor risks, and referring potential fraud to the Commerce OIG would allow it to determine if further investigation is appropriate. In addition to taking these actions, updating the antifraud strategy to include the Bureau's fraud risk tolerance and plan for OIG referral will help to ensure that the strategy is current, complete, and conforms to leading practices.

RECOMMENDATIONS FOR EXECUTIVE ACTION

We are making the following seven recommendations to the Department of Commerce and the Census Bureau:

The Secretary of Commerce should ensure that the Director of the Census Bureau develops and obtains management approval of mitigation and contingency plans for all risks that require them. (Recommendation 1)

The Secretary of Commerce should ensure that the Director of the Census Bureau updates the Bureau's decennial risk management plan to include clear time frames for developing and obtaining management approval of mitigation and contingency plans. (Recommendation 2)

The Secretary of Commerce should ensure that the Director of the Census Bureau updates the Bureau's decennial risk management plan to require that portfolio and program risk registers include a clear indication of the status of mitigation plans. (Recommendation 3)

The Secretary of Commerce should ensure that the Director of the Census Bureau updates the Bureau's decennial risk management plan to require that risk mitigation and contingency plans, including the risk register descriptions and separate plans, have the seven key attributes for helping to ensure they contain the information needed to manage risk. (Recommendation 4)

The Secretary of Commerce should ensure that the Director of the Census Bureau holds risk owners accountable for carrying out their risk management responsibilities. (Recommendation 5)

The Secretary of Commerce should ensure that the Director of the Census Bureau updates the Bureau's antifraud strategy to include a fraud risk tolerance prior to beginning the 2020 Census and adjust as needed. (Recommendation 6)

The Secretary of Commerce should ensure that the Director of the Census Bureau updates the Bureau's antifraud strategy to include the Bureau's plans for referring instances of potential fraud to the Department of Commerce Office of Inspector General for further investigation. (Recommendation 7)

AGENCY COMMENTS

We provided a draft of this chapter to the Secretary of Commerce. In its written comments, reproduced in appendix V, the Department of Commerce agreed with our findings and recommendations and said it would develop an action plan to address them. The Census Bureau also provided technical comments, which we incorporated as appropriate.

We are sending copies of this chapter to the Secretary of Commerce, the Director of the U.S. Census Bureau, and the appropriate congressional committees.

Robert Goldenkoff Director
Strategic Issues

Rebecca Shea Director
Forensic Audits and Investigative Service

List of Requesters

The Honorable Gary C. Peters
Ranking Member
Committee on Homeland Security and Governmental Affairs
United States Senate

The Honorable Elijah E. Cummings
Chairman

The Honorable Jim Jordan
Ranking Member
Committee on Oversight and Reform
House of Representatives

The Honorable Gerald E. Connolly
Chairman

The Honorable Mark Meadows
Ranking Member
Subcommittee on Government Operations
Committee on Oversight and Reform
House of Representatives

APPENDIX I: OBJECTIVES, SCOPE, AND METHODOLOGY

The objectives of this study were to examine (1) what risks to the 2020 Census the Census Bureau (Bureau) has identified, (2) the risks for which the Bureau has mitigation and contingency plans, (3) the extent to which the Bureau's mitigation and contingency plans included information needed to manage risk, and (4) the extent to which the Bureau's approach to managing fraud risks to the 2020 Census aligns with leading practices outlined in our Fraud Risk Framework.

To answer the first three objectives, we reviewed Bureau documentation regarding its approach to managing risks facing the 2020 Census, including its decennial risk management plan, operational plan, governance management plan, Risk Review Board meeting minutes and agendas, and guidance and training documents. In addition, we interviewed Bureau officials responsible for overseeing risk management for the 2020 Census.

To describe what risks to the 2020 Census the Bureau has identified and the risks for which the Bureau has mitigation and contingency plans, we also reviewed the Bureau's portfolio- and program-level decennial risk registers.

To assess the extent to which the Bureau's mitigation and contingency plans included information needed to manage risk, we selected a nongeneralizable sample of six risks from the Bureau's risk registers based on factors such as likelihood of occurrence and potential impact (see Table 3).

To select these risks, we began with the 12 risks identified by the Bureau in its 2020 Census Operational Plan as the "major concerns that could affect the design or successful implementation of the 2020 Census."[54] Next, we sorted the risks by numerical priority rating as of June 2018, a Bureau-assigned figure calculated by multiplying numerical scores for likelihood of occurrence and potential impact (see Figure 3). We then selected the six risks with the highest priority ratings. For each selected risk, we reviewed relevant Bureau documentation—including risk mitigation and contingency plans—and we conducted semistructured interviews with the Bureau officials responsible for managing the risk.

In addition, drawing principally from our Enterprise Risk Management (ERM) framework as well as secondary sources, we identified seven key attributes for risk mitigation and contingency plans to help ensure they contain the information needed to manage risks (see Figure 4). Specifically, we reviewed our ERM framework and other relevant prior work on risk management, as well as commonly used risk management publications from sources including the Office of Management and Budget, the Project Management Institute, and the Chief Financial Officers Council and Performance Improvement Council. We analyzed these publications to identify portions relevant to risk mitigation and contingency planning. Next, we synthesized the information and derived attributes that appeared most important for effective risk mitigation and contingency plans. We assessed the attributes against the essential elements laid out in our ERM framework and found that each attribute aligned with one or more of the elements. Six of the seven attributes—all

---

[54] U.S. Census Bureau, *2020 Census Operational Plan: A New Design for the 21st Century*, Version 3.0 (Washington, D.C.: Sept. 30, 2017).

but clearly defined trigger events—are applicable to mitigation plans. Each of the seven attributes are applicable to contingency plans, although two attributes—activity start and completion dates and activity implementation status—are only applicable if the risk has been realized. We assessed the risk mitigation and contingency plans entered in the Bureau's risk registers as of December 2018, as well as the separate mitigation and contingency plans for the six selected risks, against the seven key attributes.

To evaluate the extent to which the Bureau's approach to managing fraud risks to the 2020 Census aligns with leading practices outlined in our Fraud Risk Framework, we reviewed Bureau documentation related to the 2020 Census antifraud strategy. This strategy includes a fraud risk assessment that identifies and evaluates scenarios in which fraudulent activity could impact the 2020 Census results. It also includes a concept of operations that uses the fraud risk assessment to develop risk responses and its fraud detection systems. In addition, we interviewed Bureau officials responsible for antifraud efforts for the 2020 Census. We evaluated the information gathered based on the commit, assess, and design and implement components of our Fraud Risk Framework.

Our assessment was limited to a review of the presence or absence of leading practices from the framework, not whether they were sufficient. We also did not review the leading practices for the "evaluate and adapt" component of the framework. This component focuses on evaluating outcomes using a risk-based approach and then adapting activities established in the other components to improve fraud risk management. Because the census is not scheduled to start until 2020, the Bureau will not be able to implement leading practices such as:

- monitoring and evaluating the effectiveness of preventive activities;
- measuring outcomes, in addition to outputs, of fraud risk management activities;
- or using the results of monitoring and evaluations to improve the design and implementation of fraud risk management activities.

We conducted this performance audit from May 2018 to May 2019 in accordance with generally accepted government auditing standards. Those standards require that we plan and perform the audit to obtain sufficient, appropriate evidence to provide a reasonable basis for our findings and conclusions based on our audit objectives. We believe that the evidence obtained provides a reasonable basis for our findings and conclusions based on our audit objectives.

APPENDIX II: U.S. CENSUS BUREAU OPERATIONS SUPPORTING THE 2020 CENSUS

Table 5. 2020 Census Operations

Area	Operation	Purpose
Program Management	Program Management	Define and implement program management policies, processes, and the control functions for planning and implementing the 2020 Census to ensure an efficient and well-managed program.
Census/Survey Engineering	Systems Engineering and Integration	Manage the delivery of an Information Technology (IT) "System of Systems" to meet 2020 Census business and capability requirements.
	Security, Privacy, and Confidentiality	Ensure all 2020 Census operations and systems adhere to laws, policies, and regulations that ensure appropriate systems and data security, and protect respondent and employee privacy and confidentiality.
	Content and Forms Design	Identify and finalize content and design of questionnaires and other associated nonquestionnaire materials. Ensure consistency across data collection modes and operations. Provide optimal design and content of the questionnaires to encourage high response rates.
	Language Services	Assess and support language needs of non-English speaking populations. Determine the number of non-
		English languages and level of support for the 2020 Census. Optimize the non-English content of questionnaires and associated nonquestionnaire materials across data collection modes and operations. Ensure cultural relevancy and meaningful translation of 2020 Census questionnaires and associated nonquestionnaire materials.

Area	Operation	Purpose
Frame	Geographic Programs	Provide the geographic foundation to support 2020 Census data collection and tabulation activities within the Master Address File/Topologically Integrated Geographic Encoding and Referencing System. This system serves as the national repository for all spatial, geographic, and residential address data needed for census and survey data collection, data tabulation, data dissemination, geocoding services, and map production.
	Local Update of Census Addresses	Provide an opportunity for tribal, federal, state, and local governments to review and improve the address lists and maps used to conduct the 2020 Census as required by Public Law 103-430.
	Address Canvassing	Deliver a complete and accurate address list and spatial database for enumeration and determining the type and address characteristics for each living quarter.
Response Data	Forms Printing and Distribution	Print and distribute internet invitation letters, reminder cards or letters or both, questionnaire mailing packages, and materials for other special operations, as required. Other materials required to support field operations are handled in the Decennial Logistics Management operation.
	Paper Data Capture	Capture and convert data from the 2020 Census paper questionnaires, including mail receipt, document preparation, scanning, optical character and mark recognition, data delivery, checkout, and form destruction.
	Integrated Partnership and Communications	Communicate the importance of participating in the 2020 Census to the entire population of the 50 states, the District of Columbia, and Puerto Rico to support field recruitment efforts, engage and motivate people to self-respond (preferably via the internet), raise and keep awareness high throughout the entire 2020 Census to encourage response, and effectively support dissemination of Census data to stakeholders and the public.
	Internet Self-Response	Maximize online response to the 2020 Census via contact strategies and improved access for respondents. Collect response data via the internet to reduce paper and nonresponse follow-up.
Response Data	Non-ID Processing	Make it easy for people to respond anytime and anywhere to increase self-response rates by providing response options that do not require a unique Census ID. Maximize real-time matching of non-ID respondent addresses to the census living quarters address inventory, assigning nonmatching addresses to census blocks.

Table 5. (Continued)

Area	Operation	Purpose
	Update Enumerate	Update the address and feature data and enumerate respondents in person. Designated to occur in areas where the initial visit requires enumerating while updating the address frame, particularly in remote geographic areas that have unique challenges associated with accessibility.
	Update Leave	Update the address and feature data and leave a choice questionnaire package at every housing unit identified to allow the household to self-respond. Designed to occur in areas where the majority of housing units do not have a city-style address to receive mail.
	Group Quarters	Enumerate people living or staying in group quarters and provide an opportunity for people experiencing homelessness and receiving service at service-based locations, such as soup kitchens, to be counted in the census.
	Enumeration at Transitory Locations	Enumerate individuals in occupied units at transitory locations who do not have a usual home elsewhere, such as recreational vehicle parks, campgrounds, racetracks, circuses, carnivals, marinas, hotels, and motels.
	Census Questionnaire Assistance	Provide questionnaire assistance for respondents by answering questions about specific items on the census form or other frequently asked questions about the 2020 Census, and provide an option for respondents to complete a census interview over the telephone. Also provide outbound calling support of nonresponse follow-up reinterview and coverage improvement.
	Nonresponse Follow-up	Determine housing unit status for nonresponding addresses that do not self-respond to the 2020 Census and enumerate households that are determined to have a housing unit status of occupied.
	Response Processing	Create and distribute the initial 2020 Census enumeration universe, assign the specific enumeration strategy for each living quarter based on case status and associated paradata, create and distribute workload files required for enumeration operations, track case enumeration status, run postdata collection processing actions in preparation for producing the final 2020 Census results, and check for fraudulent returns.
	Federally Affiliated Count Overseas	Obtain counts by home state of U.S. military and federal civilian employees stationed or deployed overseas and their dependents living with them.
Publish Data	Data Products and Dissemination	Prepare and deliver the 2020 Census population counts to the President of the United States for congressional apportionment, tabulate and disseminate 2020 Census data products for use by the states for redistricting, and tabulate and disseminate 2020 Census data for use by the public.

Area	Operation	Purpose
	Redistricting Data	Provide to each state the legally required Public Law 94-171 redistricting data tabulations by the mandated deadline of 1 year from Census Day (April 1, 2021).
	Count Review	Enhance the accuracy of the 2020 Census through remediating potential gaps in coverage by implementing an efficient and equitable process to identify and correct missing or geographically misallocated large group quarters and their population, and positioning remaining count issues for a smooth transition to the Count Question Resolution Operation.
	Count Question Resolution	Provide a mechanism for governmental units to challenge their official 2020 Census results.
	Archiving	Coordinate storage of the materials and data and provide 2020 Census records deemed permanent, including files containing individual responses, to the National Archives and Records Administration and to the National Processing Center to use as source materials to conduct the Age Search Service. Also store data to cover in-house needs.
	Island Areas Censuses	Enumerate all residents of American Samoa, the Commonwealth of the Northern Mariana Islands, Guam, and the U.S. Virgin Islands; process and tabulate the collected data; and disseminate data products to the public.
Test and Evaluation	Coverage Measurement Design and Estimation	Develop the survey design and sample for the Post-Enumeration Survey of the 2020 Census and produce estimates of census coverage based on the Post-Enumeration Survey.
	Coverage Measurement Matching	Identify matches, nonmatches, and discrepancies between the 2020 Census and the Post-Enumeration Survey for both housing units and people in the same areas. Both computer and clerical components of matching are conducted.
	Coverage Measurement Field Operations	Collect person and housing unit information (independent from the 2020 Census operations) for the sample of housing units in the Post-Enumeration Survey to help understand census coverage and to detect erroneous enumerations.
	Evaluations and Experiments	Document how well the 2020 Census was conducted, and analyze, interpret, and synthesize the effectiveness of census components and their impact on data quality or coverage or both. Measure the success of critical 2020 Census operations. Formulate and execute an experimentation program to support early planning and inform the transition and design of the 2030 Census and produce an independent assessment of population and housing unit coverage.
Infrastructure	Decennial Service Center	Support 2020 Census field operations for decennial staff (i.e., headquarters, PDC, Regional Census Center, Area Census Office, Island Areas Censuses, remote workers, and listers/enumerators.)

Table 5. (Continued)

Area	Operation	Purpose
	Field Infrastructure	Provide the administrative infrastructure for data collection operations covering the 50 states, the District of Columbia, and Puerto Rico.
	Decennial Logistics Management	Coordinate space acquisition and lease management for the regional census centers, area census offices, and the Puerto Rico area office; and provide logistics management support services (e.g., kit assembly, supplies to field staff).
	IT Infrastructure	Provide the IT-related Infrastructure support to the 2020 Census, including enterprise systems and applications, 2020 Census-specific applications, Field IT infrastructure, mobile computing, and cloud computing.

Source: GAO analysis of U.S. Census Bureau 2020 Census Operational Plan. | GAO-19-399

APPENDIX III: 2020 CENSUS PORTFOLIO RISK MITIGATION AND CONTINGENCY PLAN TEMPLATES

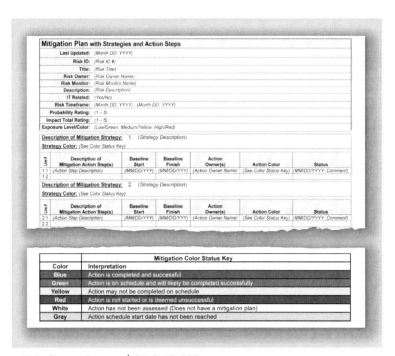

Source: U.S. Census Bureau. | GAO-19-399

Figure 7. 2020 Census Portfolio Risk Mitigation Plan Template.

SECTION I. RISK IDENTIFICATION

1. Risk ID	2. Risk Owner and Risk Monitor	3. Risk Timeframe
4. Description		

SECTION II. REALIZED RISK TRIGGER(S) & CONTINGENCY PLAN TASKS

(Copy and paste Section II for multiple triggers.)

5. Trigger Event: What event will indicate that this risk has occurred?	6. Date of the Trigger Event (*to be completed after risk becomes issue)*
7. Impacted Operations/IPTs	

8. Contingency Plan Implementation Tasks *(Insert more rows for additional tasks if needed.)*

No.	Description of the tasks to be completed if the risk occurs. Fill in dates after trigger event has occurred.	Start Date	Finish Date	Person or Area Responsible
1.				
2.				
3.				
4.				
5.				

9. What is the desired outcome of the plan? What are the results that you expect from implementing this plan?

SECTION III. CONTINGENCY PLAN STATUS

10. Is plan ready to execute? (Yes, No) If No, explain/justify why?

Please provide approval dates for Rapid Response approaches.

Source: U.S. Cenus Bureau. | GAO-19-399

Figure 8. 2020 Census Portfolio Risk Contingency Plan Template.

APPENDIX IV: LEADING PRACTICES FROM GAO'S FRAUD RISK FRAMEWORK

For the 2020 Census, the Census Bureau (Bureau) is trying to increase participation and reduce costs by offering more self-response options to households. This includes self-responses received via internet, phone, or mail. In 2018, the Self-Response Quality Assurance group finalized its antifraud strategy that includes a fraud risk assessment and risk response plan that focuses specifically on these responses. We developed a data collection instrument to structure our review of the antifraud strategy as it related to the commit, assess, and design and implement components of our Fraud Risk Framework.

Table 6. Leading Practices from GAO's Fraud Risk Framework Reflected in the Bureau's Antifraud Strategy for Self-Response Program as of February 2019

Component	Overarching concept	Leading practice	Element present
Commit	1.1 Create an Organizational Culture to Combat Fraud at All Levels of the Agency	Demonstrate a senior-level commitment to integrity and combating fraud.	Yes
		Involve all levels of the agency in setting an antifraud tone that permeates the organizational culture.	Not applicable[a]
	1.2 Create a Structure with a Dedicated Entity to Lead Fraud Risk Management Activities	Designate an entity to design and oversee fraud risk management activities that • understands the program and its operations, as well as the fraud risks and controls throughout the program; • has defined responsibilities and the necessary authority across the program; • has a direct reporting line to senior-level managers within the agency; and • is located within the agency and not the Office of Inspector General (OIG), so the latter can retain its independence to serve its oversight role.	Yes
		In carrying out its role, the antifraud entity, among other things • serves as the repository of knowledge on fraud risks and controls; • manages the fraud risk-assessment process; • leads or assists with trainings and other fraud-awareness activities; and • coordinates antifraud initiatives across the program.	Yes
Assess	2.1 Plan Regular Fraud Risk Assessments That Are Tailored to the Program	Tailor the fraud risk assessment to the program.	Yes
		Plan to conduct fraud risk assessments at regular intervals and when there are changes to the program or operating environment, as assessing fraud risks is an iterative process.	Yes

Component	Overarching concept	Leading practice	Element present
		Identify specific tools, methods, and sources for gathering information about fraud risks, including data on fraud schemes and trends from monitoring and detection activities.	Yes
		Involve relevant stakeholders in the assessment process, including individuals responsible for the design and implementation of fraud controls.	Yes
	2.2 Identify and Assess Risks to Determine the Program's Fraud Risk Profile	Identify inherent fraud risks affecting the program.	Yes
		Assess the likelihood and impact of inherent fraud risks. • Involve qualified specialists, such as statisticians and subject-matter experts, to contribute expertise and guidance when employing techniques like analyzing statistically valid samples to estimate fraud losses and frequency. • Consider the nonfinancial impact of fraud risks, including impact on reputation and compliance with laws, regulations, and standards.	Yes
Assess		Determine fraud risk tolerance.	No
		Examine the suitability of existing fraud controls and prioritize residual fraud risks.	Not applicable[b]
		Document the program's fraud risk profile.	Yes
Design and Implement	3.1 Determine Risk Responses and Document an Antifraud Strategy Based on the Fraud Risk Profile	Use the fraud risk profile to help decide how to allocate resources to respond to residual fraud risks.	Partially[c]
		Develop, document, and communicate an antifraud strategy to employees and stakeholders that describes the program's activities for preventing, detecting, and responding to fraud, as well as monitoring and evaluation.	Yes
		Establish roles and responsibilities of those involved in fraud risk management activities, such as the antifraud entity and external parties responsible for fraud controls, and communicate the role of OIG to investigate potential fraud.	Partially[d]

Table 6. (Continued)

Component	Overarching concept	Leading practice	Element present
		Create timelines for implementing fraud risk management activities, as appropriate, including monitoring and evaluations.	Yes
		Demonstrate links to the highest internal and external residual fraud risks outlined in the fraud risk profile.	Yes
		Link antifraud efforts to other risk management activities, if any.	Yes
	3.2 Design and Implement Specific Control Activities to Prevent and Detect Fraud	Focus on fraud prevention over detection and response.	Yes
		Consider the benefits and costs of control activities to address identified residual risks.	Yes
		Design and implement the following control activities to prevent and detect fraud: • data-analytics activities, • fraud-awareness initiatives, • reporting mechanisms, and • employee-integrity activities.	Yes
	3.3 Develop a Plan Outlining How the Program Will Respond to Identified Instances of Fraud	Develop a plan outlining how the program will respond to identified instances of fraud and ensure the response is prompt and consistently applied.	Yes
		Refer instances of potential fraud to the OIG or other appropriate parties, such as law-enforcement entities or the Department of Justice, for further investigation.	No
	3.4 Establish Collaborative Relationships with Stakeholders and Create Incentives to Help Ensure Effective Implementation of the Antifraud Strategy	Establish collaborative relationships with internal and external stakeholders, including other offices within the agency; federal, state, and local agencies; private-sector partners; law-enforcement entities; and entities responsible for control activities to, among other things, • share information on fraud risks and emerging fraud schemes, and • share lessons learned related to fraud control activities.	Partially[e]

Component	Overarching concept	Leading practice	Element present
		Collaborate and communicate with the OIG to improve understanding of fraud risks and align efforts to address fraud.	No
Design and Implement		Create incentives for employees to manage risks and report fraud, including • creating performance metrics that assess fraud risk management efforts and employee integrity, particularly for managers; and • balancing fraud-specific performance metrics with other metrics related to employees' duties. Provide guidance and other support and create incentives to help external parties, including contractors, effectively carry out fraud risk management activities.	Not applicable[f]

Source: GAO analysis of U.S. Census Bureau information.| GAO-19-399

[a] The Decennial Census is only one of the Bureau's programs. In this context setting an antifraud tone that permeates the organization culture would be more appropriate at the agency level and not specific to the 2020 Census.

[b] The fraud detection system is new to the 2020 Census and changes the way the Bureau will detect different fraud scenarios. As a result, all fraud risks for the 2020 Census are residual risks.

[c] Part of the fraud risk profile includes establishing a fraud risk tolerance. However, the Bureau did not define this tolerance, which affects its ability to allocate resources to respond to residual fraud risks.

[d] The Bureau did not involve the Department of Commerce (Commerce) OIG when developing their antifraud strategy.

[e] The Bureau collaborated internally with groups such as the Security Operations Center that maintain the security layer that protects Bureau systems and the nonresponse follow-up groups that visit households to collect information again. However, they did not coordinate externally with the Commerce OIG.

[f] Because the Bureau covers multiple programs, this leading practice may be more relevant across the Bureau than just the 2020 Census.

Our assessment was limited to a review of the presence or absence of leading practices from the framework, not whether they were sufficient. We also did not assess the Bureau's approach against leading practices in the "evaluate and adapt" component of the framework because the Bureau will not be able to implement practices in this component until the 2020 Census begins. The following table summarizes our comparison of the Bureau's antifraud strategy to leading practices in the fraud risk framework.

Appendix V: Comments from the Department of Commerce

UNITED STATES DEPARTMENT OF COMMERCE
The Secretary of Commerce
Washington, D.C. 20230

May 20, 2019

Mr. Robert Goldenkoff
Director, Strategic Issues
U.S. Government Accountability Office
441 G Street, NW
Washington, DC 20548

Dear Mr. Goldenkoff:

The U.S. Department of Commerce appreciates the opportunity to comment on the U.S. Government Accountability Office's (GAO) draft report titled *2020 Census: Additional Actions Needed to Manage Risk* (GAO-19-399).

The Department agrees with the GAO's findings. The U.S. Census Bureau is preparing a formal corrective action plan regarding each recommendation, including expected completion dates and our prioritization for each planned action.

Sincerely,

Wilbur Ross

APPENDIX VI: ACCESSIBLE DATA

Data Tables

Data Table for Figure 1: The Bureau Identified 330 Active Program Risks to the 2020 Census as of December 2018

Program/operation	Number of risks
Content and Forms Design	1
Enumeration at Transitory Locations	2
Archiving	3
Federally Affiliated Count Overseas	3
Language Services	3
Local Update of Census Addresses	3
Coverage Measurement Field Operations	4
Count Review	4
Integrated Partnership and Communications	4
Coverage Measurement Matching	5
Decennial Service Center	5
Island Areas Censuses	5
Paper Data Capture	5
Decennial Logistics Management	6
Update Enumerate	6
End-To-End Census Test	7
Group Quarters	7
Update Leave	7
Field Infrastructure	8
Internet Self-Response	8
Program Management	8
Redistricting Data	8
Response Processing	8
Data Products and Dissemination	9
Evaluations and Experiments	10
Address Canvassing	14
Non-ID Processing	15
Nonresponse Followup	16
Coverage Measurement Design and Estimation	18
Geographic Programs	22
Census Questionnaire Assistance	25
IT Infrastructure	37
Systems Engineering and Integration	44
Grand Total	330

Data Table for Figure 2: Active Risks to the 2020 Census as of December 2018, by Priority Classification

	Program	Portfolio	Total
High Priority	72	2	74
Medium Priority	148	23	171
Low Priority	110	5	115
Total	330	30	360

In: A Closer Look at the 2020 Census
Editor: Sille M. Schou

ISBN: 978-1-53616-508-1
© 2019 Nova Science Publishers, Inc.

Chapter 7

2020 CENSUS: BUREAU IS MAKING PROGRESS OPENING OFFICES AND RECRUITING, BUT COULD IMPROVE ITS ABILITY TO EVALUATE TRAINING[*]

United States Government Accountability Office

ABBREVIATIONS

AAAP	Automated Advanced Acquisition Program
ACO	Area Census Offices
Bureau	U.S. Census Bureau
CIS	Census Investigative Services
Commerce	Department of Commerce
e-QIP	Electronic Questionnaires for Investigations Processing System
GSA	General Services Administration

---

[*] This is an edited, reformatted and augmented version of United States Government Accountability Office; Report to Congressional Requesters, Publication No. GAO-19-602, dated July 2019.

IT	Information Technology
OF306	Optional Form 306: Declaration for Federal Employment
OIG	Office of the Inspector General
OPM	Office of Personnel Management
RCC	Regional Census Center
ROAM	Response Outreach Area Mapper
SF85	Standard Form 85: Questionnaire for Non-sensitive Positions

WHY GAO DID THIS STUDY

The decennial census is a crucial, constitutionally mandated activity with immutable deadlines. To meet these statutory deadlines, the Bureau carries out thousands of activities that need to be successfully completed on schedule for an accurate, cost-effective head count. These activities include opening area census offices, recruiting and hiring a large temporary workforce, and training that workforce.

GAO was asked to review the Bureau's plans for critical logistical support activities. This chapter (1) assesses the Bureau's progress in opening area census offices; (2) determines the extent to which the Bureau is following its field hiring and recruiting strategy for the 2020 Census; and (3) determines the extent to which the Bureau has followed its plans for training field staff, and whether this training approach is consistent with selected leading practices.

To assess the extent to which the Bureau is following its plans for opening area census offices, recruiting and hiring, and training, GAO reviewed current Bureau planning documents and schedules, and interviewed Bureau officials, including officials at the Bureau's six regional offices. GAO used its guide to training (GAO-04-546G) as criteria for selected leading practices.

WHAT GAO RECOMMENDS

The Secretary of Commerce should direct the U.S. Census Bureau to revise plans to include goals and performance measures for evaluating its new training approach. The Department of Commerce agreed with GAO's recommendation.

WHAT GAO FOUND

To help control the cost of the 2020 Census while maintaining accuracy, the Census Bureau (Bureau) is making significant changes in three areas—office space, recruiting and hiring, and training—compared to prior decennials. The Bureau is reducing its use of office space, hiring fewer census field staff, and adopting a blended training approach of instructor-led, computer-based, and hands-on training (see Figure).

Year	Office Space	Hiring For Selected Operations	Training
2010	494 offices	628,000 hired	Instructor-led
2020	248 offices	400,000 hired	Computer-based instruction

Source: GAO analysis of Census Bureau data. | GAO-19-602.

Comparison of Census Bureau 2010 and 2020 Logistical Activities.

GAO found that the Bureau generally appears to be positioned to carry out these activities as planned, if implemented properly.

Opening Offices

While the Bureau experienced early delays when regions were trying to find office space and acquire leases, Bureau officials said that the deadlines for the later phases of renovations will allow them to make up time lost. As of June 2019, there were signed leases for 247 of 248 offices.

Recruiting and Hiring

As of June 2019, the Bureau was exceeding its recruiting goals for early operations, but identified challenges in areas such as completing background checks and hiring during low unemployment, especially for partnership specialist positions. GAO will continue to monitor these challenges, as recruiting and hiring for the census continues.

Training

The Bureau generally followed its training plans for 2020 and generally followed selected leading practices for its training approach. However, GAO found that the Bureau does not have goals and performance measures for evaluating its new training approach. Without goals and performance measures the Bureau will not be able to accurately assess the cost and benefits of its new training approach.

July 19, 2019
Congressional Requesters

The decennial census is a crucial, constitutionally mandated activity with immutable deadlines.[1] The U.S. Census Bureau (Bureau) is required by law to count the population as of April 1, 2020; deliver state apportionment counts to the President by December 31, 2020; and provide

---

[1] U.S. Const. art. I, § 2, cl. 3.

redistricting data to the states by April 1, 2021. To meet these deadlines, the Bureau carries out thousands of activities that need to be successfully completed on schedule for an accurate, cost-effective head count. These activities include opening area census offices, recruiting and hiring a large temporary workforce, and training that workforce. An operation of this scale with these fixed deadlines comes at a high cost and with many risks.

The Bureau estimates the 2020 Decennial Census could cost as much as $15.6 billion after adjusting for inflation to the current 2020 Census time frame (fiscal years 2012 to 2023), which would be the most expensive decennial census to date. In February 2017, we added the 2020 Census to our High-Risk List because of operational and other issues, and the census remains on our 2019 High-Risk List as these issues have persisted.[2]

In an attempt to control escalating costs, the Bureau re-engineered its approach to the 2020 Census. Among other innovations, the Bureau is making logistical changes, such as using an electronic case management system to assign door-to-door field work for two of its largest field operations—address canvassing and nonresponse follow-up.[3] This change is intended to allow the Bureau to reduce its footprint by opening fewer offices and hiring fewer people than in 2010. The Bureau also plans to incorporate technology into its training processes, such as using web-based training.

You asked us to review the Bureau's plans for critical logistical support activities. This chapter (1) assesses the Bureau's progress in opening area census offices; (2) determines the extent to which the Bureau is following its field hiring and recruiting strategy for the 2020 Census; and (3) determines the extent to which the Bureau has followed its plans for training field staff, and whether this training approach is consistent with selected leading practices.

---

[2] GAO, *High-Risk Series: Substantial Efforts Needed to Achieve Greater Progress on High-Risk Areas,* GAO-19-157SP (Washington, D.C.: Mar. 6, 2019).

[3] The address canvassing operation has census workers verify and update addresses to ensure the Bureau has accurate address and map information for every location where a person could reside. For nonresponse follow-up, census workers visit the homes of people who did not respond to their census questionnaires and attempt to enumerate the household.

To address our objectives, we reviewed current Bureau planning documents and schedules, and we interviewed Bureau officials, including officials at the Bureau's six regional offices. To assess the status of those logistical support activities, we interviewed Bureau officials and compared the current status of the activities to the Bureau's plans, schedules, and timelines, and identified differences. We also reviewed a randomly selected non-generalizable sample of Area Census Office (ACO) files at the Philadelphia Regional Census Center (RCC) to determine whether justification was included when changes to ACO locations occurred.

As part of our analysis of the Bureau's new training approach, we compared the Bureau's planned approach to 11 selected leading practices from GAO's Guide to Assessing Strategic Training and Development Efforts in the Federal Government.[4] The guide includes four phases of training—planning/analysis, design/development, implementation, and evaluation. This chapter includes the design/development and evaluation phases of training. We did not assess the implementation phase because field staff training for the 2020 Census had not yet begun during our audit.

We also did not assess the planning/analysis phase because practices in that phase are more applicable to agency-wide rather than program-specific training development, and focus on full-time permanent employees rather than temporary employees. Within the design/development phase and evaluation phase, we did not assess all best practices because some of those best practices were also more applicable to agency-wide rather than program-specific training development, or we had already evaluated the practices such as the cost.[5] This chapter primarily focuses on training for the address canvassing and nonresponse follow-up operations. For more details on our scope and methodology, see appendix I.

---

[4] GAO, *Human Capital: A Guide for Assessing Strategic Training and Development Efforts in the Federal Government (Supersedes* GAO-03-893G*),* GAO-04-546G (Washington, D.C.: Mar. 1, 2004).

[5] GAO, *2020 Census: Census Bureau Improved the Quality of Its Cost Estimation but Additional Steps Are Needed to Ensure Reliability,* GAO-18-635 (Washington, D.C.: Aug. 17, 2018), and *2020 Census: Census Bureau Needs to Improve Its Life-Cycle Cost Estimating Process,* GAO-16-628 (Washington, D.C.: June 30, 2016).

We conducted this performance audit from August 2018 to July 2019 in accordance with generally accepted government auditing standards. Those standards require that we plan and perform the audit to obtain sufficient, appropriate evidence to provide a reasonable basis for our findings and conclusions based on our audit objectives. We believe that the evidence obtained provides a reasonable basis for our findings and conclusions based on our audit objectives.

BACKGROUND

Counting the nation's approximately 140 million households is an enormous undertaking requiring such essential logistics as the opening of hundreds of area offices to conduct essential field activities, recruiting and hiring hundreds of thousands of temporary workers to carry out those activities, and developing an approach to training those employees. To help control costs while maintaining accuracy, the Bureau is making significant changes in each of these areas compared to prior decennials.

Area Census Offices

According to Bureau planning documents, the Bureau intends to use technology to efficiently and effectively manage the 2020 Census fieldwork, and as a result, reduce the staffing, infrastructure, and brick-and-mortar footprint required for the 2020 Census. The three main components of the reengineered field operations are increased use of technology, increased management and staff productivity, and streamlined office and staffing structure.

The Bureau's 2020 Operational Plan states that 2020 Census field operations will rely heavily on automation. For example, the Bureau plans to provide most listers—temporary staff who verify and update addresses and maps—and enumerators— temporary staff who follow up with households that do not respond to the census questionnaire—with the capability to receive work assignments and perform all administrative and data collection tasks directly from a mobile device allowing them to work remotely. Supervisors will also be able to work remotely from the field and communicate with their staff via these devices—precluding them from needing access to a nearby local office.

The Bureau's 2020 Operational Plan states that these enhanced capabilities will significantly reduce the number of offices required to support 2020 Census fieldwork. In the 2010 Census, the Bureau established 12 RCCs and nearly 500 ACOs. The new design for the 2020 Census field operations includes six RCCs with 248 ACOs. Those 248 will be split into two waves, with 39 of the offices opening for Wave 1 by March 2019 to support early census operations such as in-field address canvassing, and the remaining 209 opening for Wave 2 by September 2019.

Recruiting and Hiring

Recruiting enough workers to fill the hundreds of thousands of temporary positions needed to conduct the 2020 Census is a tremendous challenge. According to Bureau plans before hiring begins, the Bureau needs to assemble an applicant pool in the millions. For the decennial census, Bureau plans indicate the Bureau will need a large and diverse workforce to ensure the accuracy of its maps and address list, and to follow up by phone or in person with households that do not respond to the questionnaire. Making these efforts even more difficult are external factors beyond the Bureau's control, such as low unemployment rate, which can make it harder to recruit.

According to Bureau plans, recruiting of potential employees will be conducted throughout the ACOs' geographic area, based on projected operational workloads and staffing models developed for 2020 Census operations. Selected candidates will be invited to be fingerprinted and submit selected appointment paperwork prior to attending classroom training. The candidates will be sworn in and hired during the first day of training.

The ACO staff model is as follows: one ACO Manager, one Lead Census Field Manager, one Administrative Manager, one Recruiting Manager, one Information Technology (IT) Manager, and Office Operations Supervisors, Clerks, and Recruiting Assistants. For data collection, it is: multiple Census Field Managers, Census Field Supervisors, and Enumerators; specific numbers based on workload; and supervisory ratios to be determined (see Figure 1).

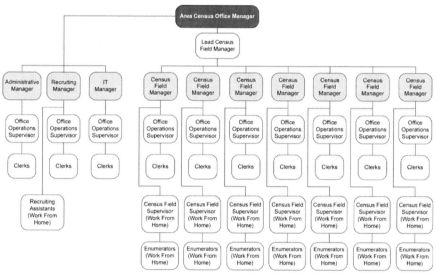

Source: GAO analysis of Census Bureau data. | GAO-19-602.

Figure 1. 2020 Census Area Census Office Structure.

Training

According to Bureau plans, the 2010 Census approach to training was predominantly instructor-led training with some hands-on training. This primarily consisted of instructors standing in front of a room of trainees and reading training materials to them from a prepared script. For 2020, the Bureau has developed training materials that use a blended training approach including instructor-led training, computer-based training, and hands-on training. This approach is intended to maximize trainee learning and on-the-job performance during the 2020 Census. According to the Bureau's Detailed Operational Plan for the Field Infrastructure and Decennial Logistics Management Operations, it has developed training materials based on the lessons learned from previous censuses, such as the need to provide computer-based training.

The Bureau's Detailed Operational Plan for the Field Infrastructure and Decennial Logistics Management Operations also states that this innovation to training combines multiple modes of training delivery designed to maximize training outcomes for various types of learning styles: visual, auditory, and hands-on, blending online training methods, instructor-led classroom training, and on-the-job training or role-playing to prepare field staff to effectively fulfill their duties. Blended training is intended to:

- Provide a standardization of training, limiting the impact of instructor interpretation.
- Allow for easily updateable training materials in the case of errors or operational changes, minimizing the burden of errata materials.
- Provide automated assessment tools to enable a more consistent and reliable way to measure learner understanding of concepts.
- Provide post-training support through easily accessible online manuals and job aids.

Training materials are designed to maximize self-paced learning. These accompanying training materials are developed to provide the most up-to- date methodologies for recruiting, onboarding, and training-the-trainer to carry out field data collection activities.

THE BUREAU'S EFFORTS TO OPEN AREA CENSUS OFFICES APPEAR ON TRACK, DESPITE SOME SCHEDULE SLIPPAGES

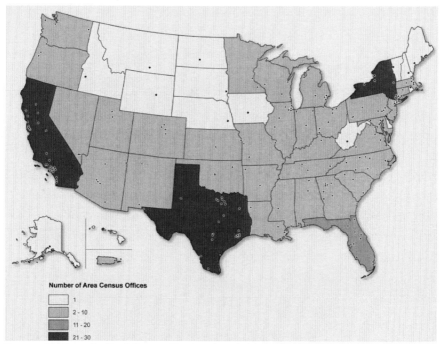

Source: GAO analysis of Census Bureau data. | GAO-19-602.

Figure 2. 2020 Census Area Census Office Locations.

For the 2020 Census, the Bureau plans to open 248 ACOs. Similar to the 2010 Census, the total number of ACOs for 2020 was derived from the projected workload for field operations based on the number of enumerators needed for nonresponse follow-up. The Bureau allotted a specific number of ACOs to each of its six regional offices.

Regions then developed boundaries for the ACO based on seven mandatory criteria that are described in a program memorandum, including that every state have at least one ACO; federally-recognized American Indian areas and military bases (regardless of county, state, or regional boundaries) will be managed by only one ACO; and ACO areas of responsibility will not cross state boundaries (with the exception of Indian reservations and military bases). See Figure 2 below for the location of the 248 offices.

Requirements for Leased Office Space for Area Census Offices

In addition to the criteria used to delineate boundaries for its ACOs, the Bureau also had requirements for the ACO leased space. These requirements, for example, included that the ACO have a certain amount of contiguous square footage depending on the ACO type, and that an ACO not be co-located in a building that also houses agencies with law enforcement responsibilities because of privacy and confidentiality concerns. The Bureau also designated an "area of consideration" for each of its ACOs. According to Bureau officials, the area of consideration, which is a smaller geographic range where they would like to house the office, was based on such factors as access to public transit, general centrality within the ACO work boundaries, and proximity to eating establishments.

In some cases, the Bureau had to deviate from its requirements for leased space or initial area of consideration. The decision to deviate from requirements usually arose from a lack of viable options in the real-estate market coupled with the Bureau's need to meet its time frames. According to RCC staff, any deviations from requirements were presented at weekly staff meetings and then subsequently approved by the Regional Director, and in some cases such as co-location with law enforcement Bureau Headquarters approval was needed.

According to Bureau officials, co-location with law enforcement is sensitive because of concerns that census data may be shared with others. Census data are kept confidential for 72 years.

However, Bureau officials told us either the law enforcement offices were deemed innocuous, for example, the office housed a public defender or the law enforcement offices operated undercover, whereby no one entering the building would have been aware of their presence.

In another case, Bureau officials told us that the Philadelphia region was struggling to find space for its ACO in Frederick, Maryland. When the General Services Administration (GSA) proposed a space in Hagerstown, Maryland, 30 miles away, the Bureau accepted it, though it was outside the initial area of consideration. According to officials at the regional office, the Bureau saved time and money by using a readily available cost-effective option by choosing Hagerstown, Maryland. The Bureau also had to expand the area of consideration for more than 31 percent or 77 of its 248 ACOs. According to Bureau officials, designating an area of consideration was an iterative process based on market availability, and having to expand the area was often necessary to secure space (see Table 1).

Table 1. Deviations from area census office requirements

Requirement	Number of Deviations
Co-location with law enforcement	11
Change from Wave 1 to Wave 2 and vice versa	3
Less square footage than initially requested	9
Co-location with other ACOs	5
Located outside ACO boundaries	6
Expanded area of consideration for ACO	77
Total	111

Source: GAO analysis of Census Bureau data. | GAO-19-602.

Note: Some ACOs had deviations from more than one requirement and summing the numbers in this table will not provide an accurate total of ACOs with deviations from requirements.

In select cases, the Bureau co-located ACOs in the same building. For example, instead of having one office in North Philadelphia and one in South Philadelphia, Bureau officials in the Philadelphia Region Census Center agreed to accept space in the same building located within the boundaries of the South Philadelphia ACO.

The Bureau hired staff for each ACO from the original designated areas and kept the two offices completely separated. Bureau officials provided documentation indicating that this compromise came with considerable cost savings.

The Bureau also abandoned other planned requirements in a number of cases to secure space, such as access to loading docks, assigned parking, and freight elevators.

When we reviewed selected ACO files at the regional offices to determine whether the files included support for when deviations from space requirements and initial areas of consideration were documented, we did not find documentation. Instead, documentation was in staff emails. Files included a checklist of documents required, such as the signed lease and design intent drawings; however, there was not a requirement that documentation of deviations from space requirements or initial areas of consideration be maintained. Bureau officials at the regional level said that all procedures for handling waivers and expansions of the area of consideration were driven by the RCCs as well as informal guidance that was not documented.

Standards for Internal Control in the Federal Government calls for documentation and records to be properly managed and maintained.[6] Based on our suggestion that the Bureau develop a procedure for documenting these deviations in ACO areas of consideration or requirements, Bureau officials sent an email requiring that staff keep documentation (electronic or paper) on deviations in ACO areas of consideration or requirements in the ACO's lease file folders. In cases where decisions are made via telephone or email, Bureau officials asked staff to write notes and scan emails, and add them to the ACO files.

Maintaining this documentation will help ensure the transparency and integrity of Bureau decision-making, and ensure the information is readily available.

---

[6] GAO, *Standards for Internal Control in the Federal Government,* GAO-14-704G (Washington, D.C.: Sept.10, 2014).

The Bureau Is Managing Schedule Slippage in Opening Area Census Offices

The Bureau experienced some early delays when regions were trying to find space and acquire leases. The Bureau attributed some of these delays to the use of the GSA's Automated Advanced Acquisition Program (AAAP) process. This procurement process provides building owners and their authorized representatives with the opportunity to offer general purpose office space for lease to the federal government. The AAAP process accepts bids the first week of each monthly cycle. Then the remaining three weeks of the month are used to evaluate submitted offers and identify a potential lessor.

According to GSA documents, in tight real estate markets, the first cycle did not always yield a suitable lessor due to lack of available inventory, and the short lease term the Bureau was seeking. Therefore, the Bureau had to wait three weeks until the start of the next cycle to re-open the bidding process. Bureau officials stated that during these 3 weeks, the Bureau regions would conduct additional market outreach and communicate outreach efforts with GSA to find a lessor.

According to GSA, they agreed that too much time was elapsing in Wave 1 trying to receive offers without making any changes to the requirements or areas of consideration. To address this issue for Wave 2, the Bureau stated that GSA provided additional training to the Bureau's regional staff, increased market outreach which included dedicated support from GSA's national office, and the development of a strategy to use all of GSA's tools, such as using GSA's contract brokers in regions with the greatest number of Wave 2 ACOs. Bureau regional staff also told us they were able to meet leasing milestones in part because of flexibility in their requirements and in the areas of consideration.

As of June 2019, there were signed leases for 247 of 248 offices. However, during our review, the Bureau reported that it had missed several construction (meaning renovations such as new electrical layouts, heating, ventilation, and air conditioning) and deployment deadlines.

According to Bureau documents, for Wave 1 offices, nine of 39 offices had missed the February 28, 2019 deadline for having furniture and IT equipment; and for Wave 2 offices, 49 of 209 offices missed the February 20, 2019 deadline for having construction drawings complete. According to Bureau officials they are managing each of these delays on an office-by-office basis, and headquarters officials meet weekly with the RCCs to discuss the status of each office. They are also actively communicating with GSA on how to best work with the landlord to meet deadlines.

Agency officials also indicated that the schedule deadlines for the later phases of construction allow for more time than may be necessary, allowing them to make up time lost from early delays. For example, at the Concord, New Hampshire ACO, the Bureau plans to make up lost time in construction with actions such as using a fence to divide two office areas instead of adding a wall, and using a "cage" for badging instead of constructing a separate room inside the space. As of June 3, 2019, 38 of 39 Wave 1 offices are ready for business. Seven of 209 Wave 2 offices are still working to finish the milestone of completing construction drawings, which had an original deadline of February 20, 2019. According to Bureau officials, the seven offices without completed construction drawings are being given priority attention by both GSA and the Bureau. We will continue to monitor the opening of ACOs in ongoing work.

THE BUREAU HAS EXCEEDED ITS EARLY RECRUITING GOALS FOR THE 2020 CENSUS; HOWEVER, IT FACES SOME CHALLENGES GOING FORWARD

The Bureau Has Exceeded Its Early Recruiting Goals

According to Bureau reporting documents, as of June 2019, the Bureau is exceeding its recruiting goals for early operations. This includes field staff for in-field address canvassing where census staff verify address and map information for housing units in selected areas of the country, office staff at the 39 Wave 1 ACOs, recruiting assistants, and partnership specialists. The Bureau had a goal of recruiting approximately 205,000 individuals for its 2020 early operations efforts by the end of June 2019, and plans to recruit between 2.4 million and 2.6 million applicants for all field operations. By comparison, in 2010, the Bureau recruited about 3.9 million applicants. As of June 17, 2019, the Bureau had processed job applications and assessments for approximately 428,000 applicants which represent about 208 percent of its roughly 205,000 recruiting goal.

For the 2020 Census, the Bureau plans to hire nearly 400,000 temporary field staff from its applicant pool for two key operations: in-field address canvassing and nonresponse follow-up, where census staff visit households that do not return census forms to collect data in person. In 2010, the Bureau hired approximately 628,000 temporary workers to conduct the address canvassing and nonresponse follow-up field operations. Below is the recruiting and hiring timeline for the in-field address canvassing and nonresponse follow-up operations (see Figure 3).

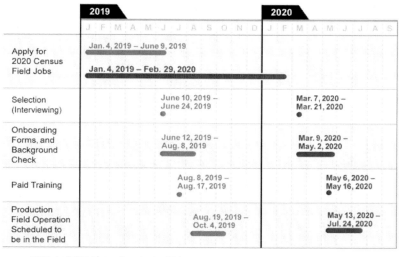

Source: GAO analysis of Census Bureau's 2020 Master Activities Schedule. | GAO-19-602.

Figure 3. Recruiting and Hiring Timeline for In-field Address Canvassing and Nonresponse Follow-up.

According to Bureau officials, they are recruiting and hiring fewer temporary staff in 2020 compared to 2010, in part, because automation has made field operations more efficient. For example, there is less paper to manage and process as daily payroll records and daily field work assignments are electronic. As a result, productivity has increased and mileage and labor costs have decreased because census field staff do not meet daily with their supervisors, as was the case in 2010. Moreover, the automation of assignment routing to housing units has optimized the time spent by enumerators driving to housing units. During the 2018 End- to- End Test, the Bureau found the productivity for in-field address canvassing had exceeded its goal at all three test sites (see Table 2). The Bureau attributes these efficiencies to the automation of work assignments.[7]

Table 2. Expected and actual productivity rates for the in-field address canvassing operation in the 2018 end-to-end test

State test site	Expected productivity rates (addresses per hour)	Actual productivity rates (addresses per hour)
Rhode Island	11.36	21.04
West Virginia	6.9	13.73
Washington	10.07	18.44

Source: GAO analysis of Census Bureau data. | GAO-19-602.

The Bureau Plans to Use Successful Recruitment Strategies from Prior Censuses while Leveraging Technology

For the 2020 Census, the Bureau plans to use some of the same strategies it used to recruit and hire all temporary workers as during the 2010 Census—because those strategies were successful—while also leveraging technology and social media. For example, according to the Bureau, the overarching strategy for hiring enumerators is to hire people who will work in the communities where they live. This strategy provides

---

[7] In May 2019, the Bureau provided revised numbers for actual productivity from what was reported in GAO, *2020 Census: Actions Needed to Improve In-Field Address Canvassing Operation,* GAO-18-414 (Washington, D.C.: June 14, 2018).

the Bureau with enumerators who are familiar with the areas where they will be working and who speak the languages of the local community. To recruit staff, recruiting assistants are to work with local partnership staff and use paid advertisements and earned media (e.g., publicity gained through promotional efforts, news reports, etc.).

The Bureau plans to also continue to use its recruiting website, http://www.2020census.gov/jobs, which provides information about the various positions, local pay rates, application materials, and job qualifications. Moreover, Bureau officials stated that a diverse multilingual workforce is needed and that the Bureau has tailored its approach to that end. For example, the website includes Spanish language pages and recruitment materials (see Figure 4).

Source: GAO analysis of Census Bureau. | GAO-19-602.

Figure 4. An Example of Census Bureau Website Spanish Language Recruitment Advertisement.

Bureau documentation indicates that similar to 2010, the Bureau will continue to use waivers and hiring exemptions to enable well-qualified individuals to work on the 2020 Census who otherwise might not have applied for jobs, particularly in hard-to-recruit areas. These waivers allow the Bureau to temporarily hire federal retirees and individuals receiving public assistance without impacting their benefits, and to hire current federal employees without impacting their job status or salary. As of February 27, 2019, the Office of Personnel Management (OPM) had given the Bureau approval to hire 44 re-employed annuitants for the 2020 Census. The Bureau also had dual employment agreements with 28 federal agencies and commissions.

For the 2010 Census, the Bureau had these agreements with a total of 81 federal agencies. To obtain waivers for individuals on public assistance, the Bureau is partnering with the Office of Management and Budget and working with Health and Human Services to obtain waivers for Temporary Assistance for Needy Families and Supplemental Nutrition Assistance Program recipients. The Bureau is also working with tribal governments to acquire similar waivers.

In addition to these previously used strategies, the Bureau is planning to leverage technology in its recruiting strategy for 2020. This technology includes the Bureau-developed Response Outreach Area Mapper (ROAM) application, a publicly available online mapping tool that Bureau staff can use to better understand the sociodemographic makeup of their assigned areas. The Bureau plans to use ROAM to identify areas where recruiting could be hard and to develop recruitment strategies such as hiring staff with specific language skills.

The new technology also includes the MOJO Recruiting Dashboard (also referred to as MOJO Recruit), which is software for Census recruiting personnel to plan and manage recruiting activities and track recruiting progress.[8] For example, MOJO Recruit includes an interactive mapping feature which lets the Bureau plan recruiting activities and track recruiting status for each census tract. The map draws attention to areas that may be experiencing recruiting problems (see Figure 5). Red indicates areas where the Bureau is less than 50 percent of the way toward meeting its recruiting goal. Yellow indicates areas where the Bureau is 50 to 79 percent of the

---

[8] MOJO is a term for the Census operational control system for re-engineered field operations.

way toward meetings its goal. Green indicates areas where the Bureau is 80 percent or higher of the way toward meetings its goal.

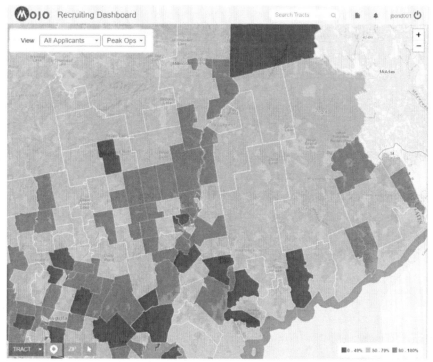

Source: Census Bureau's MOJO Recruiting Dashboard. | GAO-19-602.

Figure 5. An Example of the MOJO Recruit Interactive Map Identifying Early Operation Recruiting Status of Specific Census Tracts.

Bureau officials also stated that that they plan to increase the use of social media platforms such as Facebook, Twitter, and Instagram to promote and advertise 2020 Census job opportunities. For example, the Bureau's 2020 Census Recruitment Toolkit includes social media guidelines, tips, sample posts, and sample email messages to assist recruiting staff in providing information about 2020 Census job opportunities. It also assists recruiting staff with responding to questions and concerns or directing people to the appropriate location for more information about jobs.

The Bureau Took Steps to Improve Its Application and Assessment Process for Potential Hires

For the 2020 Census, the Bureau revised its application and assessment process to ease the burden on job applicants and to better assist the Bureau in identifying qualified applicants. Job candidates are to apply and take a skill assessment online, as opposed to attending recruiting sessions in person and taking a written test. The Bureau has also streamlined both the application and assessment process by asking fewer questions and requiring only one assessment for all nonsupervisory positions.

According to Bureau officials, the 2020 Census job application should take 10 minutes to complete, by comparison the 2010 Census job application took 30 minutes to complete. Moreover, for prior censuses, applicants had to complete one of two 45-minute assessments to determine the appropriate skill set for either working in the office or in the field. For 2020, OPM has approved the Bureau giving one assessment for all five short-term census positions: Recruiting Assistant, Clerk, Office Operations Supervisor, Enumerator, and Census Field Supervisor, thereby eliminating the need to give separate assessments for the office and field positions. Finally, for those considering a supervisor position, a separate supervisory assessment is required. For 2020, this consists of nine questions compared to 29 questions in 2010. According to Bureau officials, this supervisory assessment should take an additional 10 minutes to complete instead of 1 hour, as it did on 2010.

For 2020, the Bureau has also changed the assessment questions it asks applicants from situational-judgment questions to biodata and personality questions.[9] In making this decision, during the 2018 End-to-End Test, the Bureau asked situational-judgment questions in the assessment questionnaire, and then administered a set of biodata and personality

---

[9] OPM defines biographical data (biodata) as assessments that ask applicants questions about their past experiences. The experiences, behaviors, and events occurring throughout an individual's life can provide some indication of how an individual will perform in a job. Personality can be defined as the relatively stable pattern of thinking, feeling, and behavior that uniquely describes an individual. Personality measures that are based upon a thorough job analysis can improve the selection process over what cognitive ability measures provide by predicting how individuals will behave when faced with different situations.

questions after hiring. The Bureau conducted an analysis of both types of questions and concluded that the biodata and personality questions were a better predictor of job success. Bureau officials told us they will be evaluating their new job assessment processes for 2020, including the use of biodata.

Despite the Progress Made in Recruiting, the Bureau Still Faces Several Hiring Challenges

The Bureau has identified challenges that exist in some areas, such as: (1) delayed background checks; (2) low unemployment; and (3) language barriers.

Delayed Background Checks

Employment with the Bureau is contingent upon successfully completing a background check. The Bureau found that the process for four positions (recruiting assistants, office operation supervisors, clerks, and partnership specialists) was taking longer than it expected. These positions require a full background check because employees will have access to the Bureau's network, they will be issued expensive equipment (e.g., laptops and desktops), and their employment will likely last more than 6 months. For the full background checks, applicants must complete two security background forms—Standard Form 85: Questionnaire for Nonsensitive positions (SF85) through the Electronic Questionnaires for Investigations Processing system (e-QIP) and Optional Form 306: Declaration for Federal Employment (OF306)—and must have their fingerprints processed, in which the Federal Bureau of Investigations conducts a review for any prior arrest or convictions.[10]

---

[10] The e-QIP system is a web-based automated system that was designed to facilitate the processing of standard investigative forms used when conducting background investigations for federal security, suitability, fitness and credentialing purposes. It allows users to electronically enter, update, and transmit their personal investigative data over a secure internet connection to the requesting agency.

Once completed, the forms are reviewed by the Census Investigative Services (CIS) where OPM-trained staff make either a favorable, unfavorable, or inconclusive precheck employment determination.

According to Bureau officials, certain crimes, for example violent crimes, automatically exclude the applicant from further consideration. If the determination is inconclusive, then CIS is to send the form to the Office of Employee Relations to make a favorable or unfavorable determination. All favorable determinations are then sent to OPM for adjudication with a full background check (see Figure 6).

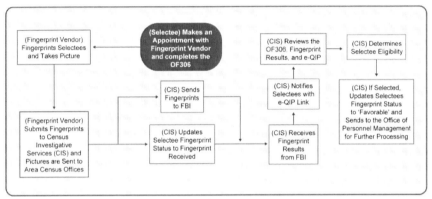

Source: GAO analysis of Census Bureau. | GAO-19-602.

Figure 6. Background Check Process for Employment with the Bureau.

According to Bureau officials, in December of 2018, they began to encounter a backlog of pre-employment background checks Bureau-wide as they began hiring some 800 recruiting assistants and about 1,970 office staff for the first wave of 39 ACO openings. As of March 21, 2019, Bureau officials told us that Bureau-wide there were 7,092 background clearances pending, of which, 4,900 were for field positions.[11] In response to the backlog, Bureau leadership said it created a team to determine the cause of the backlog and started having weekly meetings to prioritize which job positions needed to be cleared first.

---

[11] The 4,900 field positions included both the decennial census and nondecennial census surveys. However, according to Bureau officials, the majority of field positions are for the decennial census.

Bureau officials stated that the delays arose, in part, because a significant number of applicants did not completely or correctly fill out the e-QIP form. This, they said, coupled with the increase in required pre-employment background checks, resulted in a growing backlog of clearances for which the Bureau did not have the resources to clear. In response, in February 2019, the Bureau began to bring on, through a combination of new hires and reassignments, about 130 temporary staff. New staff was assigned to either review the forms for accuracy and completeness prior to being submitted to the CIS office, or help the CIS offices conduct the pre-employment background checks.

Additionally, Bureau officials told us that they meet weekly to reprioritize job positions for the clearance process. The CIS office is to process background checks for all Census employees requiring them, including decennial census field staff, decennial census contractors, and staff needed for nondecennial census surveys in headquarters and in the field. According to Bureau officials, the decennial census takes precedence and within the decennial census positions are also prioritized. For example, in January 2019, the 800 recruiting assistants were given priority and now the hiring of 1,501 partnership specialists has been given priority.

Bureau officials told us that in December 2018 they were processing 110 background checks a week, and have set a goal that each CIS analyst process 25 pre-employment packages a week. There are 40 analysts on board, giving the Bureau the ability to process 1,000 pre-employment background check packages a week. Bureau officials also told us that they anticipate the clearance process for the positions of enumerator/lister and census field supervisor will not experience the same delays because these positions only require fingerprint processing, which is quicker.

According to Bureau officials, these results can be made available within 3 hours. Moreover, although the Bureau has taken steps to address the backlog, the bulk of pre-employment background clearances has yet to be processed and Bureau officials told us that they remain concerned. In the coming months, the Bureau will need to conduct background checks for an additional 3,991 recruiting assistants and about 10,300 office staff for the remaining 209 offices. We will continue to monitor the backlog of background clearances through our ongoing work.

Low Unemployment

Although the Bureau has exceeded its recruiting goals for early operations, recruiting a sufficient number of job applicants for the job of partnership specialist is a challenge. Bureau officials told us that a robust economy and low unemployment rate have resulted in a smaller pool of applicants for that position. For example, as part of its 2020 Census efforts, the Bureau had planned to hire 1,181 partnership specialists by May 1, 2019 and 1,501 partnership specialists by June 30, 2019, to help increase awareness and participation in the 2020 Census in minority communities and hard-to-reach populations. The Bureau did not meet its goal to hire 1,181 partnership specialists by May 1, 2019.

To hire sufficient partnership staff, Bureau officials told us they have an "open and continuous" posting for partnership specialist positions instead of discrete individual job postings, and they are selecting two candidates from each certification list of qualified applicants. Moreover, Census leadership tracks the weekly progress of the partnership specialist positions.

As of July 9, 2019, the Bureau's latest biweekly reporting indicated that it had hired 813 partnership specialists as of June 22, 2019. Moreover, as of July 10, 2019 Bureau officials told us that another 830 applicants were waiting to have their background checks completed. According to Bureau officials hiring data are based on payroll dates generated biweekly, while background check data are tracked internally. Therefore, according to Bureau officials, more current hiring data were not available as of July 10, 2019 to indicate whether the Bureau had met its June 30 hiring goal. Hiring partnership specialists in a timely manner is key to the Bureau's ability to carry out its planned outreach efforts, especially for hard-to-count communities.

In addition, several RCC officials said the pay rate and the low unemployment rate in some ACO locations initially affected their ability to recruit well-qualified staff for office positions.

- Atlanta RCC officials stated it was challenging to recruit managers in the Gainesville, Florida, area. According to Bureau officials, the pay rate was too low and potential recruits were seeking employment elsewhere. The Bureau increased the managers' pay rate to be more competitive for the area.
- Philadelphia RCC officials stated that in rural ACO locations the pay rate is lower and potential recruits would rather travel to the metro areas to get the higher pay rates offered there.
- The Denver RCC reported that low unemployment rates throughout the regions make recruiting difficult, and that Census enumerators jobs are not as competitive with many other wages offered in the region.
- The Los Angeles RCC reported having difficulty recruiting local applicants in high-cost areas like Beverly Hills, the San Francisco Bay Area, and Silicon Valley.

Bureau headquarters officials acknowledge that some ACO locations have experienced some recruiting challenges, but said that the RCCs were ultimately able to fill the office positions. Headquarters officials stated that their pay rates either match or exceed the competitive pay rate in the majority of the ACO locations. According to Bureau headquarters officials, regional offices that may be experiencing challenges recruiting staff must demonstrate or prove that the pay rate for a specific ACO is causing difficulty recruiting. The Field Division is responsible for approving or denying the request to adjust pay. For the 2010 Census, the Bureau reported 124 requests for pay rate adjustments, of which 64 were approved. The Bureau stated that it will continue to monitor how low unemployment affects its ability to recruit and hire.

Language Barriers

The Bureau reports that the demographic and cultural makeup of the United States continues to increase in complexity, including a growing number of households and individuals whose proficiency in English is limited. Language barriers could make it difficult to enumerate these households, whose members may have varying levels of comfort with government involvement. Several RCC officials also mentioned that language barriers could impact their recruiting efforts:

- Both the Los Angeles and New York RCCs reported it is hard to recruit in immigrant communities where residents speak a foreign language or dialects, and often have no organizational infrastructure (such as associations of individuals of the same national origin, print news media, or radio).
- The New York RCC reported challenges in locating applicants who are bilingual in English and other languages such as Chinese, Russian, Arabic, Korean, Creole, Polish, Portuguese, Bengali, Urdu, Punjabi, Gujarati, Hindi, and Hebrew, as well as Yiddish and African languages.
- The Atlanta RCC reported challenges related to the diverse language needs (e.g., Spanish, Chinese, Vietnamese, Creole, Portuguese, etc.) in south and central Florida.
- The Chicago RCC reported recruiting outreach challenges in urban areas, including Chicago, Indianapolis, Detroit, Minneapolis/St. Paul, St. Louis, and Kansas City, that have higher minority and immigrant populations as well as in rural areas with increasing diversity.

Bureau officials responded that later this fall, in preparation for their peak operations effort, they will begin to focus recruiting efforts on foreign language recruiting. Specifically, partnership and recruiting staff plan to work with partners and advertise jobs locally (at the grassroots level) in places where persons with these skills are likely to look to ensure they are meeting recruiting goals in those areas.

THE BUREAU IS FOLLOWING ITS PLANNED TRAINING APPROACH FOR 2020, BUT HAS OPPORTUNITIES TO IMPROVE ITS ABILITY TO ASSESS PERFORMANCE

For the 2020 Census, the Bureau is following its plans to use a blended training approach combining technology-assisted training with classroom instruction.[12] According to Bureau planning documents, on the first day of in-person classroom training, the Bureau will provide orientation information and issue devices that trainees will use to conduct census operations. The Bureau plans to use local institutions such as schools, libraries, churches, and fire halls to host training. ACO staff are to coordinate the training location setup, device deliveries to training sites, and manage other logistics for large-scale field staff training.

After the first day of training, field staff will spend the next 4 to 6 days (depending on the operation) completing at-home training online using their own personal device at their own pace. This training will include, for example, operation-specific skills, use of the data collection device (smart phone or tablet), and general field processes. Trainees who complete the online portion of the training program will return to the classroom to practice what they learned through role-playing, mock interviews, or live cases (for listing operations) facilitated by managers or supervisors. According to Bureau officials, employees will also have access to just-in-time training materials on their devices for use in the field.

The Bureau Took Steps to Manage Some Challenges in Implementing Its Blended Training Approach during the 2018 End-to-End Test

The Bureau encountered a number of challenges in implementing and testing its blended training approach, but is taking steps to mitigate those

---

[12] For the 2010 Census we recommended that the Bureau consider alternate approaches to instructor-led delivery of field staff training content, such as video or computer-based instruction. The Bureau did not implement this recommendation for 2010 because it believed alternative approaches would be cost prohibitive and that instructor-led training from a script ensured consistency across training sites.

challenges. Specifically, during the 2018 End-to-End Test, the Bureau (1) experienced problems with the proper recording of online training scores for census staff, (2) was unable to test online training for one of its operations because the operation was added late, and (3) encountered challenges with census staff not always having access to the internet, which is required to complete the training.

The Bureau Is Taking Action to Ensure the Completion of Training Is Accurately Tracked

The 2018 End-to-End Test of address canvassing and nonresponse follow-up training revealed some technical challenges in using the Learning Management System. The Learning Management System is the online training system for the 2020 Census; it contains online training modules and tracks final assessment scores and training certifications.

In February 2019, the Department of Commerce (Commerce) Office of the Inspector General (OIG) noted that during the address canvassing operation there was no final assessment scores recorded for 23 trained listers. The Bureau was also unable to provide documentation that another three lister trainees who failed the final assessment had been observed by their supervisor before being permitted to work.[13] Bureau officials said they provided an action plan to the Commerce OIG in April 2019. According to Bureau officials, the action plan has not been finalized because they are incorporating changes to the action plan based on Commerce OIG comments.

In December 2018, we reported that roughly 100 enumerator trainees in the nonresponse follow-up operation were unable to transmit their final test scores because the Learning Management System had an erroneous setting.[14] According to Bureau officials, this problem delayed the start of unsupervised work for these otherwise-qualified enumerator trainees by an average of 2 days per trainee, and resulted in the attrition of some who

---

[13] Department of Commerce Office of Inspector General, *2020 Census: Issues Observed During the 2018 End-to-End Census Test's Address Canvassing Operation Indicate Risk to Address List Quality*, OIG-19-008-A (Washington, D.C.: Feb. 6, 2019).

[14] GAO, *2020 Census: Additional Steps Needed to Finalize Readiness for Peak Field Operations*, GAO-19-140 (Washington, D.C.: Dec. 10, 2018).

were able to quickly find other work. Bureau officials reported that they have fixed the system setting. Moreover, according to Bureau officials, they have also developed an alternative means to certify training by incorporating the employee final assessment into the final day of classroom training.

The Bureau was Unable to Test All Online Training, but Has Plans in Place to Conduct Dry-Runs of the Untested Training

According to Bureau officials, Update Leave online training was not tested during the 2018 End-to-End Test due to the late addition of the operation to the 2020 Census design.[15] Officials told us that the Update Leave operation was approved in May 2017, leaving just 10 months for the development team to create and implement software and the systems to support this field operation for the End-to-End Test. This left no time to develop online training that would be ready for the End-to-End Test in March 2018.

Therefore, the Bureau classroom-trained headquarters staff instead of temporary field staff for the operation. According to the Bureau's risk register, the utilization of Bureau headquarters staff did not properly simulate training conditions or staff characteristics in which new employees have no prior knowledge of census operations. Therefore, the 2018 End-to-End Test did not allow for proper training feedback or the capture of lessons learned with regard to temporary staff or the mode of training. According to Bureau officials, the Bureau plans to conduct scheduled dry runs of training in September 2019 to collect feedback and, if necessary, make changes to Update Leave-specific training.

The Bureau Has Plan to Address Trainee Access to Online Training

In June 2018, we reported that some listers had difficulty accessing the internet to take online training for address canvassing.[16] According to the

---

[15] The Update Leave operation is designed to occur in areas where the majority of housing units either do not have mail delivered to the physical location of the housing unit, or the mail delivery information for the housing unit cannot be verified.

[16] GAO-18-414.

Bureau, in addition to the Bureau-provided laptop, listers also needed a personal home computer or laptop and internet access at their home to complete the training. However, while the Bureau reported that listers had access to a personal computer to complete the training, we found some listers did not have access to the internet at their home and had to find workarounds to access the training. We recommended that the Bureau finalize plans for alternate training locations in areas where internet access is a barrier to completing training.

The Bureau took action and in March 2019 finalized its plans for identifying alternate training locations in areas where internet access is a barrier to completing training. Specifically, Bureau officials told us that in areas of known low connectivity rates, regional staff will identify sites that trainees can access to complete online components of the training. In addition, the Bureau provided us with a training module for identifying training field staff locations that emphasized training sites need to be located in areas with a good cellular connection and also have access to the internet.

The Bureau Has Generally Met the Criteria for Selected Leading Practices for Training Development, but Could Better Document Measures of Success

Effective training can enhance the Bureau's ability to attract and retain employees with the skills and competencies needed to conduct the 2020 Census. Our Guide for Assessing Strategic Training and Development Efforts in the Federal Government describes components for developing effective training in the federal government. Our strategic training guide identifies four phases of the training—planning, design/development, implementation, and evaluation. We assessed the Bureau's training approach and found that it generally aligned with selected leading practices.[17] This chapter includes the design/development and evaluation phases of training. We did not assess the implementation phase because

---

[17] GAO-04-546G.

field staff training had not yet begun during our audit, and we did not assess the planning phase because practices in that phase are more applicable to agency-wide rather than program-specific training development.

Design/Development

The design/development phase involves identifying specific training and development initiatives that the agency will use, along with other strategies, to improve individual and agency performance. According to the guide, well-designed training and development programs are linked to agency goals and to the organizational, occupational, and individual skills and competencies needed for the agency to perform effectively. Moreover, in response to emerging demands and the increasing availability of new technologies, agencies, including the Bureau for the 2020 Census, are faced with the challenge of choosing the optimal mix for the specific purpose and situation from a wide range of mechanisms, including classroom and online learning as well as structured on-the-job experiences (see Figure 7).

In developing its training approach we found the Bureau met all five selected leading practices related to design/development. Specifically,

- Bureau training aligned with achieving results for the Bureau's re-engineered field operations. Specifically, the Bureau has a formal online training program that uses the Learning Management System as a control mechanism to provide and record training results for all 2020 Census field staff who take online training.
- The Bureau's training program is integrated with other strategies to improve performance such as building team relationships. For example, the training includes modules for supervisors that focus on guiding and motivating employees, communicating effectively, and resolving conduct issues. To ensure the training is properly integrated with device issuance, for larger scale operations, the Bureau plans to stagger training sessions to help ensure there is the

- necessary support during the first day of training when census field staff receive their devices.
- The Bureau also plans to use different training delivery mechanisms. For example, the Bureau will use a blended training approach which includes a mix of computer-based and instructor-led classroom training.

Phase	Leading Practice	Assessment
Design/ development	Agency training is connected to improving individual and agency performance in achieving specific results. For example, does the agency have a formal training and professional development strategy with an assessment of needs and a control mechanism to ensure all employees receive appropriate training?	Fully Met
	The design of the training program is integrated with other strategies to improve performance. For example, is training focused on building team relationships and new ways of working?	Fully Met
	Agency considered the merits of using different delivery mechanisms to ensure efficient and cost-effective delivery of training. For example, does the agency use formal and on-the-job training opportunities that use new technologies and approaches?	Fully Met
	Training incorporates measures of effectiveness into course designs. For example, does the training include clear linkages between specific learning objectives and organizational results as well as procedures to incorporate feedback from a variety of stakeholders?	Fully Met
	Agency determined a targeted level of improved performance. For example, do specific performance improvement goals and training evaluation documents focus on achieving results?	Fully Met

● Fully Met
◐ Partially Met
○ Not Met

Source: GAO analysis of Bureau's planned training approach. | GAO-19-602.

Figure 7. Assessing the Bureau's Planned Training Approach for Design/Development against Selected Leading Practices.

- The Bureau has measures of effectiveness in its course design. The Bureau relied on an in-house training development team that worked with the data collection operations staff to develop learning objectives. We found that that the Bureau has procedures to incorporate feedback. Specifically, the Bureau incorporated lessons learned from previous census tests, such as the refinement of procedures for reassigning work in the field and emphasizing

the importance of knocking on doors to find a proxy respondent during the nonresponse follow-up operation.
- Finally, the Bureau's training documents contained goals for achieving results for its new training approach. Specifically, the Operational Assessment Study Plan for Recruiting, Onboarding, and Training for the 2018 End-to-End Test contained the following measures of success for training—reduce cost and increase efficiency over what was reported in 2010.

Evaluation

In developing its evaluation phase for training, the Bureau met five of six selected leading practices and partially met one leading practice. The evaluation phase involves assessing the extent to which training and development efforts contribute to improved performance and results. We have previously found that it is increasingly important for agencies to be able to evaluate their training and development programs, and demonstrate how these efforts help develop employees and improve the agencies' performance (see Figure 8).

Overall, we found that the Bureau has a robust evaluation plan for the 2020 Census that gathers data from multiple sources. For example,

- The Bureau has a plan to evaluate the effectiveness of training for the 2020 Census. Specifically, operational and assessment study plans set priorities for evaluations and cover the methods, timing, and responsibilities for data collection, including assessment questions, metrics, data sources and expected delivery dates, and division responsibilities.
- The Bureau has an analytical approach to assess training programs. For example, the Field Decennial Data Collection Training Branch has developed three separate training evaluation surveys which will be administered to field staff through the Learning Management System. The three evaluations provide training feedback after the completion of the online training; after the completion of the classroom training; and near the completion of

the operation. According to the Bureau, these assessments will help determine the effectiveness of training.

Phase	Leading Practice	Assessment
Evaluation	Agency systematically planned for and evaluated effectiveness of training. For example, is there a data collection analysis plan that sets priorities for evaluations and covers methods, timing, and responsibilities for data collection?	Fully Met
	Agency uses appropriate analytical approaches to assess training programs. For example, does the agency use the appropriate methods to evaluate training, guidelines for determining when and how training programs will be evaluated?	Fully Met
	Agency uses performance data to assess results achieved through training. For example, does the agency use both quantitative and qualitative measures to assess training results?	Partially Met
	Agency incorporates evaluation feedback into planning and design of training. For example, does the agency have a systematic monitoring and feedback process that is used to refine training efforts and reallocate resources?	Fully Met
	Agency incorporates different perspectives in assessing the impact of training on performance. For example, does the agency use surveys, interviews, and focus groups with stakeholders to refine training programs when necessary?	Fully Met
	Agency compares training investments, methods, or outcomes with those of other organizations. For example, does the agency compare its activities with those of other organizations and attempt to identify training efforts outside the agency for benchmarking?	Fully Met

● Fully Met
◐ Partially Met
○ Not Met

Source: GAO analysis of Bureau's planned training approach. | GAO-19-602.

Figure 8. Assessing the Bureau's Planned Training Approach for Evaluation against Selected Leading Practices.

- The Bureau incorporated evaluation feedback into planning and design of training. For example, the Bureau held debrief sessions with census workers during the 2018 End-to-End Test and told us they were also incorporating recommendations made by a training vendor. Feedback from the 2018 End-to-End Test is being used to inform training for the 2020 Census.
- The Bureau incorporates different perspectives in assessing the impact of training. Bureau officials stated that they incorporated feedback from a variety of stakeholders when evaluating the effectiveness of its training during testing, including participant

debriefs and evaluations from vendors. As previously discussed, the Bureau used three different surveys at different points in time to evaluate training, and relied on debrief sessions with census managers and staff in the field.
- Bureau officials said they considered the training methods of another organization. For example, Bureau officials told us they used training vendors that followed requirements, including e-learning content developed by the Department of Defense.

However, we found that the Bureau does not have performance goals or measures for training in its corresponding study plan for the 2020 Census. Specifically, we found that in the Detailed Operational Plan for the Field Infrastructure and Decennial Logistics Management Operations for the 2020 Census, the Bureau had planned to include the following success measures:

- Process Measures that indicate how well the process works, typically including measures related to completion dates, rates, and productivity rates.
- Cost Measures that drive the cost of the operation and comparisons of actual costs to planned budgets. Costs can include workload as well as different types of resource costs.
- Quality Measures, such as, the results of the operation, typically including rework rates, and error rates.

However, according to Bureau officials they decided not to include the measures from the study plan for training because the study plan was intended to provide descriptive information about operations rather than evaluate them.[18] We have previously reported that a fundamental element in an organization's efforts to manage for results is its ability to set

---

[18] In the design/development phase we determined the Bureau met the best practice for having goals and measures because during the 2018 End-to-End Test, when the Bureau was designing and developing online training, the 2018 End-to End test study plans for training had measures of success including a training solution that reduces cost and increases efficiency when compared to 2010.

meaningful goals for performance and to measure progress toward those goals. Thus, without specific performance goals and measures for its new blended training approach that considers cost and benefits when compared to 2010, the Bureau will not be able to determine whether its blended training approach reduced costs or increased efficiency.

Moreover, not having goals and measures in place could inhibit the Bureau's ability to develop meaningful lessons learned from the 2020 Census. Bureau officials agreed and stated they will consider including goals and measures on cost and efficiency in its plans; however, the Bureau has not yet provided us with documentation to reflect the goals and measures it will use to evaluate training, and has no time frame for doing so. Training for in-field address canvassing operation will begin in July 2019. Having performance goals and measures will help the Bureau assess the impact of its new training approach on cost, quality, and resources expended.

CONCLUSION

Successfully carrying out the thousands of activities needed to complete an accurate, cost-effective head count on schedule is an enormous and challenging task. However, for those activities we examined, the Bureau appears to be positioned to carry them out as planned, if implemented properly. While Bureau officials acknowledged there were some early delays when regions were trying to find office space and acquire leases, they said that the deadlines for the later phases of construction allow extra time—giving them a chance to make up lost time.

Regarding recruiting and hiring, the Bureau was exceeding its recruiting goals for early operations, but identified challenges in areas such as promptly completing background checks, hiring in a time of low unemployment, and overcoming language barriers. Moreover, although the Bureau has exceeded its recruiting goal for early operations, recruiting a sufficient number of job applicants for partnership specialist is a challenge. The Bureau's continued response to and management of these challenges will be important as it begins recruiting for its peak operation efforts later this fall.

The Bureau has generally followed its training plans for 2020, but has opportunities to improve its ability to evaluate training efforts. The Bureau notes that the blended training approach is intended to maximize trainee learning and on the job performance during the 2020 Census. However, 2020 Census documents do not contain performance goals or measures for determining the cost and benefits of the training when compared to 2010. Revising plans to include goals and measures will better position the Bureau to determine how its blended training approach will impact the cost, quality, and resources expended on the 2020 Census.

RECOMMENDATION FOR EXECUTIVE ACTION

We recommend that the Secretary of Commerce direct the U.S. Census Bureau to revise plans to include goals and measures for assessing the cost and benefits of the Bureau's new blended training approach. These measures might include, but are not limited to, measures of cost, quality, and resources associated with training when compared to 2010. (Recommendation 1)

AGENCY COMMENTS AND OUR EVALUATION

We provided a draft of this chapter to the Secretary of Commerce. In its written comments, reproduced in appendix II, the Department of Commerce agreed with our findings and recommendation and said it would develop an action plan to address our recommendation. The Census Bureau also provided technical comments, which we incorporated.

We are sending copies of this chapter to the Secretary of Commerce, the Under Secretary of Economic Affairs, the Director of the U.S. Census Bureau, and interested congressional committees.

Robert Goldenkoff
Director
Strategic Issues

List of Requesters

The Honorable Elijah E. Cummings
Chairman

The Honorable Jim Jordan
Ranking Member
Committee on Oversight and Reform
House of Representatives

The Honorable Gerry Connolly
Chairman

The Honorable Mark Meadows
Ranking Member
Subcommittee on Government Operations
Committee on Oversight and Reform
House of Representatives

APPENDIX I: OBJECTIVE, SCOPE, AND METHODOLOGY

This chapter assesses the extent to which the Census Bureau (Bureau) is following its plans for space acquisition, recruiting and hiring, and training. For all of our objectives, we reviewed current Bureau planning documents and schedules, and interviewed Bureau officials including officials at the Bureau's six regional offices.

To assess the Bureau's progress in opening area census offices (ACO), we obtained and reviewed current Bureau leasing agreement information and construction (meaning renovations such as new electrical layouts, heating, ventilation, and air conditioning) and deployment information. We also gathered information on the General Services Administration's role in obtaining office space. To determine whether the Bureau is on track, we compared the current status of opening, construction, and deployment of ACOs to the Bureau's plans, schedules, and timelines, and identified differences for follow-up with Bureau officials. We also reviewed a randomly selected nongeneralizable sample of ACO files at the Philadelphia RCC to determine whether justification was included when changes to ACO locations occurred.

To determine the extent to which the Bureau is following its field hiring and recruiting strategy for the 2020 Census, we reviewed Bureau documentation regarding its strategy for recruiting and hiring temporary field staff for the 2020 Census. We also reviewed output and analysis from relevant Bureau human resources systems/databases, such as MOJO Recruit. We interviewed Bureau officials in both headquarters and the field who are knowledgeable about and responsible for recruiting and hiring temporary field staff to determine the extent to which the Bureau is meeting its recruiting and hiring goals, to describe their perspectives on any challenges facing the 2020 Census, and to understand the Bureau's actions to mitigate any challenges. To understand changes from 2010, we compared the 2010 Census recruiting and hiring plans to those of the 2020 Census to determine differences, and interviewed Bureau officials to discuss what drove these changes.

Finally, to determine the extent to which the Bureau has followed its plans for training field staff, and whether this training approach is consistent with selected leading practices, we examined relevant documents and interviewed Bureau officials to determine the Bureau's planned approach for training, lessons learned from prior Census tests, the extent to which the Bureau is incorporating lessons learned as a result of its own testing, and what changes to training need to be made before the start of 2020 field operations. Additionally, we interviewed Bureau officials responsible for developing training curriculum to understand how training was developed (e.g., what courses to develop, challenges to using technology, etc.). We also reviewed federal guidance and our prior reports, and selected 11 leading practices from GAO's *Guide for Assessing Strategic Training and Development Efforts in the Federal Government* (GAO-04-546G) as leading practices for training. Our strategic training guide identifies four phases of the training development process (planning/analysis, design/development, implementation, and evaluation). We assessed the approach against leading practices in two of these phases: design/development and evaluation. We did not assess the implementation phase because field staff training for the 2020 Census had not yet begun during our audit, and we did not assess the planning/analysis phase because practices in that phase are more applicable to agency-wide rather than program-specific training development, and focus on full-time permanent employees rather than temporary employees. Moreover, within the design/development phase and evaluation phase, we did not assess all best practices because some of those best practices were also more applicable to agency-wide rather than program-specific training development, or we had already evaluated such practices as cost.[19] Moreover, this chapter primarily focuses on training for the address canvassing and nonresponse follow-up operations. We then compared the Bureau's training approach to those leading practices and identified practices being followed and any differences.

We conducted this performance audit from August 2018 to July 2019 in accordance with generally accepted government auditing standards. Those standards require that we plan and perform the audit to obtain sufficient, appropriate evidence to provide a reasonable basis for our findings and conclusions based on our audit objectives. We believe that the evidence obtained provides a reasonable basis for our findings and conclusions based on our audit objectives.

---

[19] GAO-16-628 and GAO-18-635.

APPENDIX II: COMMENTS FROM THE DEPARTMENT OF COMMERCE

July 9, 2019

Mr. Robert Goldenkoff
Director, Strategic Issues
U.S. Government Accountability Office
441 G Street, NW
Washington, DC 20548

Dear Mr. Goldenkoff:

The Department of Commerce appreciates the opportunity to comment on the U.S. Government Accountability Office's (GAO) draft report titled *2020 Census: Bureau Is Making Progress Opening Offices and Recruiting, But Could Improve Its Ability to Evaluate Training* (GAO-19-602).

The Department agrees with the findings and the recommendation. Once the GAO issues the final version of this report, the Department will prepare an action plan to document the steps we will take regarding the final recommendation.

Sincerely,

Wilbur Ross

In: A Closer Look at the 2020 Census
Editor: Sille M. Schou

ISBN: 978-1-53616-508-1
© 2019 Nova Science Publishers, Inc.

Chapter 8

2020 CENSUS: BUREAU HAS MADE PROGRESS WITH ITS SCHEDULING, BUT FURTHER IMPROVEMENT WILL HELP INFORM MANAGEMENT DECISIONS[*]

United States Government Accountability Office

WHY GAO DID THIS STUDY

The Bureau is required by law to count the population as of April 1, 2020; deliver state apportionment counts to the President by December 31, 2020; and provide redistricting data to the states within 1 year of Census Day, April 1, 2021. To meet these statutory deadlines, the Bureau carries out hundreds of projects, which it manages with an integrated master schedule. Because census operations need to proceed in concert with one another, significant delays could propagate to other activities resulting in

---

[*] This is an edited, reformatted and augmented version of United States Government Accountability Office; Report to Congressional Requesters, Accessible Version, Publication No. GAO-18-589, dated July 26, 2018.

increased costs, reduced operational quality, or changes to the design of the census in order to compensate for lost time.

This chapter determines the extent to which the Bureau is using leading practices for scheduling key projects.

GAO selected three projects for review based on their cost and in-progress status. GAO analyzed schedules and their supporting documents against GAO's Schedule Assessment Guide. GAO also spoke with relevant Bureau officials regarding the three selected projects.

GAO provided a draft of this chapter to the Department of Commerce, which agreed with the findings.

WHAT GAO FOUND

The three census project schedules GAO reviewed better reflect characteristics of a reliable schedule compared to a GAO schedule assessment performed in 2013, but weaknesses remain. GAO reviewed three projects that contribute to two of the Census Bureau's (Bureau) largest field operations—address canvassing and nonresponse follow-up. The schedules for all three projects are better constructed and more credible than previously reviewed project schedules. For example, the Bureau has improved the logic of the relationship between activities, and better ensured that all schedules are linked together in a master schedule so that their interactions can be better managed.

However, the three selected schedules have some of the same weaknesses GAO identified in other Bureau schedules in 2009 and 2013. For example, none of the selected schedules contain information on resource needs and availability. GAO has reported that such information assists program offices in forecasting the likelihood that activities will be completed as scheduled. It can also help management compute total labor and equipment hours, calculate total project and per-period cost, resolve resource conflicts, and establish the reasonableness of the plan. If the schedule does not allow insight into current or projected allocation of resources, then the likelihood is significantly increased that the program may slip or need additional resources to complete on time.

In GAO's 2009 review of the Bureau's schedule, GAO recommended that the Bureau include in the 2020 master schedule estimates of the resources, such as labor, materials, and overhead costs for each activity as the 2020 schedule was built. The Department of Commerce did not respond to the recommendation at that time. Then, regarding GAO's 2013 assessment of the Bureau's schedule, Bureau officials stated that they hoped to begin identifying the resources needed for each activity in their schedules by early 2014. However, as of May 2018, the Bureau had not taken these steps. Senior Bureau officials have now stated that it would require additional staffing in order to plan for and implement this recommendation.

Additionally, the Bureau has not conducted risk assessments for the project schedules GAO assessed. Schedule risk analysis—the systematic analysis of "what if" scenarios—is an established leading practice. Risk assessments are needed to determine the likelihood of the project's completion date; how much schedule risk contingency is needed to provide an acceptable level of certainty for completion by a specific date; risks most likely to delay the project; how much contingency reserve each risk requires; and the paths or activities that are most likely to delay the project.

In 2013, GAO recommended the Bureau conduct risk assessments for its schedules. The Bureau said it had no disagreement with this recommendation. However, while Senior Bureau officials stated that a schedule risk assessment plan and process were approved by Bureau management in late May 2018, it has not yet implemented this recommendation.

GAO believes that these prior recommendations still apply and can help the Bureau improve the reliability of its 2020 schedule.

July 26, 2018
Congressional Requesters:

The decennial census is a crucial, constitutionally mandated activity with immutable deadlines.[1] The U.S. Census Bureau (Bureau) is required by law to count the population as of April 1, 2020; deliver state apportionment counts to the President by December 31, 2020; and provide redistricting data to the states within 1 year of Census Day, April 1, 2021.[2] To meet these statutory deadlines, the Bureau carries out thousands of interrelated activities, which it manages with an integrated master schedule. The Bureau's schedule is essential to help manage the risks to preparing and implementing a successful decennial census. Because census operations need to proceed in concert with one another, significant delays could propagate to other activities and increase costs, reduce operational quality, or force the Bureau to change the design of the census in order to compensate for lost time.

Over the years, we have reported on significant weaknesses in the Bureau's scheduling practices, leading to recommendations for the Bureau to improve the comprehensiveness, construction, and credibility of its schedule, and ensure that it includes estimates of the resources and a qualitative risk assessment. The Bureau said that it had no disagreement with these recommendations, yet these recommendations have not been implemented.[3] With less than 2 years until Census Day, there is little time remaining for the Bureau to deal with any unexpected problems that may arise. Accordingly, early recognition of potential delays is essential, and

---

[1] The U.S. Constitution empowers Congress to carry out the census in "such manner as they shall by Law direct" (U.S. Const. art. I, § 2, cl. 3).

[2] 13 U.S.C. § 141(a)-(c). Although the Constitution prescribes the year in which a decennial census is to be conducted, it does not specify an actual date. The specific date for the census is established by statute. The April 1 date has been mandated by statute since the 1960 Census. The timetable for reporting population counts derived from census data is also mandated by statute. The law requires the Secretary to tabulate the "total population by States" and report these data to the President for purposes of congressional reapportionment within 9 months after the census date. The law also requires the Secretary of Commerce to send census population tabulations for redistricting to the states as expeditiously as possible, but no later than 1 year after the April 1 decennial census date.

[3] GAO, *2020 Census: Bureau Needs to Improve Scheduling Practices to Enhance Ability to Meet Address List Development Deadlines*, GAO-14-59 (Washington, D.C.: Nov. 21, 2013); and *2010 Census: Census Bureau Has Made Progress on Schedule and Operational Control Tools, but Needs to Prioritize Remaining System Requirements*, GAO-10-59 (Washington, D.C.: Nov. 13, 2009).

remaining activities need to begin and end on schedule and in the proper operational sequence.

In response to your request, our objective was to determine the extent to which the Bureau is using leading practices for scheduling key projects. In order to meet this objective, we selected the following three projects for review: 2018 End-to-End Census Test Address Canvassing, 2018 End-to-End Census Test Nonresponse Follow-up, and 2020 Census Geographic Programs. These projects are critical to the Bureau's ability to build and maintain an accurate address list, and help ensure that households respond to the census. We selected these projects based on their high cost, their significance to the 2020 Census, and that they were still in progress.

We compared the schedules for each of these projects to the leading practices in our *Schedule Assessment Guide*.[4] We spoke with relevant Bureau officials regarding these project schedules. We scored each scheduling leading practice on a five-point scale ranging from "not met" to "met." Finally, we compared these results with our prior assessments of the Bureau's schedule, particularly those where we made recommendations, and we updated the status of those recommendations.

Assessing only three key projects limits possible statements about the Bureau's entire schedule. For example, if the Bureau is not following best practices in creating and maintaining these three project schedules, we can conclude that the larger integrated schedule is unreliable. This is because an integrated master schedule consolidates lower-level project schedules. Thus, errors and reliability issues in lower levels will be transferred to higher-level schedules. However, if the selected lower-level projects are deemed reliable, we cannot definitively determine the reliability of the integrated master schedule because the other projects that were not assessed may be unreliable. For more details on our scope and methodology, see appendix I.

We conducted our performance audit from July 2017 to July 2018 in accordance with generally accepted government auditing standards.

---

[4] GAO, *Schedule Assessment Guide: Best Practices for Project Schedules*, GAO-16-89G. (Washington, D.C.: Dec. 2015).

Those standards require that we plan and perform the audit to obtain sufficient, appropriate evidence to provide a reasonable basis for our findings and conclusions based on our audit objectives. We believe that the evidence obtained provides a reasonable basis for our findings and conclusions based on our audit objectives.

BACKGROUND

A reliable schedule is critically important for a successful 2020 Census. In February 2017, we added the 2020 Census to our High-Risk List because operational and other issues including scheduling are threatening the Bureau's ability to deliver a cost-effective enumeration.[5] We reported on concerns about the quality of the Bureau's schedule and cost assessment, the Bureau's capacity to implement innovative census-taking methods, and uncertainties surrounding critical information technology systems. Underlying these issues are challenges in such essential management functions as the Bureau's ability to

- collect and use real-time indicators of schedule, cost, and performance;
- follow leading practices for scheduling, cost estimation, risk management, and IT acquisition, development, testing, and security; and
- cost effectively deal with contingencies including, for example, fiscal constraints, potential changes in design, and natural disasters that could affect the enumeration.

Reliable scheduling practices are essential for managing tradeoffs between cost, schedule, and scope. Among other things, scheduling allows program managers to decide between possible sequences of activities, determine the flexibility of the schedule according to available resources,

---

[5] GAO, *High-Risk Series: Progress on Many High-Risk Areas, While Substantial Efforts Needed on Others*, GAO-17-317 (Washington, D.C.: Feb. 15, 2017).

predict the consequences of managerial action or inaction in events, and allocate contingency plans to mitigate risk. Following changes in a program, the schedule is used to forecast the effects of delayed, deleted, and added effort, as well as possible avenues for time and cost recovery.

Scheduling is important because the cost of counting the nation's population has been escalating with each decade. The 2010 Census was the most expensive in U.S. history at about $12.3 billion, and was about 31 percent more costly than the $9.4 billion 2000 Census (in 2020 constant dollars).[6] According to the Bureau, the total cost of the 2020 Census is now estimated to be approximately $15.6 billion dollars, more than $3 billion higher than previously estimated by the Bureau.[7]

Moreover, as shown in Figure 1, the average cost for counting a housing unit increased from about $16 in 1970 to around $92 in 2010 (in 2020 constant dollars). At the same time, the return of census questionnaires by mail (the primary mode of data collection) declined over this period from 78 percent in 1970 to 63 percent in 2010. Declining mail response rates have led to higher costs because the Bureau needs to send temporary workers to each nonresponding household to obtain census data.

The schedules we reviewed for this chapter—2020 Census Geographic Programs, 2018 End-to-End Test Address Canvassing, and 2018 End-to-End Census Test Nonresponse Follow-up—relate to the key activities of developing an accurate address list and following up with households that did not mail back their census forms. The Bureau relies on a complete and accurate address list to maximize the more cost-efficient self-response rate.

---

[6] According to the Bureau, these figures rely on fiscal year 2020 constant dollar factors derived from the Chained Price Index from "Gross Domestic Product and Deflators Used in the Historical Tables: 1940–2020" table from the Fiscal Year 2016 Budget of the United States Government.

[7] The historical life-cycle cost figures for prior decennials as well as the initial estimate for 2020 provided by the Department of Commerce in October 2017 differ slightly from those reported by the Bureau previously. According to Commerce documents, the more recently reported figures are "inflated to the current 2020 Census time frame (fiscal years 2012 to 2023)," rather than to 2020 constant dollars as the earlier figures had been. Specifically, since October 2017, Commerce and the Bureau have reported the October 2015 estimate for the 2020 Census as $12.3 billion; this is slightly different than the $12.5 billion the Bureau had initially reported.

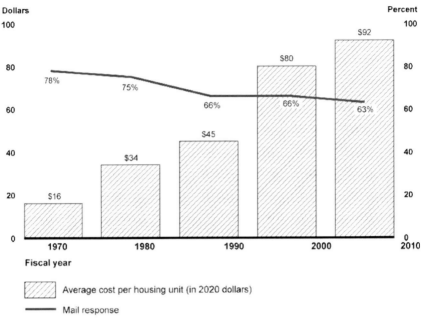

Source: GAO analysis of Census Bureau data. | GAO-18-589.

Figure 1. The Average Cost of Counting Each Housing Unit (in 2020 Constant Dollars) Has Escalated Each Decade, While the Percentage of Mail Response Rates Has Declined.

SELECTED CENSUS SCHEDULES BETTER REFLECT CHARACTERISTICS OF A RELIABLE SCHEDULE COMPARED TO PRIOR ASSESSMENT, THOUGH WEAKNESSES REMAIN

The three projects we selected contribute to two of the Census Bureau's largest field operations. The Bureau's Geographic Programs Operation maintains the Bureau's master address file and mapping data used to conduct the 2020 Census. The Bureau's Geographic Programs Operation provides the most current address list to the Bureau's Address Canvassing Operation, where Bureau staff make updates to the address list via in-office and in-field procedures. These updates are processed on an ongoing basis throughout the decade. The Bureau conducts its

Nonresponse Follow-up Operation after Census Day by having enumerators go door-to-door to determine the housing unit status for addresses that do not self-respond to the 2020 Census, and enumerate households that are determined to be occupied.

We have previously reported in our *Schedule Assessment Guide* that a reliable schedule can provide a road map for systematic execution of a program, and the means by which to gauge progress, identify and address potential problems, and promote accountability.[8] The guide identifies four characteristics of a reliable schedule:[9]

- Comprehensive: The schedule should identify all activities and resources necessary to accomplish the project. The schedule should cover the scope of work to be performed so that the full picture is available to managers.
- Well-constructed: Activities should be logically sequenced and critical activities that would affect the timelines of the schedule should be identified.
- Credible: All schedules should be linked to a complete master schedule for managers to reference and analyzed for how risk impacts the outcome of the schedule.
- Controlled: There should be a documented process for changes to the schedule so that the integrity of the schedule is assured.

For a schedule to be reliable, it must substantially or fully meet all criteria for these four characteristics. These characteristics, their related leading practices, and their criteria are described in more detail in appendix II.

In 2013, we assessed the Bureau's 2020 Research and Testing and Geographic Support System Initiative schedules using these criteria. While the results exhibited some of the characteristics of a reliable

---

[8] GAO-16-89G.
[9] Underlying these characteristics are 10 leading practices, which are described in appendix II. These characteristics and leading practices were developed based on our practices for creating a reliable cost estimate and in consultation with experts from the scheduling community.

schedule, important weaknesses remained. Both schedules substantially met one of the four characteristics (controlled) and minimally or partially met the other three characteristics (comprehensive, well-constructed, and credible).

For this review, we assessed the 2018 End-to-End Census Test Address Canvassing, 2018 End-to-End Census Test Nonresponse Follow-up, and 2020 Census Geographic Programs projects' schedules.[10] We found that overall the selected schedules better reflected two of the four characteristics of a reliable schedule compared to our 2013 assessment (see Figure 2).

Characteristic	May 2013 Census Schedule — Report GAO-14-59	December 2017 Census Schedule — 2018 End-to-End Test Address Canvassing	December 2017 Census Schedule — 2018 End-to-End Test Nonresponse Follow-up	December 2017 Census Schedule — 2020 Census Geographic Programs	Demonstrated Improvement
Comprehensive	Partially Met	Partially Met	Partially Met	Partially Met	
Well-constructed	Minimally Met	Substantially Met	Substantially Met	Partially Met	✓
Credible	Minimally Met	Partially Met	Partially Met	Partially Met	✓
Controlled	Substantially Met	Substantially Met	Substantially Met	Substantially Met	

Met: The Bureau provided complete evidence that satisfies the entire characteristic.
Substantially Met: The Bureau provided evidence that satisfies a large portion of the characteristic.
Partially Met: The Bureau provided evidence that satisfies about half of the characteristic.
Minimally Met: The Bureau provided evidence that satisfies a small portion of the characteristic.
Not Met: The Bureau provided no evidence that satisfies any of the characteristic.

Source: GAO analysis of Census Bureau December 2017 schedule data. | GAO-18-589.

Figure 2. Selected Census Bureau Schedules Show Improvement in Some Areas Compared to GAO's 2013 Assessment.

Examples of the extent to which these characteristics were met are provided below. For a more detailed explanation of our assessment results, see appendix III.

---

[10] The December 17, 2017 version of the 2020 Census integrated master schedule—from which we selected three projects for detailed analysis—consisted of 255 total projects, of which 134 were remaining. The 3 projects selected for review are 2018 End-to-End Census Test Address Canvassing, 2018 End-to-End Census Test Nonresponse Follow-up, and 2020 Census Geographic Programs. We selected these based on several criteria, including cost of the project and status of the project.

Comprehensive–Selected Schedules Partially Meet Characteristic but Do Not Identify Needed Resources

As with our 2013 schedule assessment, our 2018 analysis found that the Bureau is partially meeting the characteristics of a comprehensive schedule. For example, the projects we assessed reflect the work to be accomplished for the project schedules, and each project schedule includes estimates of the duration of each activity. Additionally, the 2018 End-to-End Census Test Address Canvassing and the 2018 End-to-End Census Test Nonresponse Follow-up project schedules contain clear start and finish milestones, and map to the census program work breakdown structure—a detailed definition of the work necessary to accomplish a program's objectives.

This leading practice of capturing all activities was substantially met, not fully met (see appendix III for a more detailed explanation), because while for each project all activities and milestones are mapped to their work breakdown structures by codes, there are no corresponding dictionaries to define the work. The absence of such a dictionary could potentially lead to confusion among staff in different census offices about the scope of the work they are responsible for performing.

Our schedule guide states that a work breakdown structure dictionary is a valuable communication tool between systems engineers, program management, and other stakeholders because it provides a clear picture of what efforts have to be accomplished. Bureau officials stated that although their 2020 Schedule Management Plan requires each project to have a schedule work breakdown structure dictionary, as project schedules are updated, they have not created these required dictionaries. As an alternative, they noted that the 2020 Census Operational Plan includes details and definitions of the projects.

Additionally, none of the three schedules we assessed include information about what levels of resources, such as labor and equipment, are required to complete the planned work—including this information is called resource loading. The Bureau's 2020 Schedule Management Plan states that it is the responsibility of a representative from a project team and the schedule staff to assign resources to an individual project schedule, and that defining and assigning resources should be done following the testing phase of the 2020 Census Lifecycle.

The Bureau is now in its implementation phase (see Figure 3 below), so according to its management plan, resource loading should have begun. But it has not. For example, the 2018 End-to-End Census Test Address Canvassing project schedule did not include any resource information on the recruiting and hiring goals for the address canvassing field work.

Instead, Bureau officials stated that they are estimating the cost of activities using a software tool separate from the current schedule management tool. They further stated that this Bureau-wide solution includes all 2020 Decennial Census staff as Decennial funded resources. However, the information in this separate tool has no effect on the durations or forecasted start and finish dates of detailed activities within individual projects. Furthermore, the separate tool does not always track all activities at the lowest level in the schedule, so that Bureau managers do not have reliable visibility with it on the efforts of the lowest level of detailed activities.

Resource loading is important for any agency, but is particularly important for the Census Bureau, given its statutorily mandated deadlines. Missed deadlines or schedule slippage can easily jeopardize the quality of the 2020 Census, and there is little room for error given that census data are used to apportion the seats of the House of Representatives, redraw congressional districts, and allocate billions of dollars each year in federal financial assistance. In our schedule guide, we reported that including resources such as labor, materials, and overhead costs can make a schedule a more useful management tool.

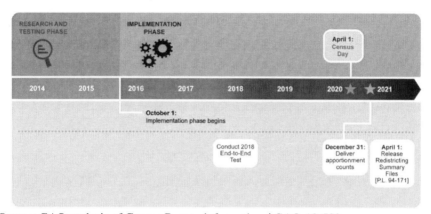

Source: GAO analysis of Census Bureau information. | GAO-18-589.

Figure 3. 2020 Census Life-Cycle.

A resource-loaded schedule can help management with things such as computing labor and equipment hours, calculating total project and per-period cost, resolving resource allocation conflicts, determining whether all required resources will be available when they are needed, and establishing the reasonableness of the plan. For example, information on the resource needs of field operations in the 2018 End-to-End Census Test would assist management in determining if the appropriate resource allocations have been made for any given test activity. It would also aide in forecasting the likelihood that those resources will be available to complete the 2018 End-to-End Census Test Address Canvassing and Nonresponse Follow-up activities as scheduled. If the schedule does not allow insight into the current or projected allocation of resources for these test activities, the Bureau's risk of key end-to-end test milestones slipping increases significantly.

In 2009, we reviewed the Bureau's schedule and recommended that the Bureau include estimates of the resources in the 2020 integrated schedule for each activity as the schedule was built.[11] The Department of Commerce did not respond to the recommendation at that time. In our 2013 assessment of the Bureau's schedule, Bureau officials stated that they hoped to begin identifying the resources needed for each activity in their

---

[11] GAO-10-59.

schedules by early 2014.[12] However, as of May 2018, the Bureau has not yet implemented this recommendation. Senior Bureau officials have now stated that the Bureau would require additional staffing in the Schedule Management Branch in the Decennial Census Management Division in order to plan for and implement resource loading. When the Bureau has resource loaded its schedule, it will be able to use the schedule more effectively as a management tool.

Well-Constructed–The Bureau Demonstrated Improvement in Selected Schedules Compared to Prior Assessment

Our 2013 assessment of the Bureau's schedule reported that the Bureau only minimally met the characteristics of a well-constructed schedule. Our 2018 assessment found that two of the selected project schedules now substantially met this characteristic and one partially met it. In this assessment, Bureau officials linked many of the activities clearly and in a straightforward sequence in the schedule, which was not always the case in prior assessments.

This improvement is important because it helps staff identify next steps as they progress through such things as acquiring and mobilizing the staff needed to conduct the address canvassing and nonresponse follow-up test field work, and helps managers identify the impact of changes in one activity on subsequent activities. For example, the schedule lays out the sequence of activities needed, such as developing training materials, recruiting field staff, training staff and equipping them with the tools needed to complete the test. Our assessment also concluded that two of the three project schedules we assessed have valid critical paths, which is the sequence of activities in the schedule that, according to their current status, lead to the program's earliest completion date. A valid critical path allows management to focus on activities that will lead to the project's success.

The 2020 Census Geographic Programs project schedule partially met the well-constructed characteristic due to problems existing within the

---

[12] GAO-14-59.

schedule's sequencing logic. In particular, we found a large number of unjustified date constraints and lags.[13] In part because of these sequencing issues, total float calculations—that is, the amount of time a predecessor activity can slip before its delay affects the program's estimated finish date—appear unreasonably high. Additionally, this project schedule has activities on the critical path with long durations. For example, the project schedule for Geographic Programs included several long-duration activities on its critical path that relate to the Bureau's collection of community boundary data—information essential to delineating geographic boundaries used in the tabulation of census data. These critical long-duration activities make it difficult to measure time-critical progress on such activities in the near term.

These issues with how the schedule is constructed can also cause schedule users to lack confidence in the forecasted dates. Bureau officials acknowledged that the 2020 Census Geographic Programs project schedule had logic issues at the time because it was in the middle of a revision. Bureau officials stated that the standard process is to update the project schedule in an offline version and then assess the quality and impacts of changes before acceptance. According to Bureau officials, the Geographic Programs project schedule did not follow this process and was instead updated in the live version of the schedule because of time constraints.

Credible–Selected Schedules Partially Meet Characteristic, but the Bureau Has Not Carried Out a Schedule Risk Analysis

Our 2013 assessment of the Bureau's schedule found that the Bureau minimally met the characteristics of a credible schedule. Our 2018 assessment of the Bureau's schedule found that the Bureau's scheduling practices for a credible schedule have improved. We found that there is now a clear relationship between lower-level activities and higher-level

---

[13] Date constraints restrict how planned dates respond to actual accomplished effort or resource availability. Lags delay a successor activity but are not associated with any effort or resources. Because constraints and lags override network logic, they should only be used when necessary and only if they are justified in the schedule documentation.

activities and milestones, and there is generally better consistency of dates between the project schedule and higher-level management documents.

However, the Bureau has not carried out a systematic quantitative risk analysis on its schedule. A schedule risk analysis is a statistical simulation of the possible effects of threats, opportunities, and general uncertainty to a program's schedule that results in a quantifiable level of confidence in meeting the program's key milestone dates. While the Bureau has identified and continues to track risks to its 2018 End-to-End Test address canvasing and nonresponse follow-up efforts in risk registers, a quantitative risk analysis would illustrate the impact of risks on the project schedule, and how those risks would affect the Bureau's ability to meet milestones on time. Such an analysis would also provide a measure of how much time contingency should be built in the schedule to help manage prioritized risks, and, implicitly, provide indications of where additional resources might be needed to stay on schedule.

In response to our 2013 schedule assessment, Bureau officials said they were waiting for decisions about scheduling software before making decisions about a schedule risk analysis. As of May 2018, the Bureau has conducted three risk analyses to prove the software's capability.

However, the Bureau still had not conducted a schedule risk assessment on the current integrated master schedule used to manage the 2020 Census program.

Without a schedule risk analysis, the Bureau cannot determine the likelihood of each project's completion date; how much schedule risk contingency is needed to provide an acceptable level of certainty for completion by a specific date; which risks are most likely to affect the schedule; how much contingency time each risk requires; and the sequence of activities that are most likely to delay the project. Senior Bureau officials stated that a schedule risk assessment plan and process was approved by Bureau management in late May 2018 and that they hope to implement this plan in summer 2018. They intend to conduct an internal review over the next couple months to determine how to best use the information this risk assessment would yield. Follow through on their plans is critical to ensuring our recommendation is implemented.

Controlled–Selected Schedules Substantially Meet the Characteristic

As with our 2013 schedule assessment, our 2018 analysis reported that the Bureau's scheduling practices are substantially meeting the characteristics of a controlled schedule. Our analysis determined that there are no date anomalies in the project schedules, such as planned dates in the past or actual dates in the future. We found the schedule was current as of the date delivered to us, and according to Bureau documents, the schedule is updated weekly following an established schedule process.

Additionally, the Bureau reported that it has a schedule management process in place and a method for logging changes to the schedule in accordance with leading practices. Bureau officials reported that they monitor schedule trends, including bi-weekly schedule reliability checks using the Defense Contract Management Agency 14-Point assessment, a commonly used set of schedule integrity and reliability measures. Bureau officials also provided the May 2014 Program Change Management Process Strategy which defines the process for initiating changes to the integrated performance measurement baseline configuration; analyzing the impact of changes to project cost, schedule and scope; approving or disapproving changes; and updating project or product specifications and baselines.

However, our assessment found that the Bureau did not fully meet this characteristic for a controlled schedule. The Bureau lacked sound documentation of the schedule in the form of a schedule basis document, and changes to the current schedules in the form of a schedule narrative. The current schedule should be documented in a schedule narrative with each update, including changes made to the schedule during status updates and changes that are justified along with their likely effect on future activities. The Bureau had not prepared such narratives. Additionally, none of the three schedules were supported by a schedule baseline document—a single document that defines the organization of a schedule, describes the logic of the network, describes the basic approach to managing resources, and provides a basis for all parameters used to calculate dates. Sound documentation helps with analyzing changes in the program schedule and identifying the reasons why actual schedule results vary from their estimates, thereby contributing to the collection of data that can be useful to evaluations of schedule efforts, and that can be used to support future estimates.

While the Bureau has made improvements to implement the recommendations regarding the comprehensiveness and construction characteristics of the Bureau's scheduling practices, the Bureau's lack of resource loading and a risk assessment of the schedule continue to affect the reliability of the Bureau's schedule. The schedule would be a more useful management tool if the Bureau increased the schedule's reliability by addressing these weaknesses. To address these remaining weaknesses, we continue to believe that these recommendations are valid in order to ensure the 2020 schedule can support key management decisions.

AGENCY COMMENTS AND OUR EVALUATION

We provided a draft of this chapter to the Department of Commerce. In its written comments, reproduced in appendix IV the Department of Commerce agreed with our findings.

We are sending copies of this chapter to the Secretary of Commerce, the Under Secretary of Economic Affairs, the Acting Director of the U.S. Census Bureau, and interested congressional committees.

Robert Goldenkoff Director
Strategic Issues

List of Requesters

The Honorable Ron Johnson
Chairman

The Honorable Claire McCaskill
Ranking Member
Committee on Homeland Security and Governmental Affairs
United States Senate

The Honorable Gary Peters
Ranking Member
Subcommittee on Federal Spending Oversight
and Emergency Management
Committee on Homeland Security and Governmental Affairs
United States Senate

The Honorable Thomas R. Carper
United States Senate

The Honorable Trey Gowdy
Chairman

The Honorable Elijah E. Cummings
Ranking Member
Committee on Oversight and Government Reform
House of Representatives

APPENDIX I. OBJECTIVE, SCOPE, AND METHODOLOGY

This chapter assesses the extent to which the Bureau is using leading practices for scheduling key projects.[14] We did this by focusing on three 2020 projects. We selected the three projects from the December 17, 2017, version of the 2020 Census integrated master schedule. That schedule

---

[14] GAO, *GAO Schedule Assessment Guide: Best Practices for Project Schedules.* GAO-16-89G (Washington, D.C.: Dec. 2015). Underlying these characteristics are 10 leading practices, which are described in appendix II. These characteristics and leading practices were developed in 2012 based on our practices for creating a reliable cost estimate and in consultation with experts from the scheduling community.

consists of 255 total projects, of which 134 were remaining to be completed. We made our selections based on the cost of the projects, their significance to the 2020 Census, and the fact that they were in progress. The 3 projects selected for review are 2018 End-to-End Census Test Address Canvassing, 2018 End-to-End Census Test Nonresponse Follow-up, and 2020 Census Geographic Programs.

We reviewed the project schedules and underlying sub-schedules to assess them against the 10 scheduling leading practices by:

- Checking for specific problems that could hinder the schedule's ability to respond to changes. For example, we:
- Examined if there are any open-ended activities (i.e., activities with no predecessor and/or successors),
- Searched for activities with poor logic:
  o For example, Start to Start successor only or Finish to Finish predecessor only which represent dangling logic, or
  o Logic on summary tasks rather than attached to detailed tasks (summary tasks are for organizing the schedule and should not drive the logic).
- Looked for activities with constraints which keep the schedule rigid (e.g., start no earlier than, finish no later than, etc.),
- Identified any lags or leads which should only be used to show how two tasks interact and not to represent work,
- Determined if activities were resource loaded—which helps to cost out the schedule—and examine whether resources are over allocated or not available when needed,
- Examined the length of activity durations and compared them to the program management review cycle,
- Checked for horizontal and vertical integration within the schedule,
- Examined the schedule critical path to determine whether or not it was reliable and logical,
- Examined schedule float and determine if it was reasonable, and

- Examined whether the schedule was baselined, its status cycle, and what deviations there were from the original plan. We also determined if there were any actual start or finish dates recorded in the future and whether there was any broken logic between planned tasks.

We also interviewed Bureau officials responsible for the 2020 schedule. We scored each scheduling leading practice on a five-point scale ranging from "not met" to "met." We determined the characteristic assessment rating by assigning each best practice rating a number and taking the average. The numerical ratings and ranges of the resulting averages are as follows.

Table 1. Scoring methodology

Rating description	Best practice rating	Characteristic (average) rating
Met	5	5.0 – 4.5
Substantially met	4	4.4 – 3.5
Partially met	3	3.4 – 2.5
Minimally met	2	2.4 – 1.5
Not met	1	1.4 – 1.0

Source: GAO-18-589.

We then compared these results with our prior assessments of the Bureau's schedule, particularly those where recommendations were made, and we updated the status of those recommendations.

Assessing only three key projects limits possible statements about the Bureau's entire schedule. For example, if the Bureau is not following best practices in creating and maintaining the three project schedules, we can conclude that the larger integrated schedule is unreliable. This is because an integrated master schedule consolidates lower-level project schedules; errors and reliability issues in lower levels will be transferred to higher-level schedules. However, if the selected lower-level projects are deemed reliable, we cannot definitively determine the reliability of the integrated master schedule because the other projects that were not assessed may be unreliable.

APPENDIX II. DESCRIPTION OF SCHEDULING LEADING PRACTICES

Characteristic	Leading Practice	Description
Comprehensive	Capturing all activities	A schedule should reflect all activities defined in the project's work breakdown structure and include all activities to be performed by the government and contractor.
	Assigning resources to all activities	The schedule should realistically reflect the resources (i.e., labor, material, and overhead) needed to do the work, whether all required resources will be available when needed, and whether any funding or time constraints exist.
	Establishing the durations of all activities	The schedule should reflect how long each activity will take to execute.
Well-constructed	Sequencing all activities	The schedule should be planned so that all activities are logically sequenced in the order they are to be carried out.
	Confirming that the critical path is valid	The schedule should identify the critical path, or those activities that, if delayed, will negatively impact the overall project completion date. The critical path enables analysis of the effect delays may have on the overall schedule.
	Ensuring reasonable total float	The schedule should identify float—the amount of time an activity can slip in the schedule before it affects other activities—so that flexibility in the schedule can be determined. As a general rule, activities along the critical path have the least amount of float.
Credible	Verifying that the schedule is traceable horizontally and vertically	The detailed schedule should be horizontally traceable, meaning that it should link products and outcomes associated with other sequenced activities. The integrated master schedule should also be vertically traceable—that is, varying levels of activities and supporting subactivities can be traced. Such mapping or alignment of levels enables different groups to work to the same master schedule.
	Conducting a schedule risk analysis	The schedule should include a schedule risk analysis that uses statistical techniques to predict the probability of meeting a completion date. A schedule risk analysis can help management identify high priority risks and opportunities.

Characteristic	Leading Practice	Description
Controlled	Updating the schedule with actual progress and logic	Progress updates and logic provide a realistic forecast of start and completion dates for program activities. Maintaining the integrity of the schedule logic at regular intervals is necessary to reflect the true status of the program. To ensure that the schedule is properly updated, people responsible for updating should be trained in critical path method scheduling.
	Maintaining a baseline schedule	A baseline schedule represents the original configuration of the program plan and is the basis for managing the project scope, the time period for accomplishing it, and the required resources. Comparing the current status of the schedule to the baseline can help managers target areas for mitigation.

Source: GAO-18-589.

Appendix III. Assessment of the Extent to Which the Bureau Followed Scheduling Leading Practices

Table 2. Assessment of the bureau's 2018 end-to-end census test address canvassing schedule

Characteristic	Overall Assessment	Leading Practice (#s refer to Schedule Guide)	Individual Assessment
Comprehensive	Partially Met	1. Capturing all activities	Substantially Met
Well-constructed	Substantially Met	2. Sequencing all activities	Substantially Met
		3. Assigning resources to all activities	Minimally Met
		4. Establishing the durations of all activities	Substantially Met
Credible	Partially Met	5. Verifying that the schedule is traceable horizontally and vertically	Substantially Met
		6. Confirming that the critical path is valid	Substantially Met
		7. Ensuring reasonable total float	Substantially Met
		8. Conducting a schedule risk analysis	Minimally Met
Controlled	Substantially Met	9. Updating the schedule with actual progress and logic	Substantially Met
		10. Maintaining a baseline schedule	Substantially Met

Source: GAO analysis of Census Bureau schedule data. | GAO-18-589.

Note: Not Met – Census provided no evidence that satisfies any of the criterion, Minimally Met – Census provided evidence that satisfies a small portion of the criterion, Partially Met – Census provided evidence that satisfies about half of the criterion, Substantially Met – Census provided evidence that satisfies a large portion of the criterion, and Met – Census provided complete evidence that satisfies the entire criterion.

Table 3. Assessment of the bureau's 2018 end-to-end census test nonresponse follow-up schedule

Characteristic	Overall Assessment	Leading Practice (#s refer to Schedule Guide)	Individual Assessment
Comprehensive	Partially Met	1. Capturing all activities	Substantially Met
		2. Sequencing all activities	Substantially Met
Well-constructed	Substantially Met	3. Assigning resources to all activities	Minimally Met
		4. Establishing the durations of all activities	Substantially Met
Credible	Partially Met	5. Verifying that the schedule is traceable horizontally and vertically	Substantially Met
		6. Confirming that the critical path is valid	Substantially Met
		7. Ensuring reasonable total float	Partially Met
		8. Conducting a schedule risk analysis	Minimally Met
Controlled	Substantially Met	9. Updating the schedule with actual progress and logic	Substantially Met
		10. Maintaining a baseline schedule	Substantially Met

Table 4. Assessment of the bureau's 2020 census geographic programs schedule

Characteristic	Overall Assessment	Leading Practice (#s refer to Schedule Guide)	Individual Assessment
Comprehensive	Partially Met	1. Capturing all activities	Substantially Met
Well-constructed	Partially Met	2. Sequencing all activities	Partially Met
		3. Assigning resources to all activities	Minimally Met
		4. Establishing the durations of all activities	Partially Met
Credible	Partially Met	5. Verifying that the schedule is traceable horizontally and vertically	Partially Met
		6. Confirming that the critical path is valid	Partially Met
		7. Ensuring reasonable total float	Minimally Met
		8. Conducting a schedule risk analysis	Minimally Met
Controlled	Substantially Met	9. Updating the schedule with actual progress and logic	Substantially Met
		10. Maintaining a baseline schedule	Substantially Met

Source: GAO analysis of Census Bureau schedule data. | GAO-18-589.

Note: Not Met – Census provided no evidence that satisfies any of the criterion, Minimally Met – Census provided evidence that satisfies a small portion of the criterion, Partially Met – Census provided evidence that satisfies about half of the criterion, Substantially Met – Census provided evidence that satisfies a large portion of the criterion, and Met – Census provided complete evidence that satisfies the entire criterion.

APPENDIX IV. COMMENTS FROM THE DEPARTMENT OF COMMERCE

UNITED STATES DEPARTMENT OF COMMERCE
The Secretary of Commerce
Washington, D.C. 20230

July 19, 2018

Mr. Robert Goldenkoff
Director, Strategic Issues
U.S. Government Accountability Office
Washington, DC 20548

Dear Mr. Goldenkoff:

The Department of Commerce appreciates the opportunity to comment on the Government Accountability Office's (GAO) draft report, *2020 Census: Bureau Has Made Progress with Scheduling, but Further Improvement Will Help Inform Management Decisions* (GAO-18-589).

The Department agrees with the findings and will continue its efforts, recognized in this draft report, to improve its scheduling practices in line with GAO's best practices. The Census Bureau acknowledges the importance of two recommendations that remain open from GAO's prior audit that call for the development of a resource-based schedule and expansion of the knowledge database.

We are keeping these recommendations in mind as we progress towards the completion of the 2020 Census. Once it is complete, the Census Bureau will focus on addressing these recommendations.

Sincerely,

Wilbur Ross

In: A Closer Look at the 2020 Census
Editor: Sille M. Schou

ISBN: 978-1-53616-508-1
© 2019 Nova Science Publishers, Inc.

Chapter 9

2020 CENSUS: CENSUS BUREAU IMPROVED THE QUALITY OF ITS COST ESTIMATION BUT ADDITIONAL STEPS ARE NEEDED TO ENSURE RELIABILITY[*]

United States Government Accountability Office

ABBREVIATIONS

Bureau	Census Bureau
CEDCaP	Census Enterprise Data Collection and Processing
Commerce	Department of Commerce
CQA	Census Questionnaire Assistance
ICE	independent cost estimate
IT	Information Technology
NRFU	non-response follow-up
OAM	Office of Acquisition Management

---

[*] This is an edited, reformatted and augmented version of United States Government Accountability Office; Report to Congressional Requesters, Publication No. GAO-18-635, dated August 2018.

OMB   Office of Management and Budget
WBS   work breakdown structure

WHY GAO DID THIS STUDY

In October 2017, the Department of Commerce (Commerce) announced that the projected life-cycle cost of the 2020 Census had climbed to $15.6 billion, a more than $3 billion (27 percent) increase over its 2015 estimate. A high-quality, reliable cost estimate is a key tool for budgeting, planning, and managing the 2020 Census. Without this capability, the Bureau is at risk of experiencing program cost overruns, missed deadlines, and performance shortfalls.

GAO was asked to evaluate the reliability of the Bureau's life-cycle cost estimate. This chapter evaluates the reliability of the Bureau's revised life- cycle cost estimate for the 2020 Census and the extent to which the Bureau is using it as a management tool, and compares the 2015 and 2017 cost estimates to describe key drivers of cost growth. GAO reviewed documentary and testimonial evidence from Bureau officials responsible for developing the 2020 Census cost estimate and used its cost assessment guide (GAO-09-3SP) as criteria.

WHAT GAO RECOMMENDS

GAO is not making any new recommendations but maintains its earlier recommendation—that the Secretary of Commerce direct the Bureau to take specific steps to ensure its cost estimate meets the characteristics of a high-quality estimate. In its response to this chapter, Commerce generally agreed with the findings related to cost estimation improvements, but disagreed that the cost estimate was not reliable. However, until GAO's recommendation is fully implemented the cost estimate cannot be considered reliable.

WHAT GAO FOUND

Since 2015, the Census Bureau (Bureau) has made significant progress in improving its ability to develop a reliable cost estimate. While improvements have been made, the Bureau's October 2017 cost estimate for the 2020 Census does not fully reflect all the characteristics of a reliable estimate. (See figure.) Specifically, for the characteristic of being well-documented, GAO found that some of the source data either did not support the information described in the cost estimate or was not in the files provided for two of its largest field operations. In GAO's assessment of the 2015 version of the 2020 Census cost estimate, GAO recommended that the Bureau take steps to ensure that each of the characteristics of a reliable cost estimate is met. The Bureau agreed and has taken steps, but has not fully implemented this recommendation.

A reliable cost estimate serves as a tool for program development and oversight, helping management make informed decisions. During this review, GAO found the Bureau used the cost estimate to inform decision making.

Factors that contributed to cost fluctuations between the 2015 and 2017 cost estimates include:

- Changes in assumptions. Among other changes, a decrease in the assumed rate for self-response from 63.5 percent in 2015 to 60.5 percent in 2017 increased the cost of collecting responses from nonresponding housing units.
- Improved ability to anticipate and quantify risk. In general, contingency allocations designed to address the effects of potential risks increased overall from $1.3 billion in 2015 to $2.6 billion in 2017.
- An overall increase in information technology (IT) costs. IT cost increases, totaling $1.59 billion, represented almost 50 percent of the total cost increase from 2015 to 2017.

August 17, 2018

Congressional Requesters:

The U.S. Census Bureau (Bureau) estimates that the 2020 Census will be the most expensive census in our nation's history, at an estimated cost of $15.6 billion after adjusting for inflation. The Bureau faces the challenge of cost effectively counting a population that is growing steadily larger, more diverse, and increasingly difficult to enumerate with a reengineered design that relies in part on automation to locate housing units and count the nation's population.[1] In an environment of constrained resources, containing costs is imperative for the 2020 Census.

In February 2017, we designated the 2020 Census as a high-risk area, in part because of uncertainty over costs and long-standing weaknesses in the Bureau's management of information technology intended to automate the census.[2] At the time the 2020 Census was designated high risk, the life-cycle cost for the 2020 Census was $12.5 billion, a figure since revised downward to $12.3 billion.[3] However, in October 2017, the Department of Commerce (Commerce) announced that it had updated its October 2015 life-cycle cost estimate and now projects the life-cycle cost of the 2020 Census will be $15.6 billion, a more than $3 billion (27 percent) increase over its earlier estimate. The higher estimated life-cycle cost is due, in part, to the Bureau's earlier failure to meet best practices for a quality cost estimate, a concern we had reported in June 2016.[4] Reliable cost estimates that appropriately account for risks facing an agency can help an agency manage large complex activities like the 2020 Census and can also help

---

[1] Counting the population is required by the U.S. Constitution. Art. I, § 2, cl. 3.
[2] GAO, *High Risk Series: Progress on Many High Risk Areas, While Substantial Efforts Needed on Others*, GAO-17-317 (Washington, D.C.: Feb. 15, 2017).
[3] The historical life-cycle cost figures for prior decennials as well as the initial estimate for 2020 provided by Commerce in October 2017 differ slightly from those reported by the Bureau previously. According to Commerce documents, the more recently reported figures are "inflated to the current 2020 Census time frame (fiscal years 2012 to 2023)," rather than to constant 2020 dollars as the earlier figures had been. Specifically, since October 2017, Commerce and the Bureau have reported the October 2015 estimate for the 2020 Census as $12.3 billion; this is slightly different from the $12.5 billion the Bureau had initially reported.
[4] GAO, *2020 Census: Census Bureau Needs to Improve Its Life-Cycle Cost Estimating Process*, GAO-16-628 (Washington, D.C.: June 30, 2016).

Congress provide oversight and make funding decisions. Having a realistic estimate of projected costs makes for effective resource allocation, and it increases the probability of a program's success.

You requested that we evaluate the reliability of the life-cycle cost estimate the Bureau submitted to Congress in October 2017. This chapter (1) evaluates the reliability of the Bureau's revised life-cycle cost estimate for the 2020 Census, and the extent to which the Bureau is using it as a management tool; and (2) compares the 2015 and 2017 life-cycle cost estimates to describe key drivers of cost growth.

For both objectives, we reviewed documentation related to the cost estimate and interviewed Bureau officials responsible for developing the 2020 Census life-cycle cost estimate. For the first question, we interviewed Bureau officials and evaluated whether the Bureau's cost estimate was generated according to best practices of our Cost Estimating and Assessment Guide.[5] We also assessed the extent to which the Bureau is using the cost estimate as a management tool. For the second question, we compared cost information included in the 2015 and 2017 cost estimates. We relied on our cost assessment guide as criteria. More information on our scope and methodology can be found in appendix I.

We conducted this performance audit from December 2017 to August 2018 in accordance with generally accepted government auditing standards. Those standards require that we plan and perform the audit to obtain sufficient, appropriate evidence to provide a reasonable basis for our findings and conclusions based on our audit objectives. We believe that the evidence obtained provides a reasonable basis for our findings and conclusions based on our audit objectives.

BACKGROUND

A high-quality, reliable cost estimate is a key tool for budgeting, planning, and managing the 2020 Census. According to OMB, programs

---

[5] GAO, *GAO Cost Estimating and Assessment Guide: Best Practices for Developing and Managing Capital Program Costs* (Supersedes GAO-07-1134SP), GAO-09-3SP (Washington, D.C.: Mar. 2, 2009).

must maintain current and well-documented estimates of program costs, and these estimates must encompass the full life-cycle of the program.[6] Among other things, OMB states that generating reliable program cost estimates is a critical function necessary to support OMB's capital programming process. Without this capability, agencies are at risk of experiencing program cost overruns, missed deadlines, and performance shortfalls.

A reliable cost estimate is critical to the success of any federal government program. With the information from reliable estimates, managers can:

- make informed investment decisions,
- formulate realistic budgets,
- allocate program resources,
- measure program progress,
- proactively correct course when warranted, and
- ensure overall accountability for results.

To be considered reliable, a cost estimate must meet the criteria for each of the four characteristics outlined in our Cost Estimating and Assessment Guide.[7] According to our analysis, a cost estimate is considered reliable if the overall assessment ratings for each of the four characteristics are substantially or fully met. If any of the characteristics are not met, minimally met, or partially met, then the cost estimate does not fully reflect the characteristics of a high-quality estimate and cannot be considered reliable. Those characteristics are:

- Well-documented: An estimate is thoroughly documented, including source data and significance, clearly detailed

---

[6] Office of Management and Budget, *Preparation, Submission, and Execution of the Budget,* Circular No. A-11 (Washington, D.C.: June 2006); *Management of Federal Information Resources,* Circular No. A-130 Revised (Washington, D.C.: Executive Office of the President, Nov. 28, 2000); and *Capital Programming Guide: Preparation, Submission, and Execution of the Budget,* Supplement to Circular A-11, Part 7 (Washington, D.C.: June 2006).

[7] GAO-09-3SP.

calculations and results, and explanations of why particular methods and references were chosen. Data can be traced to their source documents.
- Accurate: An estimate is unbiased, the work is not overly conservative or overly optimistic, and is based on an assessment of most likely costs. Few, if any, mathematical mistakes are present.
- Credible: Any limitations of the analysis because of uncertainty or bias surrounding data or assumptions are discussed. Major assumptions are varied, and other outcomes are recomputed, to determine how sensitive they are to changes in the assumptions. Risk and uncertainty analysis is performed to determine the level of risk associated with the estimate. The estimate's results are cross- checked, and an independent cost estimate (ICE) is conducted to see whether other estimation methods produce similar results.
- Comprehensive: An estimate has enough detail to ensure that cost elements are neither omitted nor double counted. All cost-influencing ground rules and assumptions are detailed in the estimate's documentation.

Past GAO Work on Census Cost Estimation

Meeting best practices outlined in our Cost Estimating and Assessment Guide for a reliable cost estimate has been a long-standing challenge for the Bureau. In 2008 we reported that the 2010 Census cost estimate was not reliable because it lacked documentation and was not comprehensive, accurate, or credible. For example, in our 2008 report on the Bureau's cost estimation process, Bureau officials were unable to provide documentation that supported the assumptions for the initial 2001 life-cycle cost estimate as well as the updates.[8] Consequently, we recommended that the Bureau

---
[8] GAO, *2010 Census: Census Bureau Should Take Action to Improve the Credibility and Accuracy of Its Cost Estimate for the Decennial Census*, GAO-08-554 (Washington, D.C.: June 16, 2008).

establish guidance, policies, and procedures for estimating costs that would meet best practices criteria. The Bureau agreed with the recommendation and said at the time that it already had efforts underway to improve its future cost estimation methods and systems. Moreover, weaknesses in the life-cycle cost estimate were one reason we designated the 2010 Census a GAO High- Risk Area in 2008.[9]

In 2012 we reported that, while the Bureau was taking steps to strengthen its life-cycle cost estimates, it had not yet established guidance for developing cost estimates. We recommended that the Bureau finalize its guidance, policies, and procedures for cost estimation in accordance with best practices.[10] The Bureau agreed with the overall theme of the report but did not comment on the recommendation. During this review we found that the Bureau took steps to address this recommendation, which is discussed later in this chapter. Such guidance can help to institutionalize best practices and ensure consistent processes and operations for producing reliable estimates.

In a 2016 report we found that the October 2015 version of the Bureau's life-cycle cost estimate for the 2020 Census was not reliable.[11] Overall, we reported that the 2020 Census life-cycle cost estimate partially met two of the characteristics of a reliable cost estimate (comprehensive and accurate) and minimally met the other two (well-documented and credible). We recommended that the Bureau take specific steps to ensure its cost estimate meets the characteristics of a high-quality estimate. The Bureau agreed with this recommendation, and took steps to improve the reliability of its cost estimate, which we focus on later in this chapter. Consequently, an unreliable life-cycle cost estimate is one of the reasons we designated the 2020 Census a GAO High-Risk Area in 2017.[12]

---

[9] GAO, *Information Technology: Significant Problems of Critical Automation Program Contribute to Risks Facing 2010 Census*, GAO-08-550T (Washington, D.C.: Mar. 5, 2008). Other factors contributing to the 2008 high risk designation included long-standing weaknesses in the Bureau's management of information technology and the fact that the Bureau delayed the dress rehearsal and dropped several operations.

[10] GAO, *Decennial Census: Additional Actions Could Improve the Census Bureau's Ability to Control Costs for the 2020 Census*, GAO-12-80 (Washington, D.C.: Jan. 24, 2012).

[11] GAO-16-628.

[12] GAO-17-317.

Development of the 2020 Cost Estimate

In October 2015, the Bureau estimated the cost of the 2020 Census to be $12.3 billion. According to the Bureau, the October 2015 version was the Bureau's first attempt to model the life-cycle cost of its planned 2020 Census, in contrast to its earlier 2011 estimate, which the Bureau said was intended to produce an approximation of potential savings and to begin developing the methodology for producing decennial life-cycle cost estimates covering all phases of the decennial life cycle. To help control costs while maintaining accuracy, the Bureau introduced significant change to how it conducts the decennial census in 2020. Its planned innovations include reengineering how it builds its address list, improving self-response by encouraging the use of the Internet and telephone, using administrative records to reduce field work, and reengineering field operations using technology to reduce manual effort and improve productivity. In contrast to the estimated $12.3 billion in 2015, the 2020 Census would cost $17.8 billion in constant 2020 dollars if the Bureau repeated the 2010 Census design and methods, according to the Bureau's estimates.

In October 2017, Commerce announced that it had updated the October 2015 life-cycle cost estimate, projecting the life-cycle cost of the 2020 Census to be $15.6 billion, an increase of over $3 billion (27 percent) over its 2015 estimate. (See Figure 1.) In developing the 2017 version of the cost estimate, Bureau cost estimators identified cost inputs, their ranges for possible outcomes, and overall cost estimating relationships (i.e., logical or mathematical formulas, or both). To identify cost inputs and the ranges of potential outcomes, the Bureau worked with subject matter experts and used historical data to support assumptions and generate inputs. The Bureau's cost estimation team used a software tool to generate the cost estimate.[13]

---

[13] TM1 is an IBM software tool that enables the generation of cost estimates with capabilities for detailed modeling of the cost of complex programs comprised of multiple products and operations with thousands of variables. The software also supports cost model sensitivity and uncertainty analysis around key input variables by defining simple statistical distributions around a central estimate for each variable (i.e., minimum, median, and

Because cost estimates predict future program costs, uncertainty is always associated with them.[14] For example, data from the past (such as fuel prices) may not always be relevant in the future. Risk and uncertainty refer to the fact that because a cost estimate is a forecast, there is always a chance that the actual cost will differ from the estimate. One way to determine whether a program is realistically budgeted is to perform an uncertainty analysis, so that the probability associated with achieving its point estimate can be determined, usually relying on simulations such as those of Monte Carlo methods. This can be particularly useful in portraying the uncertainty implications of various cost estimates.

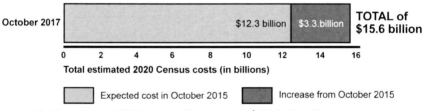

Source: GAO analysis of U.S. Census Bureau data. | GAO-18-635.

Figure 1. Increases to the 2020 Census Life-Cycle Costs Estimated by the Census Bureau.

Consistent with cost estimation practices outlined in our Cost Estimating and Assessment Guide, the estimate was compared with two independent cost estimates (ICE), developed by Commerce's Office of Acquisition Management (OAM) and the Bureau's Office of Cost Estimation, Analysis, and Assessment. The offices producing the ICEs and the cost estimate team worked together to examine the process each used, an effort known as the reconciliation process. Through this reconciliation, the Bureau identified areas where discrepancies existed and elements that could require additional review and possible improvement.

---

maximum), as well as an interface to support quick model re-estimation and Monte Carlo simulations. DBiT is an integrated set of applications on the TM1 platform for cost modeling and estimation, budget planning, and formulation and execution; as well as for analysis and interactive reporting.

[14] Uncertainty is the indefiniteness about the outcome of a situation. It is assessed in cost estimate models to estimate the risk (or probability) that a specific funding level will be exceeded.

According to Bureau documentation the estimate will be updated as the program meets milestones and to reflect changes in technical or program assumptions. Figure 2 details the Bureau's cost estimation process. OAM was involved extensively in the development of the 2017 estimate, an increased involvement compared to 2015, according to Bureau officials. OAM participated in regular review meetings throughout the development of the estimate and also developed an independent cost estimate, as shown in the figure.

End-to-end system testing activities for the 2020 Census are currently underway in Providence, Rhode Island. According to the Bureau, information collected from the test, such as overall response rates and the use of administrative records to inform census records, will inform future versions of the life-cycle cost estimate. Some updates from the test will be incorporated into the next cost estimate, which will be available in the first quarter of the coming fiscal year.

CENSUS BUREAU HAS MADE PROGRESS BUT HAS NOT TAKEN ALL THE STEPS NEEDED TO ENSURE THE RELIABILITY OF 2020 COST ESTIMATE

Since our June 2016 report, in which we reviewed the Bureau's 2015 version of the cost estimate, the Bureau has made significant progress.[15] For example, the Bureau has put into place a work breakdown structure (WBS) that defines the work, products, activities, and resources necessary to accomplish the 2020 Census and is standardized for use in budget planning, operational planning, and cost estimation. However, the Bureau's October 2017 cost estimate for the 2020 Census does not fully reflect characteristics of a high-quality estimate as described in our Cost Estimating and Assessment Guide and cannot be considered reliable.[16]

Our Cost Estimating and Assessment Guide describes best practices for developing reliable cost estimates. For our reporting needs, we

---

[15] GAO-16-628.
[16] GAO-09-3SP.

collapsed these best practices into four characteristics for sound cost estimating— comprehensive, well-documented, accurate, and credible— and identified specific best practices for each characteristic. To be considered reliable, an organization must meet or substantially meet each characteristic. Our review found the Bureau met or substantially met three out of the four characteristics of a reliable cost estimate, while it partially met one characteristic: well-documented. When compared to the October 2015 estimate, the 2017 estimate shows considerable improvement. (See Figure 3 below.)

Well-Documented

Cost estimates are considered valid if they are well-documented to the point they can be easily repeated or updated and can be traced to original sources through auditing, according to best practices.

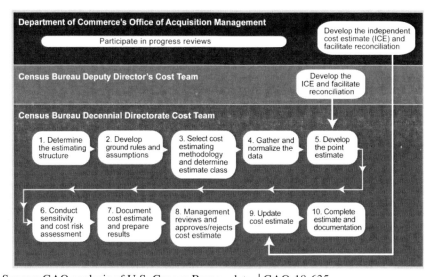

Source: GAO analysis of U.S. Census Bureau data. | GAO-18-635

Figure 2. Census Bureau's Cost Estimation Process.

Characteristic	2015 Assessment	2017 Assessment
Well-Documented	Minimally Met	Partially Met
Accurate	Partially Met	Substantially Met
Credible	Minimally Met	Substantially Met
Comprehensive	Partially Met	Met

● Met   ◕ Substantially Met   ◐ Partially Met   ◔ Minimally Met   ○ Not Met

Source: GAO analysis of U.S. Census Bureau data. | GAO-18-635.

Note: Not Met – Census Bureau provided no evidence that satisfies the criterion; Minimally Met – Census Bureau provided evidence that satisfies a small portion of the criterion; Partially Met – Census Bureau provided evidence that satisfies about half of the criterion; Substantially Met – Census Bureau provided evidence that satisfies a large portion of the criterion; and Met – Census Bureau provided complete evidence that satisfies the entire criterion.

Figure 3. Overview of the Census Bureau's 2017 Cost Estimate Compared to Characteristics of a Reliable Cost Estimate.

The Bureau only partially met the criteria for well-documented, as set forth in our Cost Estimating and Assessment Guide. A cost estimate that does not fully meet the criteria for well-documented cannot be used by management to make informed and effective implementation decisions. The well-documented characteristic comprises five best practices. The Bureau substantially met two out of five best practices (as shown in Figure 4). First, the estimate describes in sufficient detail the calculations performed and the estimating methodology used to derive each element's cost, and the cost estimate had been reviewed by management. Since cost estimates can inform key decisions and budget requests, it is vital that management review and understand how the estimate was developed, including risks associated with the underlying data and methods.

Characteristic	Best Practice	Individual Assessment
Well-Documented	The documentation should capture the source data used, the reliability of the data, and how the data were normalized.	Partially Met
	The documentation describes in sufficient detail the calculations performed and the estimating methodology used to derive each element's cost.	Substantially Met
	The documentation describes step by step how the estimate was developed so that a cost analyst unfamiliar with the program could understand what was done and replicate it.	Partially Met
Overall Assessment Partially Met	The documentation discusses the technical baseline description and the data in the baseline is consistent with the estimate.	Partially Met
	The documentation provides evidence that the cost estimate was reviewed and accepted by management.	Substantially Met

● Met ◕ Substantially Met ◐ Partially Met ◔ Minimally Met ○ Not Met

Source: GAO analysis of U.S. Census Bureau data. | GAO-18-635.

Figure 4. Assessment of Census Bureau's Cost Estimate for Well-Documented.

The cost estimate only partially met three best practices for the characteristic of being well-documented. In general, some documentation was missing, inconsistent, or difficult to understand. First, we found that source data did not always support the information described in the basis of estimate document or could not be found in the files provided for two of the Bureau's largest field operations: Address Canvassing and Non-Response Follow-Up (NRFU).[17] For example, the cost estimate documentation referred to actual data from the 2010 Census and information obtained from experts as sources for address canvassing rework rates.[18] However, the folder source documents provided as support

---

[17] The basis of estimate document describes in detail the scope of the estimate, the cost approaches and ground rules, the data sources, main assumptions, and cost estimating relationships.

[18] The address canvassing rework rate refers to the percentage of housing units that will need to be revisited during initial in-field data collection. The Bureau's address canvassing operation updates its address list and maps, which are the foundation of the decennial census, through data collection efforts conducted both in the office and through in-field visits to address locations.

for the basis of estimate did not include this information. Next, in several cases, we could not replicate calculations, such as for mileage costs, using the description provided. Lastly, we found that some of the cost elements did not trace clearly to supporting spreadsheets and assumption documents.

Failure to document an estimate in enough detail makes it more difficult to replicate calculations, or to detect possible errors in the estimate; reduces transparency of the estimation process; and can undermine the ability to use the information to improve future cost estimates or even to reconcile the estimate with another independent cost estimate. The Bureau told us it would continue to make improvements to ensure the estimate is well- documented. For the estimate to be considered well-documented, the Bureau will need to address these issues.

Accurate

An accurate cost estimate supports measurement of program progress by providing unbiased and correct data, which can help management ensure accountability for scheduled results. We found the Bureau's cost estimate substantially met the criteria for accuracy. As shown in Figure 5, and in line with best practices outlined in our Cost Estimating and Assessment Guide, the estimate was not overly optimistic; appeared to be free of errors; was based on historical data or input from subject matter experts; and, according to Bureau officials, is updated regularly as information becomes available.

The Bureau can enhance the accuracy of their estimate by increasing the level of detail included in the documentation, such as detail on specific inflation indices used, and by monitoring actual costs against estimates. We identified areas for improvement, which, according to Bureau officials, will be addressed as part of its ongoing efforts. For example, while the basis of estimate document describes different inflation indexes, it was not clear exactly which indexes were applied to the various cost elements in the estimate. Also, evidence of how variances between estimated costs and actual expenses would be tracked over time was not available at the time of our analysis. Tools to track variance enable management to measure progress against planned outcomes. Bureau officials stated that they already have systems in place that can be adapted for tracking estimated and actual costs.

Characteristic	Best Practice	Individual Assessment
Accurate	The cost estimate results are unbiased, not overly conservative or optimistic, and based on an assessment of most likely costs.	Substantially Met
	The estimate has been adjusted properly for inflation.	Partially Met
	The estimate contains few, if any, minor mistakes.	Met
	The cost estimate is regularly updated to reflect significant changes in the program so that it is always reflecting current status.	Met
Overall Assessment	Variances between planned and actual costs are documented, explained, and reviewed.	Minimally Met
Substantially Met	The estimate is based on a historical record of cost estimating and actual experiences from other comparable programs.	Met

● Met   ◕ Substantially Met   ◐ Partially Met   ◑ Minimally Met   ○ Not Met

Source: GAO analysis of U.S. Census Bureau data. | GAO-18-635.

Figure 5. Assessment of Census Bureau's Cost Estimate for Accurate.

Credible

All estimates include a certain amount of informed judgment about the future. Assumptions made at the start of a program can turn out to be inaccurate. Credible cost estimates identify limitations due to uncertainty or bias surrounding data or assumptions, and control for these uncertainties by identifying and quantifying cost elements that represent the most risk. We found that the Bureau's cost estimate substantially met the criteria for credible, as shown in Figure 6 below.

The Bureau's cost estimate clearly identifies risks and uncertainties, and describes approaches taken to mitigate them. In line with best practices outlined in our Cost Estimating and Assessment Guide, the Bureau did the following:

Characteristic	Best Practice	Individual Assessment
Credible	The cost estimate includes a sensitivity analysis that identifies a range of possible costs based on varying major assumptions, parameters, and data inputs.	Met
	A risk and uncertainty analysis was conducted that quantified the imperfectly understood risks and identified the effects of changing key cost driver assumptions and factors.	Substantially Met
	Major cost elements were cross-checked to see whether results were similar.	Partially Met
Overall Assessment: Substantially Met	An independent cost estimate was conducted by a group outside the acquiring organization to determine whether other estimating methods produce similar results.	Met

● Met ◕ Substantially Met ◐ Partially Met ◔ Minimally Met ○ Not Met

Source: GAO analysis of U.S. Census Bureau data. | GAO-18-635.

Figure 6. Assessment of Census Bureau's Cost Estimate for Credible.

- Sensitivity analysis. The Bureau conducted sensitivity analysis to identify possible changes to estimated costs for the 2020 Census based on varying major assumptions, parameters, and data inputs.[19] For example, the Bureau calculated the likely cost implications for a range of possible response rates to identify a range of projected costs and to calculate appropriate reserves for risk. Bureau officials

---

[19] Sensitivity analysis first identifies key elements that drive cost and their associated assumptions and then calculates the estimate's sensitivity to changes in the underlying assumptions.

stated that they also identified the estimate input parameters that contributed the most to estimate uncertainty.
- Risk and uncertainty analysis. A cost estimate is a forecast, and as such, there is always a chance that the actual cost will differ from the estimate. Uncertainty is the indefiniteness about the outcome of a situation. Uncertainty is assessed in cost estimate models to estimate the risk (or probability) that a specific funding level will be exceeded. We found the Bureau performed an uncertainty analysis on a portion of the estimate to determine whether estimated costs were realistic and to establish the probability of achieving projections outlined in the estimate. The Bureau used a combination of modeling based on Monte Carlo analysis and allocations of funding for risks.[20] The Monte Carlo simulation was performed on a portion of the estimate to account for uncertainty around various operational parameters for which a range of outcomes was possible, including Internet response rates and the extent to which data collection issues might be resolved using administrative records. To account for the inherent uncertainty of assumptions included within the life-cycle cost estimate, the Bureau added funding to the cost estimate totaling approximately $292 million to account for risks based on the results of the Monte Carlo analysis.

For other risks, such as acquisition lead time and the possibility of delays in information technology (IT) development, contingency funding was added to the estimate to reflect the potential cost of resolving these issues, through use of a backup system or an alternative approach. These are described as "special risks" in the Bureau's basis of estimate, and total approximately $171 million.

---

[20] The Monte Carlo simulation randomly samples parameters from a probability distribution for each variable (using parameters that define a statistical distribution, such as minimum, most likely, and maximum) and then uses those values to calculate an output distribution, preserving the logical and mathematical relationship among inputs and outputs. Typically, after thousands of simulation runs, an output distribution is generated as a result of the analysis.

Based on additional sensitivity analysis, the Bureau added approximately $965 million to the cost estimate to reflect discrete risks outlined in the risk register as well as those associated with (1) variability in self-response rates, (2) the effect of fluctuations in the size and wage rate of the temporary workforce on the cost of field operations, and (3) the potential need to reduce the enumerator-to-manager staffing ratio in case expected efficiencies in field operations are not realized.

In addition to these provisions, the Secretary of Commerce added a contingency amount of about $1.2 billion to account for what the Bureau refers to as unknown-unknowns. Bureau documentation states that conducting a decennial census is an extremely complex, high-risk operation. In order to mitigate some of the risk, contingency funding must be available to initiate ad hoc activities necessary to overcome unforeseen issues. According to Bureau documentation these include such risks as natural disasters or cyber-attacks. The Bureau provides a description of how the general risk contingency is calculated. However, this description does not clearly link calculated amounts to the risks themselves.

In our June 2016 report we reported the Bureau had not properly accounted for risk and recommended the Bureau, in part; improve control over how risk and uncertainty are accounted for. We continue to believe the prior recommendation from our June 2016 report remains valid and should be addressed: that the Bureau properly account for risk in the 2020 Census cost estimate, among other things. As such, risks need to be linked to the $1.2 billion general risk contingency fund.

- Independent cost estimate. According to best practices outlined in our Cost Estimating and Assessment Guide, an independent cost estimate should be performed to determine whether alternate estimate approaches produce similar results. The Bureau compared their estimate with two independent cost estimates, developed by Commerce's Office of Acquisition Management and the Bureau's Office of Cost Estimation and Assessment. As part of their process for finalizing the cost estimate, Bureau officials reconciled differences between the estimates in discussions with the two offices, resulting in more conservative assumptions by the Bureau around risk and uncertainty in both cases.

In addition to implementing our recommendation to properly account for risk, going forward, while the Bureau substantially met the credibility characteristic it will be important for them to also integrate regular cross-checks of methodology into their cost estimation process.[21] In our analysis we observed that no specific cross-checks of cost methodology were performed. According to the Bureau, cross-checks were not performed because the Bureau considered the independent cost estimates as overall cross-checks on the reliability of their methodology and did not conduct additional cross-checks. The main purpose of cross-checking is to determine whether alternative methods for specific cost elements within the cost estimate could produce similar results. An independent cost estimate, though important for the credibility of an estimate, does not fulfill the same function as a targeted cross-check of individual elements.[22]

Comprehensive

Comprehensive estimates have enough detail to ensure that cost elements are neither omitted nor double-counted, all cost-influencing assumptions are detailed in the estimate's documentation, and a work breakdown structure is defined.[23] Our analysis of the 2017 cost estimate

---

[21] To cross-check is to apply a different method for cost estimation for cost drivers. If the alternative method produces similar results, then confidence in the estimate increases leading to greater credibility.

[22] Cross-checks and independent cost estimates are two different techniques for ensuring the credibility of a cost estimate. Cross-checking is performed by the original cost estimating team, on individual cost elements, to validate their primary estimating methodologies. Independent cost estimates are typically performed by organizations higher in the decision-making process than the office performing the baseline estimate. They provide an independent view of expected program costs that tests the program office's estimate for reasonableness.

[23] A WBS defines in detail the work necessary to accomplish a program's objectives. It describes the products and activities necessary to complete the program and provides a basis for identifying resources and tasks needed.

demonstrates improvement over the 2015 cost estimate when the Bureau's cost estimate only partially met the criteria for comprehensive.[24]

Characteristic	Best Practice	Individual Assessment
Comprehensive	The cost estimate includes all life cycle costs.	● Met
	The cost estimate completely defines the program, reflects the current schedule, and is technically reasonable.	● Met
	The cost estimate work breakdown structure is product-oriented, traceable to the statement of work/objective, and at an appropriate level of detail to ensure that cost elements are neither omitted nor double-counted.	● Met
Overall Assessment: ● Met	The estimate documents all cost-influencing ground rules and assumptions.	◐ Substantially Met

● Met ◐ Substantially Met ◐ Partially Met ◐ Minimally Met ○ Not Met

Source: GAO analysis of U.S. Census Bureau data. | GAO-18-635.

Figure 7. Assessment of Census Bureau's Cost Estimate for Comprehensive.

We found the Bureau met or substantially met all four best practices for the comprehensive characteristic, as shown in Figure 7. For example, all life-cycle costs are included in the estimate along with a complete description of the 2020 Census program and current schedule. We also found that the Bureau substantially met criteria for documenting cost influencing ground rules and assumptions. A standardized WBS (as detailed in Table 1) with supporting dictionary outlines the major work of the program and describes the activities and deliverables at the project

---

[24] If the cost estimate is not comprehensive, then it cannot fully meet the well-documented, accurate, or credible best practice characteristics. For instance, if the cost estimate is missing some cost elements, then the documentation will be incomplete, the estimate will be inaccurate, and the result will not be credible due to the potential for underestimating costs and the lack of a full risk and uncertainty analysis.

level where costs are tracked. In 2016, the Bureau's WBS did not contain sufficient detail and we found significant differences in the presentation of the work between sources. In 2017, based on our review of Bureau documentation and interviews with Bureau officials, we found that the WBS is standardized and cost elements are presented in detail. The WBS is a necessary program management tool because it provides a basic framework for a variety of related tasks like estimating costs, developing schedules, identifying resources, determining where risks may occur, and providing the means for measuring program status.

Table 1. Census Work Breakdown Structure Elements

Program Management	Policies, processes, and control functions for planning and implementing the 2020 Census.
Census Survey and Engineering	Scientific, technical, and managerial efforts needed to evolve, verify, or deploy and support a census.
Frame	Activities related to the development of a geospatial frame (addresses and maps) to serve as the universe for enumeration activities.
Response	Deliverables and activities required to access, maintain, and process the response data.
Published Data	Activities related to preparing and disseminating publishable data.
Test and Evaluation	To ensure all systems and activities meet the technical and operational needs of the Bureau.
Infrastructure	Administrative functions, service, logistics, information technology, and operational support.

Source: GAO analysis of U.S. Census Bureau documents. | GAO-18-635.

Although the Bureau's updated life-cycle cost estimate reflects three of the four characteristics of a reliable cost estimate, we are not making any new recommendations to the Bureau in this chapter. We continue to believe the prior recommendation, made in 2016, remains relevant: that the Secretary of Commerce ensure that the Bureau finalizes the steps needed to fully meet the characteristics of a high-quality estimate, most notably in the well-documented area. The Bureau told us it has used our best practices for cost estimation to develop their cost estimate, and will focus on those best practices that require attention moving forward. Without a reliable cost estimate, the Bureau is limited in its ability to make informed decisions about program resources and to effectively measure progress against operational objectives.

Life-Cycle Cost Estimate is Used by Management to Inform Decisions

OMB, in its guidance for preparing and executing agency budgets, cites that credible cost estimates are vital for sound management decision making and for any program or capital project to succeed.[25] A well-developed cost estimate serves as a tool for program development and oversight, supporting management to make informed decisions.

According to the Bureau, the 2020 Census cost estimate is used as a management tool to guide decision making. Bureau officials stated the cost estimate is used to examine the cost impact of program changes. For example, the cost estimate served as the basis for the fiscal year 2019 funding request developed by the Bureau. The Bureau also said it used the 2020 Census life-cycle cost estimate to establish cost controls during budget formulation activities and to monitor spending levels for fiscal year 2019 activities. According to the Bureau, as detailed operational and implementation plans are defined, the 2020 Census life- cycle cost estimate has been and will continue to be used to support ongoing "what-if" analyses in determining the cost impacts of design decisions. Specifically, using the cost estimate to model the impact of changes on overall cost, the Bureau adjusted the scope of the Census Enterprise Data Collection and Processing (CEDCaP) operation.[26]

Census Bureau Guidance to Develop Cost Estimates Meets Best Practices

The processes for developing and updating estimates are designed to inform management about program progress and the use of program resources, supporting cost-driven planning efforts and well-informed decision making. Our work has identified a number of best practices for use in developing guidance related to cost estimation and analysis that are

---

[25] Office of Management and Budget, *Capital Programming Guide: Supplement to Circular A-11, Planning, Budgeting and Acquisition of Capital Assets*. (Washington, D.C.: July 2016).
[26] CEDCap is an enterprise-wide initiative intended to deliver a system-of-systems to support all of the Bureau's survey data collection and processing functions.

the basis of effective program cost estimating and should result in reliable and valid cost estimates that management can use for making informed decisions.[27]

In 2012 we reported that the Bureau had not yet established guidance for developing cost estimates.[28] We recommended that the Bureau establish guidance, policies, and procedures for developing cost estimates that would meet best practice criteria. The Bureau agreed with the theme of the report but did not specifically agree with the recommendation. Moreover, in June 2016, we also reported that the cost estimation team did not record how and why it changed assumptions that were provided to it and did not document the sources of all data it used.[29] The documentation of these changes to assumptions did not happen because the Bureau lacked written guidance and procedures for the cost estimation team to follow. During this review we found the Bureau has since established reliable guidance, processes, and policies for developing cost estimates and managing the cost estimation process. The following documents, shown in Table 2, establish roles and responsibilities for oversight and approval of cost estimation processes, provide a detailed description of the steps taken to produce a high-quality cost estimate, and clarify the process for updating the cost estimate and associated documents over the life of a project.

The Decennial Census Program's Cost Estimate and Analysis Process, which provides a detailed description of the steps taken to produce a high-quality estimate, is reliable as it met the criteria for 8 steps and substantially met the criteria for 4 steps of the 12 best steps outlined in our Cost Estimating and Assessment Guide, as shown below in Figure 8. To avoid cost overruns and to support high performance, it will be important for the Bureau to abide by their newly developed policies and guidance and continue to use the life-cycle cost estimate as a management tool.

---

[27] GAO-09-3SP.
[28] GAO-12-80.
[29] GAO-16-628.

Table 2. Cost Estimation Guidance and Policy Documents

Title	Description
Cost Estimation and Analysis Guidance	Establishes the overall authority, requirements, activities, roles, and responsibilities for cost estimation and supporting analysis specifically within the Decennial Census Programs Directorate.
Cost Center of Excellence Charter	Charter for the core cost estimation body responsible for coordinating, facilitating, and supporting cost estimation and analysis activities across the 2020 Census Program.
Cost Estimate and Analysis Process	Step-by-step guidance and a framework for how the 2020 Census Program conducts cost estimation and analysis.
2020 Life-Cycle Cost Estimate Version Control Plan	Establishes a disciplined approach to cost estimate updates, changes, and releases.

Source: GAO analysis of U.S. Census Bureau documents. | GAO-18-635.

GAO 12 Step Cost Estimating Process — Assessment of Census guidance

Phase	Step	Assessment
Initiation and Research	1. Define the estimate's purpose	Substantially Met
	2. Define the estimating plan	Substantially Met
Assessment	3. Define the program characteristics	Substantially Met
	4. Determine the estimating structure	Met
	5. Identify ground rules and assumptions	Met
	6. Obtain the data	Met
	7. Develop the point estimate and compare it to an independent cost estimate	Met
Analysis	8. Conduct sensitivity analysis	Met
	9. Conduct a risk and uncertainty analysis	Met
	10. Document the estimate	Met
Presentation	11. Present estimate to management for approval	Substantially Met
	12. Update the estimate to reflect actual costs/changes	Met

● Met   ◐ Substantially Met   ◐ Partially Met   ◐ Minimally Met   ○ Not Met

Source: GAO analysis of U.S. Census Bureau data. | GAO-18-635.

Figure 8. Assessment of Census Bureau Cost Estimation Guidance.

INCREASED COSTS ARE DRIVEN BY AN ASSUMED DECREASE IN SELF-RESPONSE RATES AND INCREASES IN CONTINGENCY FUNDS AND IT COST CATEGORIES

The 2017 life-cycle cost estimate includes significantly higher costs than those included in the 2015 estimate. In 2015, the Bureau estimated that they could conduct the operation at a cost of $12.3 billion in constant 2020 dollars. The Bureau's latest cost estimate, announced in October 2017, reflects the same design, but at an expected cost of $15.6 billion. Figure 9 below shows the change in cost by WBS category for 2015 and 2017. The largest increases occurred in the Response, Managerial Contingency, and Census/Survey Engineering categories. Increased costs of $1.3 billion in the response category (costs related to collecting, maintaining, and processing survey response data) were in part due to reduced assumptions for self-response rates, leading to increases in the amount of data collected in the field, which is more costly to the Bureau. Contingency allocations increased overall from $1.35 billion in 2015 to $2.6 billion in 2017, as the Bureau gained a greater understanding of risks facing the 2020 Census. Increases of $838 million in the Census/Survey Engineering category were due mainly to the cost of an IT contract for integrating decennial survey systems that was not included in the 2015 cost estimate. Bureau officials attribute a decrease of $551 million in estimated costs for Program Management to changes in the categorization of costs associated with risks: In the 2017 version of the estimate, estimated costs related to program risks were allocated to their corresponding WBS element.

More generally, factors that contributed to cost fluctuations between the 2015 and 2017 cost estimates include:[30]

---

[30] Many of these factors are interrelated and their contribution to increases in certain cost categories may overlap. As one example, IT increases overlap with the Bureau's ability to define their contract requirements. Though we recognize the interconnection between these factors, we describe these separately for ease of explanation.

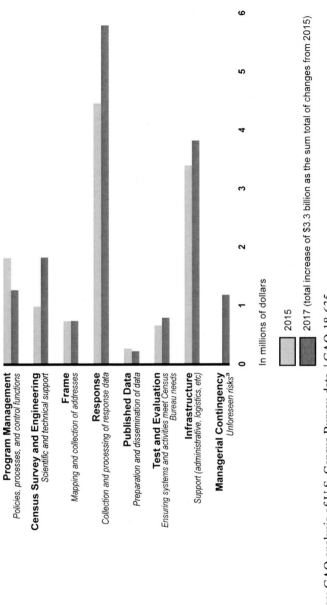

Source: GAO analysis of U.S. Census Bureau data. | GAO-18-635.

[a] The 2015 cost estimate also included managerial contingency amounts totaling $829 million; however, these were not presented as a separate work breakdown structure category.

Figure 9. Change in 2020 Census Cost Estimate by Work Breakdown Structure Category, 2015 vs. 2017.

- changes in assumptions for census operations,
- improved ability to anticipate and quantify risk,
- an overall increase in IT costs, and
- more defined contract requirements.

Changes in Assumptions

Several assumptions for the implementation of the 2020 Census have changed since the 2015 cost estimate. Some assumptions contributing to cost changes, mainly in the Response (related to collecting and processing response data) and Frame (the mapping and collecting addresses to frame enumeration activities) categories, include the following:

- Self-response rates. Changes in assumptions for expected self-response rates contributed to increases in the response category, as the assumed rate decreased from 63.5 percent in 2015 to 60.5 percent in 2017, thereby increasing the anticipated percentage and associated cost of nonresponse follow-up.[1] When the Bureau does not receive responses by mail, phone, or Internet, census enumerators visit each nonresponding household to obtain data. Thus, reduced self-response rates lead to increases in the amount of data collected in the field, which is more costly to the Bureau. Bureau officials attributed this decrease to a forecasted reduction in Internet response due to added authentication steps at log in and the elimination of the function allowing users to save their responses and return later to complete the survey.
- Productivity rates. The productivity of enumerators collecting data for NRFU is another variable in the cost estimate that was updated, contributing to cost increases in the response category. Expected productivity rates for NRFU decreased from the 2015 estimate of 4 attempts per hour to 2.9. According to Bureau documentation, this

---

[1] NRFU refers to enumerators personally visiting households that did not respond to the census through mail, phone or Internet.

more conservative estimate is based on historical data, rather than research and test data.
- In-office address canvassing rates. The Bureau will not go door-to-door to conduct in-field address canvassing across the country to update address and map information for every housing unit, as it has in prior decennial censuses. Rather, some areas would only need a review of their address and map information using computer imagery and third-party data sources—what the Bureau calls "in-office" address canvassing procedures. However, in March 2017, citing budget uncertainty the Bureau decided to discontinue one of the phases of in-office review address canvassing for the 2020 Census. The cancellation of that phase of in-office review is expected to increase the number of housing units canvassed in-field by 5 percent (from 25 to 30 percent of all canvassed housing units). In-field canvassing is more labor intensive compared to in office procedures. The 2017 version of the cost estimate reflects this increase in workload for in-field address canvassing, though overall changes in estimated costs for the Frame category, of which Address Canvassing is a part, were minimal.
- Staffing. Updated analysis resulted in changes to several staffing assumptions, which resulted in decreases across WBS categories. Changes included reduced pay rates for field data collection staff based on current labor market conditions and reductions in the length of staff engagement.

Anticipation of Risk

In general, contingency allocations increased overall from $1.35 billion in 2015 to $2.6 billion in 2017. This increase in contingency can be attributed, in part, to the Bureau gaining a clearer understanding of risk and uncertainty in the 2020 Census as it approaches. The Bureau developed some of its contingency based on proven risk management techniques, including Monte Carlo analysis and allocated funding for known risk scenarios. The 2017 estimate includes close to $1.4 billion in estimated costs for these risks, almost three times the amount included in the 2015 estimate. The basis of estimate contains detail on the various risks and the process for calculating the associated contingency. The 2017 version also includes a contingency amount of $1.2 billion for general risks, or unknown-unknowns, such as natural disasters and cyber-attacks.

Contingency amounts were reallocated within the WBS to more closely reflect the nature of the risk: Bureau officials attribute a decrease from the 2015 estimate of $551 million in estimated costs for program management to changes in the categorization of costs associated with risks. Officials stated that, in 2015, discrete program risks were previously consolidated as program management costs. In 2017, these discrete costs were reallocated to associate risks with the appropriate WBS element. For example, contingency amounts related to the likelihood of achieving a certain response rate previously included in the program management work breakdown category are now a part of the "response" work breakdown category.

Increased IT Costs

Increases in IT costs, totaling $1.59 billion, represented almost 50 percent of the total cost increase from 2015 to 2017. The total share of IT costs as a percentage of total census costs increased from 28 percent in 2015 to 32 percent in 2017, or from $3.41 billion to approximately $5 billion. Increases in IT costs are spread across seven cost categories. Figure 10 shows the IT and non-IT cost by WBS for the 2017 cost estimate. IT costs in infrastructure, response data, and census/survey WBSs account for the majority of the approximately $5 billion.

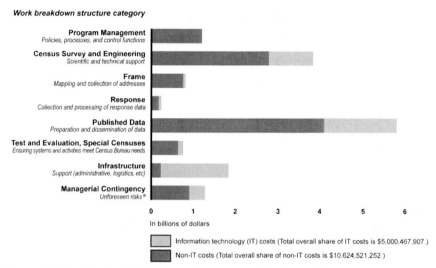

Source: GAO analysis of U.S. Census Bureau data. | GAO-18-635.

[a] The managerial contingency fund is included as a provision for unforeseen risks, which may or may not include IT related risks.

Figure 10. 2017 Cost Estimate, IT vs. Non IT Costs.

The Bureau's October 2015 cost estimate included IT costs for, among other things, system engineering, test and evaluation, and infrastructure, as well as for a portion of the Census Enterprise Data Collection and Processing (CEDCaP) program. The 2017 estimated IT cost increases were due, in large part, to the Bureau (1) updating the cost estimate for CEDCaP; (2) including an estimate for technical integration services that contributed to increases in the Census and Survey Engineering category; and (3) updating costs related to other major contracts (such as mobile device as a service, field IT services, and payroll systems).

Contract Requirements

Bureau documents described an overall improvement in the Bureau's ability to define and specify contract requirements. This resulted in updated estimates for several contracts, including for the Census

Questionnaire Assistance (CQA) contract.[2] Assumptions regarding call volume to the CQA were increased by 5 percent to account for expected response by phone after the elimination of the option to save Internet responses and return to complete the form later. The Bureau also cited updated cost data and the results of reconciliation with independent cost estimates as factors contributing to the increased costs of other major contracts, including for the procurement of data collection devices.

AGENCY COMMENTS AND OUR EVALUATION

The Secretary of Commerce provided comments on a draft of this chapter on August 2, 2018. The comments are reprinted in appendix II. The Department of Commerce generally agreed with our findings regarding the improvements the Census Bureau has made in its cost estimates. However, Commerce did not agree with our assessment that the Bureau's 2017 lifecycle cost estimate is "not reliable." Commerce noted that it had conducted two independent cost analyses and was satisfied that the cost estimate was reliable. The Bureau also provided technical comments that we incorporated, as appropriate.

We maintain that, to be considered reliable, a cost estimate must meet or substantially meet the criteria for each of the four characteristics outlined in our Cost Estimating and Assessment Guide. These characteristics are derived from measures consistently applied by cost estimating organizations throughout the federal government and industry and are considered best practices for the development of reliable cost estimates. Without a reliable cost estimate, the Bureau is limited in its ability to make informed decisions about program resources and to effectively measure progress against operational objectives. Thus, while the Bureau has made considerable progress in all four of the characteristics, it has only partially met the criteria for the characteristic of

---

[2] CQA has two primary functions: to provide 1) questionnaire assistance by telephone and email for respondents by answering questions about the census in general and regarding specific items on the census form, and 2) an option for respondents to complete a census interview over the telephone.

being well-documented. Until the Bureau meets or substantially meets the criteria for this characteristic, the cost estimate cannot be considered reliable.

As agreed with your offices, unless you publicly announce the contents of this chapter earlier, we plan no further distribution until 30 days from the report date. At that time, we will send copies of the report to the appropriate congressional committees, the Secretary of Commerce, the Under Secretary of Economic Affairs, the Acting Director of the U.S. Census Bureau, and other interested parties.

Robert Goldenkoff
Director, Strategic Issues

List of Requesters

The Honorable Claire McCaskill
Ranking Member
Committee on Homeland Security and Governmental Affairs
United States Senate

The Honorable Gary Peters
Ranking Member
Subcommittee on Federal Spending Oversight and Emergency Management
Committee on Homeland Security and Governmental Affairs
United States Senate

The Honorable Elijah E. Cummings
Ranking Member
Committee on Oversight and Government Reform
House of Representatives

The Honorable John A. Culberson
Chairman

The Honorable José Serrano
Ranking Member
Subcommittee on Commerce, Justice, Science, and Related Agencies
Committee on Appropriations
House of Representatives

APPENDIX I: OBJECTIVES, SCOPE, AND METHODOLOGY

The purpose of our review was to evaluate the reliability of the Census Bureau's (Bureau) life-cycle cost estimate using our Cost Estimating and Assessment Guide.[3] We reviewed (1) the extent to which the Bureau's life-cycle cost estimate and associated guidance met our best practices for cost estimation using documentation and information obtained in discussions with the Bureau related to the 2020 life-cycle cost estimate and (2) compared the 2015 and 2017 life-cycle cost estimates to describe key drivers of cost growth. For both objectives we reviewed documentation from the Bureau on the 2020 life-cycle cost estimate and interviewed Bureau and Department of Commerce officials.

For the first objective, we relied on our Cost Estimating and Assessment Guide as criteria. Our cost specialists assessed measures consistently applied by cost-estimating organizations throughout the federal government and industry and considered best-practices for developing reliable cost estimates. We analyzed the cost estimating practices used by the Bureau against these best practices and evaluated them in four categories: comprehensive, well-documented, accurate, and credible.

---

[3] GAO-09-3SP.

- Comprehensive. The cost estimate should include both government and contractor costs of the program over its full life-cycle, from inception of the program through design, development, deployment, and operation and maintenance to retirement of the program. It should also completely define the program, reflect the current schedule, and be technically reasonable. Comprehensive cost estimates should be structured in sufficient detail to ensure that cost elements are neither omitted nor double counted. Specifically, the cost estimate should be based on a product-oriented work breakdown structure (WBS) that allows a program to track cost and schedule by defined deliverables, such as hardware or software components. Finally, where information is limited and judgments are made, the cost estimate should document all cost-influencing assumptions.
- Well-documented. A good cost estimate—while taking the form of a single number—is supported by detailed documentation that describes how it was derived and how the expected funding will be spent in order to achieve a given objective. Therefore, the documentation should capture in writing such things as the source data used, the calculations performed and their results, and the estimating methodology used to derive each WBS element's cost. Moreover, this information should be captured in such a way that the data used to derive the estimate can be traced back to, and verified against, their sources so that the estimate can be easily replicated and updated. The documentation should also discuss the technical baseline description and how the data were normalized. Finally, the documentation should include evidence that the cost estimate was reviewed and accepted by management.
- Accurate. The cost estimate should provide for results that are unbiased, and it should not be overly conservative or optimistic. An estimate is accurate when it is based on an assessment of most likely costs; adjusted properly for inflation; and contains few, if any, minor mistakes. In addition, a cost estimate should be updated regularly to reflect significant changes in the program—such as

when schedules or other assumptions change—and actual costs, so that it is always reflecting current status. During the update process, variances between planned and actual costs should be documented, explained, and reviewed. Among other things, the estimate should be grounded in a historical record of cost estimating and actual experiences on other comparable programs.
- Credible. The cost estimate should discuss any limitations of the analysis because of uncertainty or biases surrounding data or assumptions. Major assumptions should be varied, and other outcomes recomputed to determine how sensitive they are to changes in the assumptions. Risk and uncertainty analysis should be performed to determine the level of risk associated with the estimate. Further, the estimate's cost drivers should be cross-checked, and an independent cost estimate conducted by a group outside the acquiring organization should be developed to determine whether other estimating methods produce similar results.

If any of the characteristics are not met, minimally met, or partially met, then the cost estimate does not fully reflect the characteristics of a high- quality estimate and cannot be considered reliable.

We also analyzed the Bureau's cost estimation and analysis guidance and evaluated them against a 12-step process outlined in our Cost Estimation and Assessment Guide. A high-quality cost estimating process integrates the following:

1. Define estimate's purpose.
2. Develop estimating plan.
3. Define program characteristics.
4. Determine estimating structure.

5. Identify ground rules and assumptions.
6. Obtain data.
7. Develop point estimate and compare it to an independent cost estimate.
8. Conduct sensitivity analysis.
9. Conduct risk and uncertainty analysis.
10. Document the estimate.
11. Present estimate to management for approval.
12. Update the estimate to reflect actual costs and changes.

These 12 steps, when followed correctly, should result in reliable and valid cost estimates that management can use for making informed decisions. If any of the steps in the Bureau's process do not meet, minimally meet, or partially meet the 12 steps, then the cost estimate guidance does not fully reflect best practices for developing a high-quality estimate and cannot be considered reliable.

Lastly, to describe key drivers of cost growth, we compared cost information included in the 2015 and 2017 cost estimates. We analyzed both summary and detailed cost information to assess key changes in totals overall, by WBS category, and by information technology (IT) vs. Non-IT costs. We used this analysis in conjunction with information received from the Bureau during interviews and through document transfers to describe overall changes in the cost estimate from 2015 to 2017.

We conducted this performance audit from December 2017 to August 2018 in accordance with generally accepted government auditing standards. Those standards require that we plan and perform the audit to obtain sufficient, appropriate evidence to provide a reasonable basis for our findings and conclusions based on our audit objectives. We believe that the evidence obtained provides a reasonable basis for our findings and conclusions based on our audit objectives.

Appendix II: Comments from the Department of Commerce

UNITED STATES DEPARTMENT OF COMMERCE
The Secretary of Commerce
Washington, D.C. 20230

August 2, 2018

Mr. Robert Goldenkoff
Director, Strategic Issues
U.S. Government Accountability Office
441 G Street, NW
Washington, DC 20548

Dear Mr. Goldenkoff:

The U.S. Department of Commerce appreciates the opportunity to comment on the U.S. Government Accountability Office's (GAO) draft report, *"2020 CENSUS: Census Bureau Improved the Quality of its Cost Estimation but Additional Steps Are Needed to Ensure Reliability"* (GAO-18-635).

The Department agrees with GAO's findings regarding the improvements the U.S. Census Bureau has made in its cost estimations. However, the Department does not agree with GAO's assessment that the Census Bureau's October 2017 lifecycle cost estimate is "not reliable" because the GAO believes additional documentation best practices could be followed. The Department conducted two independent cost analyses in producing the October 2017 lifecycle cost estimate, and we are satisfied that the estimate is comprehensive, credible, accurate, and reliable.

Our disagreement over this one aspect notwithstanding, the Department agrees that efforts to document the Census Bureau's cost estimates according to GAO's best practices must continue, and we are working with the GAO to that end.

Sincerely,

Wilbur Ross

In: A Closer Look at the 2020 Census
Editor: Sille M. Schou

ISBN: 978-1-53616-508-1
© 2019 Nova Science Publishers, Inc.

Chapter 10

2020 CENSUS: ADDITIONAL STEPS NEEDED TO FINALIZE READINESS FOR PEAK FIELD OPERATIONS[*]

United States Government Accountability Office

ABBREVIATIONS

Bureau	Census Bureau
IT	Information Technology
NRFU	Non-Response Follow-Up

WHY GAO DID THIS STUDY

The cost of the decennial census has steadily increased over the past several decades, with self-response rates declining over the same period. The largest and costliest operation that the Bureau undertakes, NRFU is the

---

[*] This is an edited, reformatted and augmented version of the United States Government Accountability Office Report to Congressional Requesters, Publication No. GAO-19-140, dated December 2018.

Bureau's attempt to enumerate households not initially self-responding to the census.

GAO was asked to review NRFU implementation during the 2018 Census Test as well as the Bureau's overall readiness for peak field operations, which cover the actual enumeration of residents. This chapter examines (1) how peak field operations, including NRFU, were implemented during the test; and (2) the extent to which prior test implementation issues have been addressed. GAO reviewed test planning and training documentation, as well as production and payroll data. At the test site, GAO observed and interviewed enumerators, field supervisors, and managers conducting peak operations.

WHAT GAO RECOMMENDS

GAO recommends that the Bureau (1) determine procedures for late-NRFU data collection; (2) align census field supervisor screening, authorities, and information flows; (3) prepare for targeted mid-operation training or guidance as needed; and (4) improve training on reporting cases that need supervisory attention and alternative ways to communicate these cases.

The Department of Commerce agreed with GAO's findings and recommendations, and the Bureau provided technical comments that were incorporated as appropriate.

WHAT GAO FOUND

In preparation for the 2020 census, the Census Bureau (Bureau) set out to enumerate over 140,000 housing units during the 2018 Census Test at a site in Providence County, Rhode Island. The 2018 Census Test marked the Bureau's last chance to test enumeration procedures for peak field operations under census-like conditions before 2020. Implementation of this test identified the following concerns:

- The Bureau experienced operational issues during implementation of the Non-Response Follow-Up (NRFU) as part of the 2018 Census Test. For example, the Bureau had not finalized procedures for data collection during late phases of NRFU (e.g., after multiple attempts to interview had been made) until after the work had already started. As a result, enumerators and their supervisors did not have standardized procedures during the test, which made it difficult to evaluate the effectiveness of the test procedures. GAO also observed a range of other NRFU implementation issues during the test, such as the Bureau's use of progress reporting that overstates the number of NRFU cases not needing any additional fieldwork and the Bureau having fewer of its enumerators work Saturdays, which can be among the most productive interview days. The Bureau is taking steps to assess and mitigate these and other issues that GAO identified.
- The Bureau's field workforce was not fully prepared to face all of the enumeration challenges that arose during the test. For instance, the Bureau expects census field supervisors to provide front-line coaching to enumerators but did not screen these employees to ensure they had the needed skills. Moreover, it did not provide them with the authorities and information that would have helped them serve that role. As a result, we believe that supervisors did not have the casework expertise, information, or authority to help enumerators with procedural questions, and higher-level census field managers ended up providing direct support to enumerators.
- While the Bureau provided extensive online and in-person training to enumerators prior to NRFU fieldwork for the 2018 Census Test, the Bureau lacked any standardized form of mid-operation training or guidance as new procedures were implemented. GAO observed that during the test some enumerators continued to have questions and were uncertain about procedures. Developing targeted, location-specific training could help ensure that, in 2020, enumerators receive the guidance they need to collect census data consistently and in accordance with NRFU procedures.

The Bureau has made progress addressing prior test implementation issues but still faces challenges. For example, the Bureau improved its collection of enumerator case notes, which reflect real-time knowledge gained during enumeration. However, enumerators did not always report cases using flags built in to their interviewing device that would benefit from supervisory review, such as for language barriers. Moreover, supervisors were not systematically analyzing case notes to identify cases not flagged properly. As a result, critical data on fieldwork challenges were not being communicated effectively to those who could analyze and use them.

December 10, 2018
Congressional Requesters

The cost of the decennial census has steadily increased over the past several decades, with enumeration costs rising from about $16 per household in 1970 to around $92 in 2010 (all in constant 2020 dollars). The Census Bureau (Bureau) estimates that overall decennial costs will increase by over $3 billion from the 2010 Census to $15.6 billion in 2020 (in current decennial time frame costs).[1] During this period of increasing costs, the percentage of households self-responding to mailed census questionnaires has declined from 78 percent in 1970 to 63 percent in 2010. The Bureau anticipates that the self-response rate will further decline to roughly 60 percent in 2020, in part because, as the Bureau has noted, the population is overloaded with requests for information and has become increasingly concerned about sharing information.

When a household does not initially respond to the census, the Bureau attempts to enumerate the residents through Non-Response Follow-Up (NRFU), an operation where enumerators personally visit to count the household. NRFU is labor intensive and is the largest and costliest operation that the Bureau undertakes. Another enumeration operation happening at about the same time is Group Quarters, when the Bureau

---

[1] According to October 2017 Commerce documents, the reported figures are "inflated to the current 2020 Census time frame (fiscal years 2012 to 2023);" the Bureau had cited constant 2020 dollars for prior figures.

counts residents of group facilities (such as skilled nursing facilities and correctional facilities).

The Bureau planned its 2018 Census Test in Providence County, Rhode Island, to rehearse most of the operations, systems, and procedures that it will implement during the 2020 Census.[2] Previously, the Bureau conducted operational tests from 2013 through 2017, as well as multiple small-scale tests designed to demonstrate specific functionalities (such as submitting census data over the Internet). The 2018 test is the last opportunity for the Bureau to demonstrate readiness for its major operations in 2020 and to apply lessons learned from prior tests.[3]

You asked us to review implementation of NRFU testing during the 2018 Census Test as well as the Bureau's overall readiness for peak operations, which cover the actual enumeration of residents. This chapter examines (1) the implementation of peak operations during the 2018 Census Test at the Providence County, Rhode Island, site; and (2) the extent to which implementation issues raised in prior 2020 Census tests have been addressed and what actions the Bureau could take to address these issues.[4]

To address both of these research objectives, we visited the test site in Rhode Island to observe implementation of the peak operations being tested between May and August 2018. These visits included nongeneralizable observations of door-to-door field enumeration and office clerical work, as well as interviews with local managers. We also observed debrief sessions held with multiple levels of the census field workforce after the operations. From each of these visits, we documented

---

[2] Address canvassing, another decennial field operation, was also tested in Pierce County, Washington, and the Bluefield-Beckley-Oak Hill area of West Virginia earlier during the test.

[3] In November 2018 Bureau officials told us they plan to conduct a randomized control test for the 2020 Census using the American Community Survey infrastructure in the summer of 2019 for the purposes of informing NRFU and the Integrated Partnership and Communications Campaign for the 2020 Census. The test will ask the 2020 questions, including a question on citizenship in one panel of the test and excluding it from the test's second panel.

[4] Peak operations include self-response and other enumeration activity. Due to the timing of our work and the schedule of the 2018 Census Test, we specifically reviewed the NRFU and Group Quarters operations.

observations and provided feedback to Bureau managers in near real time so that the Bureau could mitigate and adapt to issues raised by the test's implementation in a timely manner. Implementation issues are a natural part of the testing environment and are what testing is intended to uncover. We also discussed any mitigation or evaluation strategies developed in response to our observations with the cognizant Bureau headquarters officials.

In addition to our fieldwork, we collected real-time production data on the tested operations. These data included tallies of case outcomes, transactional case activity by enumerators, and hours worked by Bureau employees. After testing the case tallies and distributions and interviewing cognizant officials, we determined that these data were sufficiently reliable for our reporting purposes. We also received daily progress reports from the Bureau throughout the test, and we reviewed Bureau test-planning documentation and our work from prior tests to examine how, if at all, the Bureau planned to address prior implementation issues.

We conducted this performance audit from April 2018 to December 2018 in accordance with generally accepted government auditing standards. Those standards require that we plan and perform the audit to obtain sufficient, appropriate evidence to provide a reasonable basis for our findings and conclusions based on our audit objectives. We believe that the evidence obtained provides a reasonable basis for our findings and conclusions based on our audit objectives.

BACKGROUND

NRFU is a field-based operation that the Bureau administers following the self-response period so that it can (1) determine the occupancy status of individual non-responsive housing units and (2) enumerate them. In most instances, the Bureau typically allows up to six enumeration attempts for each nonresponsive housing unit, or case. If the Bureau is unable to enumerate the housing unit in the field, it may have to impute attributes of the household based on the demographic characteristics of surrounding housing units as well as administrative records.

Within the test site in Providence County, Rhode Island, the Bureau set up an area census office to administer field operations. Figure 1 provides an overview of the managerial hierarchy of the area census office. The *area census office manager* oversees day-to-day operations within the office and acts as a liaison with the Bureau's New York Regional Census Center, which is a Bureau regional office with jurisdiction over the Providence area census office. *Census field managers* are to monitor operational progress and performance indicators to understand any areas of concern and shift resources as needed within the test site. *Census field supervisors* are to act as front-line supervisors for individual performance and payroll processes and receive procedural questions from *enumerators*, who conduct the count.

The Bureau has another operation—Group Quarters—to enumerate those living or staying in a group facility that provides housing or services. Such facilities can include skilled nursing facilities, college and university student housing, and correctional facilities. Within the Group Quarters enumeration, the Bureau also enumerates places such as soup kitchens, homeless shelters, and other service-based enumeration facilities.

Table 1. Time Frames for Operational Activities Observed during 2018 Census Test

Operation	Testing period
Non-Response Follow-Up	May 9 through July 31, 2018
Group Quarters Advance Contact	June 18 through July 10, 2018
Group Quarters	July 25 through August 24, 2018
Service-based Enumeration	July 25through July 27, 2018

Source: Census Bureau planning documentation. | GAO-19-140.

Prior to Group Quarters enumeration in the field, the Bureau attempts to establish the facilities' approximate population count and preferred enumeration method through the Advance Contact operation. These facilities can choose among methods including paper listing, where the facility provides a roster of residents as of census day to the Bureau, and in-person enumeration, where a team of enumerators count residents. For the 2020 cycle, the Bureau is also adding an "eResponse" option, tested on a small scale in 2016, whereby facility administrators can electronically submit enumeration data at a date of their choosing within operational time frames.

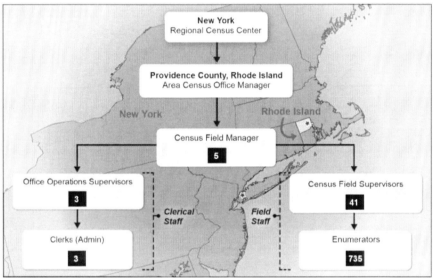

Source: GAO analysis of Census report data. | GAO-19-140.

Figure 1. Non-Response Follow-Up Was Implemented in a Multi-Tiered Structure at the Test Site.

The Bureau's testing of the peak operations that we observed during the 2018 Census Test was intended to test collection of census data from those either not responding themselves via paper, telephone, or over the Internet or those living in group quarters. Prior to the start of NRFU during the 2018 test, roughly 45 percent of anticipated housing units in the test area of Providence County, Rhode Island, self-responded, leaving more than 140,000 remaining housing units to be attempted by NRFU itself, which took place between May 9 and July 31, 2018. The Bureau conducted a test of its Group Quarters enumeration from July 25 through August 24, 2018, including service-based enumeration. Both portions of Group

Quarters fieldwork were preceded by the Advance Contact activity. Dates for the peak operations we observed during the 2018 test are listed in table 1.

The Bureau's operational plans for this phase of the fieldwork for the 2018 test incorporated two innovation areas that the Bureau hopes will produce savings for 2020.

- Reengineered field operations. For most of NRFU during the 2018 test, the Bureau relied on automated data collection methods, including a system-based, automated process for assigning work to enumerators, a smartphone-based application for collecting enumeration data in the field, and system-generated supervisory alerts.[5]
- Use of administrative records. To help reduce costly NRFU visits during the 2018 test, the Bureau reviewed and, where appropriate, applied administrative records—information already provided to the government as it administers other programs, such as Social Security, the Selective Service, or the Special Supplemental Nutrition Program for Women, Infants, and Children—to determine the occupancy status of housing units and thus remove vacant housing units from the NRFU workload, as well as to provide population counts of households not responding.[6]

The Bureau also tested multiple operational features for the first time this decennial cycle under full census-like production conditions in 2018:

- NRFU Closeout. During the 2018 test, the Bureau tested how best to relax certain business rules and enumeration procedures late in the NRFU operation so that it can enumerate persistently non-

---

[5] Consistent with the 2016 Census Test, the Bureau had designed traditional NRFU, which began in May 2018, to involve a maximum of six enumeration attempts per non-responding housing unit. In most cases during this phase, the Bureau used its automated process for case assignments, whereby the system was to assign and route cases by geographic clusters based on multiple factors including: enumerator work availability; the likeliest time of day to successfully make contact with a resident; and spatial relationship with other open cases.

[6] For more information on the Bureau's use of Administrative Records, see: GAO, *2020 Census: Bureau Is Taking Steps to Address Limitations of Administrative Records,* GAO-17-664 (Washington, D.C.: July 26, 2017).

responsive housing units. Examples of procedural modifications include increasing the maximum allowable number of enumeration attempts for each housing unit and manually assigning cases to the highest-performing enumerators.

- Office-Based Group Quarters Advance Contact. In the 2010 Census, the Bureau sent enumerator crews in person to each facility in advance of enumeration to establish the facility's preferred method of enumeration and to obtain an approximate population count. In the 2018 Census Test, the Bureau implemented a new method for 2020 that instead involved clerical staff contacting facilities by telephone and updating the group quarters address list and enumeration information remotely to reduce expenses associated with field visits for its enumerator crews.

THE BUREAU EXPERIENCED OPERATIONAL PLANNING, WORKFORCE MANAGEMENT, AND OTHER ISSUES DURING ITS 2018 TEST OF PEAK OPERATIONS

The Bureau Did Not Determine Procedures for Late-NRFU Data Collection until after It Started the Work

The Bureau began the last phase of NRFU data collection in the 2018 test without having yet determined the procedures it would use for that critical phase.[7] Bureau planning documentation from February 2018 described a late-operation "closeout" phase of NRFU that would attempt to resolve cases that had not yet responded. However, we found that the Bureau had not determined the procedural modifications this phase would involve, either in terms of rules enumerators followed or business rules for how cases were to be assigned. By late May, nearly 3 weeks into the operation, the Bureau issued a set of closeout procedures to census areas where most cases had either been completed or where at least four of the

---

[7] Every decennial, some housing units do not respond to the Bureau's multiple attempts to count them. In the 2018 test, NRFU included separately what it referred to as "closeout" and "final attempt" phases to maximize the participation rate of these housing units.

six allowable enumeration attempt day assignments had been made. The Bureau also placed a priority on having high-performing enumerators—in terms of their ability to complete cases—available to work these cases during this phase of the NRFU testing.

Table 2 summarizes the chronology for when the Bureau implemented and documented procedural changes governing the transition from early to late-NRFU data collection, as well as the nature of those changes.

In late June 2018, the Bureau began testing the third phase of NRFU data collection, what it referred to as the "final attempt" phase, with officials citing a high incidence of non-interviews during prior phases as the reason. However, the Bureau had also begun this phase's data collection before it had established the procedural modifications it would be using. The modifications were intended to further increase the chances of enumerators completing cases in the field, such as by removing the limit on the number of attempts enumerators could make at each remaining case before NRFU ended.

Table 2. Census Bureau Established Procedures for Late Non-Response Follow-Up (NRFU) after Test Implementation Had Begun

Operational Phase	Initial data collection	Final attempt
Initial scope of workload for the phase of data collection	Entire NRFU workload	NRFU areas with >3% of cases visited maximum number of times without getting a population count
Date that test data collection began for the phase	May 9, 2018	June 23, 2018
Datethat test data collection procedures were documented for the phase	January 4, 2018	July 13, 2018
Method of assigning cases	Automated assignment	Experimented with mix of manual and automated assignments
Notable changes to enumerator procedures relative to initial data collection	—	Unlimited number of attempts per day during time remaining; enumerators could sequence cases on their own

Source: GAO analysis of Bureau documentation. | GAO-19-140.
Legend: — refers to not applicable.

Standards for Internal Control in the Federal Government states that agencies should implement control activities by, for example, documenting policies.[8] However, the Bureau did not determine procedures for the final attempt phase until after testing for this phase of NRFU had begun. Enumerators and census field supervisors thus began working closeout and final attempt cases without a standardized set of test procedures.

Without determining the procedural changes the Bureau would be testing—or the business rules guiding when to make those changes—the Bureau was not well positioned to collect data to assess the alternatives it used during the test to inform planning for 2020. Bureau officials shared with us that they believed their automated case assignment approach is most effective during initial data collection but that it is less effective at targeting the toughest cases to resolve late in NRFU data collection. Yet, in part because the Bureau had not established when the transition from automated to manual case management would occur—or the business rules for determining when—some of the highest-performing enumerators were unavailable to receive assignments when the Bureau needed to begin the final attempt phase, according to the area census office manager. By not establishing the scope and timing of procedural changes for late-NRFU data collection in 2020, the Bureau may not be in a position to efficiently shift from its automated assignment approach to a manual one at the right time and position its most effective enumerators to receive assignments when needed.

In November 2018, the Bureau provided a draft contact strategy for NRFU in 2020 that included an outline of a multi-phase strategy for late-NRFU data collection. By including multiple phases of (1) shifting away from a fully-automated case assignment process and (2) relaxing management controls to complete as much casework as possible in areas with continued high non-response rates, this strategy appears to follow what the Bureau ultimately implemented during the 2018 test. It will be important, however, for the Bureau to determine the business rules for procedural changes and their timing in advance so that it can maximize the

---

[8] GAO, Standards for Internal Control in the Federal Government, GAO-14-704G (Washington, D.C.: Sept. 10, 2014).

value of NRFU in reducing the number of housing units that have to be imputed for the 2020 Census.

The Bureau Did Not Fully Ready Its Field Workforce for Enumeration Challenges

Census Field Supervisors Were Not Integrated into Casework Management

As described in the Bureau's training and operational planning documents, census field supervisors were to be the primary points of contact in fielding and addressing enumerator questions. Census field managers—the next step above census field supervisors— were to focus their efforts on monitoring progress in completing the caseload, reviewing cases flagged by enumerators as problematic in one of a small number of pre-defined ways (e.g., dangerous addresses), and resolving significant performance issues. Among field supervisors' key responsibilities, according to the Bureau's plan for NRFU, were providing guidance to help enumerators understand procedural matters and to offer coaching and problem-solving support to enumerators who may need it. They also led enumerator training prior to the beginning of NRFU and generally were to train their specific team of enumerators.

However, census field managers and enumerators indicated that census field supervisors were often not the primary actors involved in fielding and addressing enumerator questions. Instead, enumerators and census field managers reported having direct contact with each other over procedural questions. Moreover, seven of the nine enumerators participating in the Bureau's operational debrief focus group who responded said they thought finding someone who could answer their questions was either difficult or very difficult.

We found that census field supervisors went underutilized in part because the Bureau did not recruit and position them to assume front-line supervising and coaching responsibilities. As outlined in training documentation, the Bureau vested supervisory review authority (for special cases, such as resident refusals and language barrier issues) within census field managers, the area census office manager, clerks, and office operations supervisors instead of census field supervisors. Additionally, as part of the Bureau's reengineered field operations for 2020, census field supervisors are given automated tools to monitor enumerators, and enumerators we observed told us that they generally did not interact in person with their supervisors apart from training. We believe that the combination of these factors resulted in census field supervisors having limited exposure to NRFU casework and any problematic situations enumerators might encounter. Officials also told us that the Bureau did not screen census field supervisors for their supervisory or coaching skillsets, though officials noted that this has been the practice in prior censuses, too. Rather, they hired census field supervisors based on their scores on the online enumerator training and because they reported an interest in supervising.

Additionally, census field supervisors lacked access to certain data streams from the test that could have helped them answer or troubleshoot enumerator questions. According to two census field managers, the Bureau did not regularly share consolidated records of procedural changes with census field supervisors. Information technology (IT) and census field managers also noted that the Bureau did not share or compare observations between the census field supervisor hotline and the decennial IT hotline, even though enumerators could potentially call either or both with technical or procedural questions. As a result, without sharing how best to respond to similar questions across support lines, enumerators could receive different answers for related questions depending on which hotline they contacted.

Standards for Internal Control in the Federal Government states that agency management should demonstrate a commitment to recruit, develop, and retain competent individuals.[9] Management should establish expectations for competence in key roles and should consider the level of assigned responsibility and delegated authority when establishing expectations. Yet, the role the Bureau envisioned census field supervisors having was not aligned with the authority supervisors were given, the skills

---

[9] GAO-14-704G.

for which the Bureau hired them, or the access to information that they had for the 2018 test.

When we raised this issue related to using census field supervisors, Bureau officials agreed and cited feedback they had received that census field managers felt inundated with the combination of the volume of supervisory review cases that flowed to them and with troubleshooting day-to-day enumerator questions. In October 2018, the Bureau provided documentation to us proposing a set of questions that they could use in screening applicants for the census field supervisor position to identify supervisory skills. Officials also said they were still evaluating options for granting census field supervisors more supervisory review authority. As the Bureau continues to learn from the 2018 test as part of its planning for 2020, it will be important to align census field supervisor roles with their authorities, skills, and information flows so that the Bureau does not underutilize a key portion of its field management chain. Doing so could also lessen the operational burden on higher-level census field managers.

Enumerators Did Not Receive Training to Address Mid-Operation Issues

Prior to the start of 2018 NRFU testing, the Bureau trained enumerators with a series of online training modules and assessments and one full day of in-person training facilitated by census field supervisors. The training included modules on data stewardship requirements, payroll responsibilities, and procedural directions for conducting respondent interviews. However, officials acknowledged that when the Bureau implemented its closeout and final attempt phases of NRFU, it did not provide standardized training to enumerators on the rollout of procedural changes. Five enumerators we observed during these stages said they relied on informal communications from their census field supervisors or census field managers for guidance. The initial practice had been for enumerators to receive daily assignments and follow pre-specified case sequencing and routing based on the Bureau's automated system. During the final attempt phase, enumerators were given discretion over the sequencing, routing, and number of attempts to make for cases that could be manually assigned, yet they were not given standardized training on how to handle this shift.

During our field observations, some enumerators we spoke with said they were uncertain about core procedures. For example, enumerators were not consistently aware that they had some discretion in large multi-unit settings to deviate from the assigned sequence of their cases provided by the automated system. Enumerators we observed and spoke to were also not always clear on how to flag within their field enumeration application the commonly occurring cases with confusing address markings and numberings. For example, enumerators had the option of selecting a case outcome of "missing unit designation," but they were not always sure whether this selection would capture the nuances of what they were seeing on the ground or how it differed from other selection options.[10]

Standards for Control in the Federal Government states that agencies should demonstrate a commitment to competence by, for example, tailoring training based on employee needs and helping personnel adapt to an evolving environment.[11] Targeted informational training would help the Bureau ensure that staff understand mid-operation procedural changes, and the training could be an opportunity for the Bureau to address commonly-observed and persistent implementation issues that may be arising. By developing brief, targeted mid-operation training, either as formal modules, guidance, or other standardized job aids, such as "frequently asked questions" worksheets, the Bureau could better position itself to react nimbly to enumerator feedback.

We have previously reported challenges the Bureau faces with its field work in other locations, such as connecting to the Internet during testing of address canvassing in rural West Virginia in 2017 and dealing with language barriers and other circumstances in unincorporated communities in southern Texas or with migrant and seasonal farmworkers in southern

---

[10] "Missing unit designation" is one of several case outcomes that refer to multi-unit address frame discrepancies. Other examples include "does not exist," "uninhabitable," and "nonresidential." Bureau officials indicated that they are reviewing the categorization of these outcomes in preparation for 2020.

[11] GAO-14-704G.

California during the 2000 Census.[12,13] All challenges are not universal to all locations. Given that some of the enumeration challenges enumerators encountered in 2018 NRFU testing might not occur everywhere, and that some other areas of the country will have their own types of challenges, locally- or regionally-specific training or guidance may better address some needs. By relying solely on pre-NRFU training, the Bureau risks having little opportunity to course-correct with enumerators who may not have absorbed all of the training and are experiencing difficulty completing interviews or not collecting quality data.

The Bureau Is Assessing Other Implementation Issues That Arose during the 2018 Test

We observed and discussed with Bureau officials in real time several other implementation issues that occurred during the 2018 test. Bureau officials acknowledged these issues and, as of September 2018, were assessing them and developing mitigation strategies as part of their test evaluation process. These issues include:

- *Training certification.* Census field managers estimated that roughly 100 enumerators were unable to transmit their final test scores because the Bureau's online learning management system had an erroneous setting. According to Bureau officials, this problem delayed the start of unsupervised work for these otherwise-qualified enumerators by an average of 2 days per enumerator and resulted in the attrition of some who were able to quickly find other work. Bureau officials told us they have fixed the system setting and are considering an alternative means to certify training, such as by having the option of trainees taking and verifying their final assessment as part of their final capstone day

---

[12] GAO, 2020 Census: Actions Needed to Improve In-Field Address Canvassing, GAO-18-414 (Washington, D.C.: June 14, 2018).
[13] GAO, Decennial Census: Lessons Learned for Locating and Counting Migrant and Seasonal Farm Workers, GAO-03-605 (Washington, D.C.: July 3, 2003).

of classroom training. According to Bureau officials, development of this backup strategy will begin in December 2018.

- *Assigning cases manually in batches.* During the 2018 test, the Bureau's automated case management system was not configured for non-Headquarters staff to manually assign multiple cases to an enumerator at once. Rather, according to officials, census field managers were faced with having to manually assign thousands of cases individually during latter stages of NRFU. According to field management, this problem presented an unexpected burden on them, delayed assignments of the hardest-to-count cases, and contributed to high-performing enumerators not receiving work timely and in some cases for days in a row. Officials told us that, as a work-around, the Bureau shifted responsibility for assigning cases to a headquarters official with access rights in the system to assign large numbers of cases at once. Bureau officials acknowledge the unsustainability of this work-around if needed at a national level and the importance of resolving this before the 2020 Census. As of October 2018, Bureau officials showed us system screenshots of how census field managers would be able to manually assign batches of cases and indicated that this functionality would be ready for the 2020 Census.

- *Monitoring operational progress.* The Bureau's reporting on its progress in completing the NRFU casework for the 2018 test emphasized a process-oriented measure that overstated the extent to which the NRFU efforts were resulting in completed workload. In planning documentation, the Bureau listed the outcomes of interview attempts that it considered complete and thus not in need of further enumeration assignments. These outcomes—such as a full interview of the household or confirmation of a housing unit being vacant or nonexistent—would also result directly in reduction in the number of incomplete cases needing to have some of their missing data imputed by the Bureau later.

Yet the daily Bureau progress report and "dashboard" the Bureau provided us for the 2018 test, which decennial leadership also identified as their primary monitoring report, did not reflect these pre-planned definitions of completed workload. Rather, as officials acknowledged, it included cases that the Bureau had unsuccessfully attempted to enumerate the maximum number of allowable times for the initial phase of NRFU being tested, even though those cases could still—and did— receive additional attempts during later phases of NRFU. Officials noted that the measure reported could be helpful during early stages of the operation in determining whether enough employees had been hired, or whether case assignments were being worked quickly enough.

Figure 2 demonstrates the gap that arose during 2018 NRFU test implementation between the reported progress measure and the number of cases actually being completed. The totals reflected in the Bureau's reported measure include those that either have to be re-worked in the field during the final attempt phase as discussed or have their data imputed after fieldwork had ended. By contrast, an outcome-based measure of operational progress, like the one the Bureau designed, would capture only those cases where the Bureau had completed enumeration of the nonresponding housing units and thus be a more accurate representation of the operation's status.[14]

Bureau officials acknowledged the need to maintain measures that focus on process as well as outcomes—such as avoiding having to impute data for cases after field work—when measuring progress completing NRFU. They said that managers in the field and in Bureau headquarters had access to alternative measures and reports that more closely identified outcomes. The officials noted that the reporting mechanism expected to be used in 2020 was not fully available in time for the beginning of NRFU testing in 2018, so the reporting format and measures will likely differ. In addition, in October 2018, the Bureau provided a draft dashboard for 2020 that included greater detail on the number of cases that could still require

---

[14] The Bureau-designed, outcome-oriented measure that we report also includes cases that, while not enumerated in the field, were successfully enumerated using the Bureau's sources of administrative records.

work to enumerate. Such detail could help assist with determining when to transition to the final-attempt phase of the operation to address cases without sufficient information yet collected.

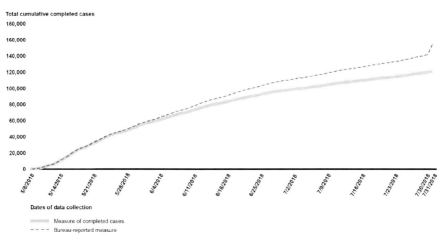

Source: GAO analysis of Census report data. | GAO-19-140.

Figure 2. The Bureau's Regular Reporting on Non-Response Follow-up Progress during the 2018 Census Test Overstated the Number of Cases Not Needing Additional Fieldwork.

Integrating Key Systems Settings

At the beginning of NRFU test implementation, the Bureau's case assignment and case sequencing systems were operating as if they were on time zones 4 hours apart. Bureau officials said that this resulted in enumerators receiving mismatched case assignment times, which hampered early NRFU production, and census field supervisors having to process erroneous "work not started" supervisory alerts. Bureau officials said they addressed the problem within the first week of the operation and that they would ensure that future updates and key settings would be coordinated across systems.

Tracking Employees and Equipment

The Bureau used two different sets of employee identification numbers to track their payroll status and use of Bureau-issued equipment (e.g., smart phones), respectively, without cross-walking them. According to census field managers, this resulted in extra work when trying to monitor changes in enumerators' employment statuses and whether enumerators had returned their equipment to the Bureau. The managers noted that office staff had to spend extra time comparing different lists of staff, while one manager developed a spreadsheet listing all staff by their two different identification numbers. Bureau officials said they considered this a priority issue to be resolved during final systems development for 2020 and had already developed a fix within their case management system so that the crosswalk between the two systems would be integrated within their management system. This would eliminate the need for manually reconciling the differing identification numbers.

Having More Enumerators Work Weekends

Until the latter stages of 2018 NRFU testing, the Bureau assigned cases to enumerators based on the alignment of the Bureau's estimated probability of finding respondents at home at certain times and enumerator-reported work availability. Bureau officials told us that Saturdays are generally one of the best days to find a household member home to respond to the census. However, during the test, our analysis showed that Saturdays had the second-fewest number of enumerators assigned to cases of any day of the week. Bureau officials said that they would review whether the incentive structure for working on Saturdays should be altered and that they would examine ways to ensure that more enumerators are working on those days. This includes exploring the feasibility of hiring and assigning work to applicants who may only want to work weekends and being clearer with enumerators about what the expected peak enumeration hours are.

Increasing Electronic Completion Rates for Group Quarters

The Bureau hopes to reduce field costs for Group Quarters (such as skilled nursing homes, college and university student housing, and correctional facilities) by, for the first time, encouraging facilities to self-enumerate electronically, when possible. As previously discussed, clerical staff first establish facility enumeration preferences during Group Quarters

Advance Contact, and enumeration (either in person or otherwise) takes place afterward. During the 2018 test, the Bureau reported that only 25 of the 75 facilities that selected the "eResponse" enumeration option during Advance Contact submitted responses by the enumeration deadline. As of September 2018, Bureau officials said they were still evaluating potential causes of the low response rate by Group Quarters facilities but noted that issues with the required format for the submission of response files may have prevented some submissions. Bureau officials also acknowledged the need to conduct more active follow-up with these facilities during the eResponse period to ensure a full and accurate count of Group Quarters facilities.

THE BUREAU HAS MADE PROGRESS BUT CONTINUES TO FACE CHALLENGES ADDRESSING IMPLEMENTATION ISSUES IDENTIFIED IN PRIOR TESTS

The Bureau Has Improved Its Collection of Case Notes, but Enumerators Remain Unclear on How to Report Fieldwork Issues

We reported to the Bureau during the 2015 Census Test that information enumerators were typing into their case notes did not appear to be systematically used by their managers.[15] We also reported that, during the 2016 Census Test, the Bureau was not reviewing case notes written by enumerators providing respondent information on better times-of-day for future NRFU visits to their housing unit, and enumerators did not always have this note-taking feature available.[16] During the 2018 test, enumerators were trained to take notes and, when appropriate, identify special cases that would later require supervisory review. We also observed that enumerators appeared to be consulting case notes from prior enumerator visits when

---

[15] GAO, 2020 Census: Additional Actions Would Help the Bureau Realize Potential Administrative Records Cost Savings, GAO-16-48 (Washington, D.C.: Oct. 20, 2015).

[16] GAO, 2020 Census: Additional Actions Could Strengthen Field Data Collection Efforts, GAO-17-191 (Washington, D.C.: Jan. 26, 2017).

planning NRFU visits to the same housing unit. Enumerators can use markings within their automated interview instrument to describe certain types of cases (e.g., hearing barriers and dangerous situations), which the automated system would then route to receive supervisory review. Enumerators could select other case outcomes that the automated system would apply predetermined business rules to either reassign the cases (e.g., refusal, no one home) or treat them as completed (verified vacant or not a housing unit).

However, we identified multiple scenarios in which enumerators had described cases in their case notes but for which the enumerators had not selected the corresponding case flag for the situation that would have resulted automatically in a supervisory review. One census field manager described discovering several dozen cases that had been inactive where enumerators had written case notes describing language barriers encountered but had not specifically marked the flag within the device for "language barrier." Because these cases thus were not triggered for supervisory review, they were eligible to be reassigned by the Bureau's standard automated system. As a result, the Bureau was not controlling for the requisite language skills in assigning the cases for subsequent enumeration attempts.

The Bureau's use of automated systems to apply business rules to efficiently manage field casework for 2020—including identifying which cases receive supervisory review—relies critically on field staff understanding how to reflect what they are seeing on the ground within the choices provided to them with which to flag cases in their interview device. The Bureau's use of remote management as part of reengineered field operations also relies on enumerators knowing when and how to report issues to their supervisors.

We observed multiple field scenarios that called these conditions into question, however. For example, enumerators we observed during NRFU told us that they indicated address listing issues in their case notes, such as if the unit designation was missing or incorrectly marked. Yet, these enumerators did not know how to flag such cases in their interview instrument to trigger supervisory review. According to Bureau officials, this type of address listing issue turned out to be a broadly experienced challenge within the test area. Additionally, during Group Quarters, an enumerator we observed received supplemental information about the number of residents at a neighboring facility after that facility had been enumerated. The enumerator made note of this discrepancy and included the original facility's identifying information but was uncertain about how, if at all, to alert the supervisor about the discrepancy.

Moreover, we saw little evidence that census field supervisors or managers were systematically reviewing case notes for the purpose of identifying either cases not being marked properly or for which the selected flags may not have been fully describing the case characteristics. For example, a census field manager confirmed that case notes recorded at Group Quarters facilities that were enumerated would not be reviewed during clerical processing, leaving the possibility—such as we observed— that if enumerators relied on case notes to communicate information about the accuracy of data collected, it would not be acted on. Bureau officials told us that reviewing all case notes could require more staff time than budgeted for, and changing the automation process to selectively present unflagged cases for supervisory review could necessitate requirements changes to systems whose development is already pressed for time.

Standards for Internal Control in the Federal Government states that agencies should use quality information by, for example, processing reliable information to help it make informed decisions.[17] Bureau enumerators can record useful local knowledge about their cases with their choice of case type flags and within their descriptive case notes. While the Bureau has anticipated a broad range of types of cases for enumerators to select from when documenting their casework, enumerators we observed did not uniformly understand those options, and the descriptors did not fully anticipate what enumerators were encountering. Improving training and guidance to field staff on the intended use of case notes and on alternative ways to communicate their concerns about cases, such as flags for different types of cases, can help ensure the Bureau has reliable data on

---

[17] GAO-14-704G.

the cases during its field operations relying on automated interviewing instruments.

Leveraging Information on Enumerator-Reported Technical and Procedural Issues Remains a Challenge

During the 2015 Census Test, we reported that certain technical and procedural problems that enumerators were encountering in the field were going unreported and that enumerators did not always know who to contact for assistance. We further noted that the Bureau was not systematically assessing or tracking the extent of these issues during testing, and we recommended that it enable such capture of information by training enumerators on where to record issues and whom to contact.[18] The Bureau agreed with our recommendation.

During the 2018 test, the Bureau had both an information technology (IT) hotline and a census-field-supervisor hotline established for technical and procedural questions, respectively. Yet, enumerators we observed told us they did not always report to their support lines the technical issues that they were easily able to resolve by, for example, turning their devices on and off to reset. This lack of reporting kept the Bureau from getting information on commonly-occurring challenges that might be useful real-time feedback in the testing environment. Moreover, a Bureau IT manager noted that the Bureau does not formally review and share observations and troubleshooting notes from IT hotline and census field supervisor hotline calls. Because enumerators may call either or both hotlines when having difficulty operating their Bureau-issued smart phone, operators of these hotlines could be unaware of the prevalence of or solutions to a given problem if the Bureau does not monitor troubleshooting information across the two operational silos. For the Bureau to be informed on any additional training needs or other operational decisions for 2020, it will need to continue to expand its efforts in collecting information on enumerator-reported problems per our 2015 recommendation.

---

[18] GAO-16-48.

The Bureau Continues to Assess How to Ensure Efficient Staffing Levels for Group Quarters

Depending on the size of a Group Quarters facility (e.g., skilled nursing facility, college and university student housing), the Bureau can use varying sizes of enumerator crews to conduct an onsite count. During the 2010 Census, we observed overstaffing during the service-based enumeration (e.g., homeless shelters and soup kitchens) portion of Group Quarters. While determining staffing levels at these facilities can be challenging, such overstaffing can lead to poor productivity and unnecessarily high labor costs. We recommended that the Bureau determine and address the factors that led to this overstaffing prior to 2020.[19] The Bureau agreed with our recommendation.

However, the Bureau has faced challenges determining the right staffing ratios in light of complications with the Advance Contact phase of Group Quarters. As previously noted, the Bureau used this phase to establish facilities' enumeration method preferences. For the 2018 test, most Group Quarters facilities selected the facility-provided paper listing and the eResponse enumeration options. Therefore, the Bureau allocated a large share of its enumerator and census field supervisor workforce in the test area to the 44 known service-based enumeration facilities, which were restricted in terms of the enumeration options they could select and tended to select in-person enumeration. However, only 11 of these facilities responded to initial inquiries, so the Bureau had less work than anticipated for its enumerator crews. At multiple sites we observed in the test area, enumerators appeared either idle or underutilized. Moreover, several of the Group Quarters facilities we observed had changed their initial choice of enumeration method on the day of enumeration.

Enumerator crews thus ran the risk of either being overstaffed (in the case of switching to a facility-provided paper listing) or understaffed (in the case of switching to an in-person enumeration).

---

[19] GAO, 2010 Census: Key Efforts to Include Hard-to-Count Populations Went Generally As Planned; Improvements Could Make the Efforts More Effective for Next Census, GAO-11-45 (Washington, D.C.: Dec. 14, 2010).

The Bureau's Advance Contact activities have a potential benefit—if the Bureau can get accurate information on the method of enumeration and approximate population within a facility ahead of time, Bureau managers and enumerator crews can more proactively allocate resources and prepare for the count. Bureau officials said they are still assessing outcomes of Advance Contact to see if these gains were realized and may have completed the assessment by as early as January 2019. Doing so will help the Bureau determine appropriate staffing sizes and thus address our prior recommendation.

The Bureau Is Working to Determine the Causes of Elevated Non-Interview Rates

According to preliminary data from the 2018 Census Test, the Bureau experienced similarly high rates of cases coded as non-interviews as it did during its last major field test of NRFU in 2016. Non-interviews are cases where enumerators collect no data or insufficient data from households either because enumerators made the maximum number of visits without a successful interview, or because of special circumstances like language barriers or dangerous situations.[20] When this happens, the Bureau may have to impute the census data for the case, such as whether the housing unit is vacant or not, the population counts of the households, or demographic characteristics of their residents. In January 2017, we reported that, during the 2016 Census Test, the Bureau incurred what it considered high non-interview rates (31 and 22 percent across the two test sites, respectively, as the Bureau preliminarily reported at the time), and we recommended that the Bureau determine the causes of these rates.[21]

Using the same method to calculate the rate of non-interviews for the test as in 2016, the 2018 Census Test had similarly high non-interview rates— 33 percent of all NRFU cases. Bureau officials said they are still

---

[20] According to the Bureau, it needs to collect a combination of data fields during field interviews in order to consider the interview complete.
[21] GAO-17-191.

examining causes of these elevated non-interview rates and whether final attempts helped to mitigate the non-interview rate and will report out on what they learn as part of their comprehensive assessment of the test, planned for December 2018. A draft of the Bureau's revised contact strategy for NRFU, provided in November 2018, indicates that as part of enumerator training in 2020 the Bureau will need to incorporate messaging that emphasizes the importance of obtaining sufficient data from interview attempts. Officials noted that any interim lessons learned from this assessment process would inform updates to the field enumeration contact strategies for 2020.

The Bureau Experienced a Programming Error While Implementing Procedures for Proxy Interviews

Enumerators are directed to try and complete a NRFU case by interviewing a proxy for a household respondent, like a neighbor, after multiple failed attempts have been made to contact someone in the household for that case. We previously observed in the 2016 Census Test that enumerators did not seem to understand the procedures for conducting these interviews and, as a result, underutilized the interviewing method. In our January 2017 report, we therefore recommended that, as part of determining the causes of its non-interview rate, the Bureau revise and test any needed changes to proxy procedures and associated training.[22] The Bureau agreed with our recommendation and subsequently developed automated supervisory performance alerts for census field supervisors and census field managers that would inform them when an enumerator was not following prompts to conduct proxy interviews for eligible cases.

However, in implementing proxy interview procedures for the 2018 Census Test, the Bureau experienced a technical glitch resulting in some confusion among some enumerators and their supervisors about related procedures. Early in NRFU data collection for the test, a programming error within the field enumeration application was prompting enumerators

[22] GAO-17-191.

to make more than the allowable three attempts to interview a proxy respondent.[23] The Bureau reported promptly implementing a technical fix to this issue; yet, enumerators we observed reported receiving varying guidance from their supervisors on whether to abide by the erroneous prompts. While some of these enumerators appeared to understand the importance of attempting proxy interviews, some did not appear to understand Bureau guidance that enumerators should make no more than three attempts to interview a proxy respondent, and some appeared conditioned to follow the erroneous prompts.

Proxy interviews can be a substantial portion of completed interviews during the census. In 2018 NRFU testing, interviews of proxy respondents accounted for 27 percent of all successful interview-based enumerations of occupied housing units—compared to 24 percent during the 2010 Census and 9 percent during the 2016 Census Test. Given the role that proxy interviews play in completing census data collection, it will be important for the Bureau to fully implement our recommendation so that enumerators are properly pursuing and conducting these interviews.

Enumerators We Observed Were Uncertain of How to Proceed When Property Managers Were Unavailable

Initial visits to property managers of multi-unit residences can help the Bureau identify vacant and occupied housing units before sending enumerators to individual units within the facilities. We have previously reported that property managers can also be a helpful source of information on respondents who are not at home, thereby making subsequent follow-up visits to individual units more productive.[24] During the 2016 Census Test, we observed that enumerators were uncertain of how to handle individual cases within a multi-unit once they were unsuccessful in contacting a property manager initially. As a result, we recommended in January 2017

---

[23] The 2020 NRFU operational plan indicates that enumerators should, in most cases, only attempt three proxy interviews per visit. These interviews can be conducted with neighbors, relatives, landlords, or other sources with connections to the respondent or housing unit.

[24] GAO-17-191.

that the Bureau revise and test procedural and training modifications as needed to aid enumerators and their supervisors in these cases.[25] The Bureau agreed with this recommendation and indicated that the evaluations of the 2018 test would inform its strategies for 2020.

However, we observed a similar issue during the 2018 Census Test in that enumerators were unclear on what, if any, proxies to attempt if they were unsuccessful in finding the listed property manager. Additionally, we observed multiple enumerators leave voicemails with their contact information—not a central number—for the listed property manager, but it was unclear how these voicemails would produce a successful interview because, later, the automated system could reassign other enumerators to visit the manager. When we raised this concern with Bureau officials, they acknowledged that they need to continue to refine procedures for handling initial property manager visits for 2020.

The Bureau Provided Enumerators Access to Incomplete Closed Cases, but Enumerators Were Not Consistently Aware They Had Access

Previously, during the 2016 Census Test, we observed that enumerators were unable to re-open closed non-interview cases even if they happened upon the respondent in question soon after and nearby. We noted this inefficiency, since these cases would get re-assigned later, and in January 2017, we recommended that the Bureau revise and test procedures that would grant flexibility to enumerators to access cases in these circumstances.[26] The Bureau agreed with our recommendation.

For the 2018 Census Test, the Bureau provided a list in the field enumeration application of the cases that had been worked by the enumerator that day but that had not been submitted for processing or reassignment. Training for enumerators described this enumeration option, and enumerators were authorized to access these cases when needed, but

---

[25] GAO-17-191.
[26] GAO-17-191.

not all enumerators we observed were consistently aware of how to do so. Enumerators we spoke with cited uncertainty over how to access these cases and whether enumerators were allowed to do so as considerations. Continuing to review the procedures and guidance to enumerators on this flexibility for completing interviews, consistent with our prior recommendation, will help the Bureau make better use of it in 2020.

The Bureau May Add an Extra Check on NRFU Addresses Identified by Administrative Records as Vacant or Nonexistent

As we reported in 2017, the Bureau previously modified how it would treat some of the households that did not respond to the 2020 Census and that the Bureau's use of administrative records had determined to be not occupied. The Bureau's earlier testing had determined that the Bureau should require two—instead of just one—notices from the United States Postal Service that mail could not be delivered to these households before removing their addresses from the NRFU workload.[27] After we provided a draft of this chapter to the Department of Commerce to obtain agency comments, Bureau officials provided us with findings from an evaluation of the 2018 Census Test. In the evaluation, Bureau officials observed that there were households for which they had received multiple notices from the United States Postal Service that mail was undeliverable but that Bureau enumerators recorded as occupied. While Bureau officials believe, based on their follow-up research, that these addresses may likely be vacant or not housing units, they are concerned about possible undercounting from not enumerating people who may be at these addresses. As of November 2018, the Bureau was considering adding one physical visit for each of these cases. Bureau officials said they are continuing to analyze these evaluation results and expect to document and include changes within its final operational plan for the 2020 Census due in January 2019.

---

[27] GAO-17-664.

CONCLUSION

The 2018 Census Test offered the Bureau its last opportunity to test key procedures, management approaches, and systems under decennial-like conditions prior to the 2020 Census. As the Bureau studies the results of its NRFU and Group Quarters testing to inform 2020, it will be important that it address key program management issues that arose during implementation of the test. Namely, by not establishing the intended procedural changes for late-NRFU data collection ahead of time, the Bureau risked not getting the most out of NRFU to minimize the number of housing units having to have their information imputed by the Bureau later. Additionally, by not aligning the skills, responsibilities, and information flows for census field supervisors, the Bureau limited their role in support of enumerators within the reengineered field operation. The Bureau also lacks mid-operation training or guidance, which, if implemented in a targeted, localized manner, could further help enumerators navigate procedural modifications and any commonly-encountered problems when enumerating. Finally, without enumerators understanding how to use case notes and flags for various types of cases in their enumeration device and to report enumeration challenges to supervisors and managers, the Bureau may be unaware of field work issues that could affect the efficiency of its operations and the quality of its data.

We provided near real-time feedback to the Bureau across a range of test implementation issues. Some, such as those related to staffing ratios for the Group Quarters operation, build on long-standing implementation issues that, if addressed, can contribute to the efficiency and effectiveness of 2020 field operations. Others, like not having NRFU progress measures that provide true indications of completed workload, are issues specific to this test that the Bureau is assessing as part of its 2018 Census Test evaluations. It will be important for the Bureau to prioritize its mitigation strategies for these implementation issues so that it can maximize readiness for the 2020 Census.

RECOMMENDATIONS FOR EXECUTIVE ACTION

We are making four recommendations to the Department of Commerce and the Census Bureau:

The Secretary of Commerce should ensure that the Director of the Census Bureau determines in advance of Non-Response Follow-Up what the procedural changes will be for the last phases of its data collection and what the business rules will be for determining when to begin those phases, which cases to assign, and how to assign them. (Recommendation 1)

The Secretary of Commerce should ensure that the Director of the Census Bureau identifies and implements changes to align census field supervisor screening, authorities, and information flows to allow greater use of the census field supervisor position to provide supervisory support to enumerators. (Recommendation 2)

The Secretary of Commerce should ensure that the Director of the Census Bureau enables area census offices to prepare targeted, mid-operation training or guidance as needed to address procedural changes or implementation issues encountered locally during Non-Response Follow-Up. (Recommendation 3)

The Secretary of Commerce should ensure that the Director of the Census Bureau improves training and guidance to field staff on the intended use of case notes and flags, as well as on alternative ways to alert supervisors and managers when case characteristics are not readily captured by those flags. (Recommendation 4)

AGENCY COMMENTS AND OUR EVALUATION

We provided a draft of this chapter to the Secretary of Commerce. In its written comments, reproduced in appendix II, the Department of Commerce agreed with our findings and recommendations and said it would develop an action plan to address them. The Census Bureau also provided technical comments and an update on their evaluation of the test, which we incorporated as appropriate.

We are sending copies of this chapter to the Secretary of Commerce, the Undersecretary of Economic Affairs, the Acting Director of the U.S. Census Bureau, and the appropriate congressional committees.

Robert Goldenkoff
Director
Strategic Issues

List of Congressional Requesters

The Honorable Trey Gowdy
Chairman

The Honorable Elijah E. Cummings
Ranking Member
Committee on Oversight and Government Reform
House of Representatives

The Honorable Mark Meadows
Chairman

The Honorable Gerald E. Connolly
Ranking Member
Subcommittee on Government Operations
Committee on Oversight and Government Reform
House of Representatives

APPENDIX I: OBJECTIVES SCOPE & METHODOLOGY

This chapter examines (1) how peak field operations were implemented during the 2018 Census Test; and (2) the extent to which implementation issues raised in prior 2020 Census tests have been addressed, and what actions the Census Bureau (Bureau) is taking to address them.

To address these objectives, we reviewed 2018 Census Test and 2020 Census operational planning and training documentation. We also reviewed our prior reports and documentation on prior census testing operations. Non-Response Follow-Up (NRFU) operations took place from May 8 through July 31, 2018, while Group Quarters took place from July 25, 2018 through August 24, 2018, with the service-based enumeration portion taking place July 25, 2018 through July 27, 2018.

To review the Bureau's test implementation and mitigation strategies for previously-identified implementation issues for peak operations, we visited Providence, Rhode Island, multiple times between May and August 2018 to observe enumerators, census field supervisors, and management operations. NRFU visits took place between mid-May and late-July 2018, while we also conducted two iterations of visits of Group Quarters in late July and early-August 2018. These multiple iterations both across and within operations enabled us to see how, if at all, implementation of procedures varied over time. It also enabled us to get direct feedback from Bureau field managers on how various phases of test operations were proceeding. These visits consisted of non-generalizable observations of field enumeration and office clerical work, as well as interviews with local managers. For each of these visits, we developed data collection instruments to structure our interviews and to cover topics that were pertinent to the given phase of the operation we were observing. We also observed debrief sessions with multiple levels of the Bureau's field workforce following the field work.

To translate our observations into actionable feedback for the Bureau, we shared high-level observations in near real-time to Bureau headquarters management overseeing the operations so that the Bureau could mitigate and adapt to known issues in a timely manner.

We also discussed any mitigation or evaluation strategies developed in response to our observations with the cognizant Bureau headquarters officials. For objective two specifically, we reviewed Bureau test planning documentation and our work from prior tests to examine how, if at all, the Bureau planned to address known implementation issues.

To gain insight into how implementation was proceeding when we were not directly observing test implementation, we received daily management progress reports from the Bureau throughout the NRFU operation testing that included information on the total number of NRFU cases, the final outcomes of each case, and the number of cases that the Bureau reported as completed for each day of the NRFU operation. We also received Periodic Management Reports that summarized high level outcomes of both the NRFU and Group Quarters workload.

To fully understand the source of the Bureau's daily progress reports, we requested and received all transactional data collected during NRFU production. We reconciled case totals and outcomes with the final numbers in the NRFU progress reports and then used these data to analyze the Bureau's progress during NRFU production. We also received and analyzed Bureau payroll data on enumerator hours worked during NRFU operations. Specifically, we assessed the number of enumerators working each day, the number of enumerator' hours paid each day, and the days of the week that were worked the most by enumerators. We found the Bureau's transactional and payroll data sources to be sufficiently reliable for our reporting purposes.

We conducted this performance audit from April to December of 2018 in accordance with generally accepted government auditing standards. Those standards require that we plan and perform the audit to obtain sufficient, appropriate evidence to provide a reasonable basis for our findings and conclusions based on our audit objectives. We believe that the evidence obtained provides a reasonable basis for our findings and conclusions based on our audit objectives.

APPENDIX II: COMMENTS FROM THE DEPARTMENT OF COMMERCE

December 3, 2018

Mr. Robert Goldenkoff
Director, Strategic Issues
U.S. Government Accountability Office
441 G Street, NW
Washington, DC 20548

Dear Mr. Goldenkoff:

The U.S. Department of Commerce appreciates the opportunity to comment on the U.S. Government Accountability Office's (GAO) draft report titled *2020 Census: Additional Steps Needed to Finalize Readiness for Peak Field Operations* (GAO-19-140).

The Department agrees with the findings and recommendations in this draft report. Once the GAO issues the final version of this report, the Department will prepare an action plan to document the steps we will take regarding the final recommendations.

Sincerely,

Wilbur Ross

In: A Closer Look at the 2020 Census ISBN: 978-1-53616-508-1
Editor: Sille M. Schou © 2019 Nova Science Publishers, Inc.

Chapter 11

2020 CENSUS: ACTIONS NEEDED TO IMPROVE IN-FIELD ADDRESS CANVASSING OPERATION[*]

United States Government Accountability Office

ABBREVIATIONS

CFS	Census Field Supervisor
GPS	Global Positioning System
LiMA	Listing and Mapping Application
MCM	Mobile Case Management System
Standards for Internal Control	Standards for Internal Control in the Federal Government
UTS	Unified Tracking System

---

[*] This is an edited, reformatted and augmented version of United States Government Accountability Office, Report to Congressional Requesters, Publication No. GAO-18-414, dated June 2018.

WHY GAO DID THIS STUDY

The success of the decennial census depends in large part on the Bureau's ability to locate every household in the United States. To accomplish this monumental task, the Bureau must maintain accurate address and map information for every location where a person could reside. For the 2018 Endto-End Test, census workers known as listers went door-to-door to verify and update address lists and associated maps in selected areas of three test sites—Bluefield-Beckley-Oak Hill, West Virginia; Pierce County, Washington; and Providence County, Rhode Island.

GAO was asked to review in-field address canvassing during the End-toEnd Test. This chapter determines whether key address listing activities functioned as planned during the Endto-End Test and identifies any lessons learned that could inform pending decisions for the 2020 Census. To address these objectives, GAO reviewed key documents including test plans and training manuals, as well as workload, productivity and hiring data. At the three test sites, GAO observed listers conducting address canvassing.

WHAT GAO RECOMMENDS

GAO is making seven recommendations to the Department of Commerce and Bureau including to: (1) finalize procedures for reassigning work, (2) continue to evaluate workload and productivity data, (3) fix software problem, or determine and address why procedures were not followed, and (4) finalize report requirements to ensure data are accurate. The Department of Commerce agreed with GAO's recommendations, and the Bureau provided technical comments that were incorporated, as appropriate.

WHAT GAO FOUND

The Census Bureau (Bureau) recently completed in-field address canvassing for the 2018 End-to-End Test. GAO found that field staff known as listers generally followed procedures when identifying and updating the address file; however, some address blocks were worked twice by different listers because the Bureau did not have procedures for reassigning work from one lister to another while listers work offline. Bureau officials told GAO that they plan to develop procedures to avoid duplication but these procedures have not been finalized. Duplicating work decreases efficiency and increases costs.

GAO also found differences between actual and projected data for workload, lister productivity, and hiring.

- For the 2020 Census, the Bureau estimates it will have to verify 30 percent of addresses in the field. However, at the test sites, the actual workload ranged from 37 to 76 percent of addresses. Bureau officials told GAO the 30 percent was a nationwide average and not site specific; however, the Bureau could not provide documentation to support the 30 percent workload estimate.
- At all three test sites listers were significantly more productive than expected possibly because a design change provided better quality address and map data in the field, according to the Bureau.
- Hiring, however, lagged behind Bureau goals. For example, at the West Virginia site hiring was only at 60 percent of its goal. Bureau officials attributed the shortfall to a late start and low unemployment rates. Workload and productivity affect the cost of address canvassing. The Bureau has taken some steps to evaluate factors affecting its estimates, but continuing to so would help the Bureau refine its assumptions to better manage the operation's cost and hiring.

Listers used laptops to connect to the Internet and download assignments. They worked offline and went door-to-door to update the address file, then reconnected to the Internet to transmit their completed assignments. Bureau officials told GAO that during the test 11 out of 330 laptops did not properly transmit address and map data collected for 25 blocks. Data were deleted on 7 laptops. Because the Bureau had known there was a problem with software used to transmit address data, it created an alert report to notify the Bureau staff if data were not properly transmitted. However, Bureau officials said that either responsible staff did not follow procedures to look at the alert reports or the reports were not triggered. The Bureau is working to fix the software problem and develop new alert reports, but has not yet determined and addressed why these procedures were not followed.

The Bureau's data management reporting system did not always provide accurate information because of a software issue. The system was supposed to pull data from several systems to create a set of real-time cost and progress reports for managers to use. Because the data were not accurate, Bureau staff had to rely on multiple systems to manage address canvassing. The Bureau agreed that not only is inaccurate data problematic, but that creating workarounds is inefficient. The Bureau is developing new requirements to ensure data are accurate but these requirements have not been finalized.

June 14, 2018
Congressional Requesters

The federal government is constitutionally mandated to undertake the decennial census, a complex and costly activity—estimated at $15.6 billion (dollars inflated to the current 2020 Census time frame fiscal years 2012-2023) for the 2020 Census. The data that the census produces are used to apportion the seats of the U.S. House of Representatives; realign the boundaries of the legislative districts of each state; allocate hundreds of billions of dollars in federal financial assistance; and provide a social, demographic, and economic profile of the nation's people to guide policy decisions at each level of government.

The success of the census depends largely on the ability of the Census Bureau (Bureau) to locate every person residing in the United States. To accomplish this monumental task, the Bureau must maintain accurate address and map information for every person's residence. If the Bureau's address list and maps are inaccurate, people can be missed, counted more than once, or included in the wrong location. In an effort to help control costs, the Bureau is using new procedures to build its address list for 2020. As these procedures have not been used in prior decennials, the Bureau has conducted several tests in the last few years to help ensure the new approach will function as planned and produce a complete and accurate address database. The 2018 End-to-End Test is the last opportunity to demonstrate census technology and procedures— including new methods for building the address list—across a range of geographic locations, housing types, and demographic groups under census-like conditions before the 2020 Census.

On August 28, 2017, the Bureau began what it calls the "in-field" address canvassing operation for the End-to-End Test where temporary census employees known as listers walked the streets of designated census blocks. In three test sites—Bluefield-Beckley-Oak Hill, West Virginia; Pierce County, Washington; and Providence County, Rhode Island— listers knocked on doors and, using laptops connected to the internet, verified the address and geographic location of assigned housing units and identified any additions, deletions, and any other changes that need to be made to the address list. For example, they would add converted basements, attics, and other "hidden" housing units to the list.

You asked us to review how the address canvassing operation performed as part of the 2018 End-to-End Test. This chapter (1) determines the extent to which key "in-field" address listing activities functioned as planned and (2) identifies any lessons learned that could potentially affect pending decisions for the 2020 Census.

To address these objectives, we reviewed key documents including the 2018 End-to-End Test plan that discussed the goals and objectives for the test, as well as training manuals and other related documents for address canvassing. We interviewed Bureau staff at the three 2018 Census test sites including census field supervisors (CFS), address listers, and office personnel to discuss what went well and what challenges they faced during address canvassing. At each test site, the Bureau selected Census field staff for us to interview and observe from among those working on the days of our visits. At all three test sites, we observed listers conduct address canvassing. In addition, we used the training manuals to determine whether listers collected address information as prescribed by the Bureau. In total we conducted 18 in-field observations of listers and used a data collection instrument to document our observations. These observations are not generalizable. We also interviewed Bureau headquarters officials to discuss the use of management reports for monitoring and overseeing the operation.

We reviewed workload estimates, address lister productivity rates, and hiring information for each test site in order to report how many housing units were included at each test site, how many addresses the Bureau expected to canvass per hour, and how many people they needed to hire. To assess the reliability of these data, we reviewed available documentation and interviewed knowledgeable officials. We found the data to be sufficiently reliable for the purposes of our reporting objectives. We also met periodically with Bureau headquarters staff to discuss progress of the operation.

We conducted this performance audit from July 2017 to June 2018 in accordance with generally accepted government auditing standards. Those standards require that we plan and perform the audit to obtain sufficient, appropriate evidence to provide a reasonable basis for our findings and conclusions based on our audit objectives. We believe that the evidence obtained provides a reasonable basis for our findings and conclusions based on our audit objectives.

BACKGROUND

The Bureau's address canvassing operation updates its address list and maps, which are the foundation of the decennial census. An accurate address list both identifies all households that are to receive a notice by mail requesting participation in the census (by Internet, phone, or mailed-in questionnaire) and serves as the control mechanism for following up with households that fail to respond to the initial request. Precise maps are critical for counting the population in the proper locations—the basis of congressional apportionment and redistricting.

Our prior work has shown that developing an accurate address list is challenging—in part because people can reside in unconventional dwellings, such as converted garages, basements, and other forms of hidden housing. For example, as shown in Figure 1, what appears to be a single-family house could contain an apartment, as suggested by its two doorbells.

During address canvassing, the Bureau verifies that its master address list and maps are accurate to ensure the tabulation for all housing units and group quarters is correct.[1] For the 2010 Census, the address canvassing operation mobilized almost 150,000 field workers to canvass almost every street in the United States and Puerto Rico to update the Bureau's address list and map data—and in 2012 reported the cost at nearly $450 million. The cost of going door-to-door in 2010, along with the emerging availability of imagery data, led the Bureau to explore an approach for 2020 address canvassing that would allow for fewer boots on the ground.

Traditionally, the Bureau went door-to-door to homes across the country to verify addresses. This "in-field address canvassing" is a labor-intensive and expensive operation. To achieve cost savings, in September 2014 the Bureau decided to use a reengineered approach for building its address list for the 2020 Census and not go door-to-door (or "in-field") across the country, as it has in prior decennial censuses.[2] Rather, some

---

[1] A group quarters is a place where people live in a group living arrangement that is owned or managed by an entity or organization providing housing or services for the residents (e.g., college residence halls, residential treatment centers, nursing/skilled nursing facilities, group homes, correctional facilities, workers' dormitories, and domestic violence shelters).

[2] This change to how the Bureau builds its address list is one of four broad innovation areas for the 2020 Census. The other three innovation areas are (1) seeking to improve self-response by encouraging the use of the Internet and telephone, (2) using administrative records to reduce field work, and (3) reengineering field operations using technology to reduce manual effort and improve productivity, among other things.

areas (known as "blocks") would only need a review of their address and map information using computer imagery and third-party data sources—what the Bureau calls "in-office" address canvassing procedures.

Source: GAO. | GAO-18-414.

Figure 1. Determining an Accurate Address List Includes Identifying Whether a Dwelling Is Single or Multi-unit Housing.

According to the Bureau's address canvassing operational plan, in-office canvassing had two phases:

- During the first phase, known as "Interactive Review," Bureau employees use current aerial imagery to determine if areas have housing changes, such as new residential developments or repurposed structures, or if the areas match what is in the Bureau's master address file. The Bureau assesses the extent to which the number of housing units in the master address file is consistent with the number of units visible in the current imagery. If the housing shown in the imagery matches what is listed in the master address file, then those areas are considered to be resolved or stable and would not be canvassed in-field.

- During the second phase, known as "Active Block Resolution," employees would try to resolve coverage concerns identified during the first phase and verify every housing unit by virtually canvassing the entire area. As part of this virtual canvass, the Bureau would compare what is found in imagery to the master address file data and other data sources in an attempt to resolve any discrepancies. If Bureau employees still could not reconcile the discrepancies, such as housing unit count or street locations with what is on the address list, then they would refer these blocks to in-field address canvassing.

However, in March 2017, citing budget uncertainty the Bureau decided to discontinue the second phase of in-office review for the 2020 Census. According to the Bureau, in order to ensure that the operations implemented in the 2018 End-to-End Test were consistent with operations planned for the 2020 Census, the Bureau added the blocks originally resolved during the second phase of in-office review back into the in-field workload for the test. The cancellation of Active Block Resolution is expected to increase the national workload of the in-field canvassing workload by 5 percentage points (25 percent to 30 percent).

During in-field address canvassing, listers use laptop computers to compare what they see on the ground to what is on the address list and map. Listers confirm, add, delete, or move addresses to their correct map positions. At each housing unit, listers are trained to speak with a knowledgeable resident to confirm or update address data, ask about hidden housing units, confirm the housing unit location on the map, (known as the map spot) and collect a map spot using global positioning systems (GPS). If no one is available, listers are to use house numbers and street signs to verify the address data. The data are transmitted electronically to the Bureau.

The Census Bureau expects that the End-to-End Test for address canvassing will identify areas for improvement and changes that need to be made for the 2020 Census. Our prior work has shown the importance of robust testing. Rigorous testing is a critical risk mitigation strategy because it provides information on the feasibility and performance of individual census-taking activities, their potential for achieving desired results, and the extent to which they are able to function together under full operational conditions.

In February 2017, we added the 2020 Census to GAO's High-Risk List because operational and other issues are threatening the Bureau's ability to deliver a cost-effective enumeration.[3] We reported on concerns about the Bureau's capacity to implement innovative census-taking methods, uncertainties surrounding critical information technology systems, and the quality of the Bureau's cost-estimates. Underlying these issues are challenges in such essential management functions as the Bureau's ability to:

- collect and use real-time indicators of cost, performance, and schedule;
- follow leading practices for cost estimation; scheduling; risk management; IT acquisition, development, testing, and security; and
- cost-effectively deal with contingencies including, for example, fiscal constraints, potential changes in design, and natural disasters.

THE LISTERS GENERALLY FOLLOWED PROCEDURES, BUT THE BUREAU EXPERIENCED SOME ISSUES REASSIGNING WORK, ESTIMATING WORKLOAD AND LISTER PRODUCTIVITY, AND MANAGING TO STAFFING GOALS

The Bureau completed in-field address canvassing as scheduled by September 29, 2017, canvassing approximately 340,400 addresses. Most of the listers we observed generally followed procedures. For example, 15 of

---

[3] GAO, *High-Risk Series: Progress on Many High-Risk Areas, While Substantial Efforts Needed on Others*, GAO-17-317 (Washington, D.C.: Feb. 15, 2017).

18 listers knocked on doors, and 16 of 18 looked for hidden housing units, which is important for establishing that address lists and maps are accurate and for identifying hard-to-count populations. Those procedures include taking such steps as:

- comparing the housing units they see on the "ground" to the housing units on the address list,
- knocking on all doors so they could speak with a resident to confirm the address (even if the address is visible on the mailbox or house) and to confirm that there are no other living quarters such as a basement apartment,
- looking for "hidden housing units,"
- looking for group quarters such as group homes or dormitories, and
- confirming the location of the housing unit on a map with GPS coordinates collected on the doorstep.

To the extent procedures were not followed, it generally occurred when listers did not go up to the door and speak with a resident or take a map spot on the doorstep. Failure to follow procedures could adversely affect a complete count, as addresses could be missed or a group quarter could be misclassified as a residential address. After we alerted the Bureau to our observations, the Bureau agreed moving forward, to emphasize the importance of following procedures during training for in-field address canvassing.

Some Listers Duplicated Each Other's Work Due to a Lack of Operational Procedures for Reassigning Work

Address canvassing has tight time frames, so work needs to be assigned efficiently. Sometimes this means the Bureau needs to reassign work from one lister to another. During address canvassing, the Bureau discovered that reassigned census blocks sometimes would appear in both the new and the original listers' work assignments. In some cases, this led to blocks being worked more than once, which decreased efficiency, increased costs, and could create confusion and credibility issues when two different listers visit a house.

According to Bureau procedures, listers were instructed to connect to the Bureau's Mobile Case Management (MCM) system to download work assignments (address blocks) and to transmit their completed work at the beginning and end of the work day but not during the work day.[4] Thus during the work day, they were unaware when unworked blocks had been reassigned to another lister. Bureau officials also told us that the Listing and Mapping Application (LiMA)[5] software used to update the address file and maps was supposed to have the functionality to prevent blocks from being worked more than once, but this functionality was not developed because of budget cuts.

For 2020, Bureau officials told us they plan to create operational procedures for reassigning work. According to Bureau officials, they plan to require supervisors to contact the original lister when work is reassigned. We have requested a copy of those procedures; however, the Bureau has not finalized them. Standards for Internal Control in the Federal Government (Standards for Internal Control) call for management to design control activities, such as policies and procedures to achieve objectives.[6] Finalizing these procedures should help prevent blocks from being canvassed more than once.

---

[4] MCM provides mobile device-level survey case management and dashboards. MCM also manages data transmissions and other applications on the mobile device. Listers use MCM to view assignment information about blocks. MCM enables listers to receive block assignments, launch the listing and mapping application in order to work a block assignment, and transmit completed block assignments.

[5] Listing and Mapping Application (LiMA) is a single instrument that enables field users to capture and provide address listing and mapping updates to the Master Address File/Topologically Integrated Geographic Encoding and Referencing System.

[6] GAO, *Standards for Internal Control in the Federal Government*, GAO-14-704G, (Washington, D.C.: Sep.10, 2014).

The Bureau Has Not Evaluated Workload, Productivity Rates, and Staffing Assumptions for Address Canvassing

The Bureau conducts tests under census-like conditions, in part, to verify 2020 Census planning assumptions, such as workload, how many houses per hour a lister can verify (also known as a lister's productivity rate), and how many people the Bureau needs to hire for an operation. Moreover, one of the objectives of the test is to validate that the operations being tested are ready at the scale needed for the 2020 Census. For the 2018 End-to-End Test, the Bureau completed in-field address canvassing on time at two sites and early at one site; despite workload increases at all three test sites and hiring shortfalls at two sites. The Bureau credits this success to better than expected productivity. As the Bureau reviews the results of address canvassing, evaluating the factors that affected workload, productivity rates, and staffing and making adjustments to its estimates, if necessary, before the 2020 Census would help the Bureau ensure that address canvassing has the appropriate number of staff and equipment to complete the work in the required time frame.

Workload

For the 2020 Census, the Bureau estimates it will have to send 30 percent of addresses to the field for listers to verify. However, at the three test sites, the workload was higher than this estimate (see Table 1). At one test site, the percent of addresses verified through in-field address canvassing was 76 percent or 46 percentage points more than the Bureau's expected 2020 Census in-field address canvassing workload estimate of 30 percent.

Bureau officials told us that the 30 percent in-field workload estimate is a national average and is not specific to any of the three test sites. Prior to the test, officials said that the Bureau also knew that the West Virginia site was assigning new addresses to some of the test site's housing units due to local government emergency 911 address conversion and that the in-field workload would be greater in West Virginia when compared to the other test sites.

Table 1. Workload for the Address Canvassing Operation in the 2018 End-to-End Test

Test site	Addresses canvassed in the office	Addresses sent to the field to be canvassed	Percent of addresses canvassed in the field
Rhode Island	271,643	101,635	37%
Washington	335,544	175,226	52%
West Virginia	83,446	63,512	76%

Source: GAO analysis of Census Bureau data. | GAO-18-414.

We requested documentation for the Bureau's original estimate that 30 percent of the 133.8 million expected addresses would be canvassed infield for the 2020 Census. However, the Bureau was unable to provide us with documentation to support how they arrived at the 30 percent estimate. Instead, the Bureau provided us with a November 2017 methodology document that showed three in-field address canvassing workload scenarios, whereby, between 41.9 and 45.1 percent of housing units would need to go to the field for address canvassing. The three scenarios consider a range of stability in the address file as well as different workload estimates for in-field follow-up. At 30 percent the Bureau would need to canvass about 40.2 million addresses; however, at 41.9 and 45.1 percent the Bureau would need to canvass between 56 million and 60.4 million addresses, respectively. According to Bureau officials, they are continuing to assess whether changes to its in-office address canvassing procedures would be able to reduce the in-field address canvassing workload to 30 percent, while at the same time maintaining address quality. However, Bureau officials did not provide us with documentation to show how the in-field address canvassing workload would be reduced because the proposed changes were still being reviewed internally.

Workload for address canvassing directly affects cost – the greater the workload the more people as well as laptop computers needed to carry out the operation. We found that the 30 percent workload threshold is what is reflected in the December 2017 updated 2020 Census cost estimate that was used to support the fiscal year 2019 budget request. Thus, if the 30 percent threshold is not achieved then the in-field canvassing workload will likely increase for the 2020 Census and the Bureau would be at risk of exceeding its proposed budget for the address canvassing operation.

Standards for Internal Control call for organizations to use quality information to achieve their objectives. Thus, continuing to evaluate and finalize workload estimates for in-field address canvassing with the most current information will help ensure the Bureau is well-positioned to conduct addressing canvassing for the 2020 Census. For example, according to Bureau officials, preliminary workload estimates will need to be delivered by January 2019 for hiring purposes and the final in-field workload numbers for address canvassing will need to be determined by June 2019 for the start of address canvassing, which is set to begin in August 2019. Moreover, by February 2019 the Bureau's schedule calls for it to determine how many laptops will be needed to conduct 2020 Census address canvassing.

Lister Productivity

At the test sites, listers were substantially more productive than the Bureau expected. The expected production rate is defined as the number of addresses expected to be completed per hour, and it affects the cost of the address canvassing operation. This rate includes time for actions other than actually updating addresses, such as travel time. In the 2010 Census the rates reflected different geographic areas, and the country was subdivided into three areas: urban/suburban, rural, and very rural.

Table 2. Expected and Actual Productivity Rates for the In-Field Address Canvassing Operation in the 2018 End-to-End Test

Test site	Expected productivity rates (addresses per hour)	Actual productivity rates (addresses per hour)
Rhode Island	11.36	13.84
West Virginia	6.9	10.21
Washington	10.07	13.94

Source: GAO analysis of Census Bureau data. | GAO-18-414.

According to Bureau officials, for the 2020 Census the Bureau will have variable production rates based on geography, similar to the design used in the 2010 Census. The Bureau told us they have not finalized the 2020 Census address canvassing production rates.

Table 2 shows the expected and actual productivity rates (addresses per hour) for the in-field address canvassing operation at all three test sites.

To ensure address canvassing for the test was consistent with the 2020 Census, Bureau officials told us they included the blocks resolved during the now discontinued second phase of in-office review, into the in-field workload for the test. The Bureau attributed the greater productivity to this discontinued second phase. Bureau officials told us that they believe that listers spent less time updating those blocks because they had already been resolved, and any necessary changes were already incorporated. Moreover, while benefitting from the second phase of in-office address canvassing may be one explanation for why listers were more productive, Bureau officials told us that they are unable to evaluate the differences in expected versus actual productivity for blocks added to the workload as a result of the discontinued second phase because of limitations with the data. However, there could be other reasons as well such as travel time and geography. Standards for Internal Control require that organizations use quality information to achieve their objectives. Therefore, continuing to evaluate other factors from the 2018 End-to-End Test that may have increased or could potentially decrease productivity will be important for informing lister productivity rates for 2020, as productivity affects the number of listers needed to carry out the operation, the number of staff hours charged to the operation, and the number of laptops to be procured.

Hiring

For the 2018 End-to-End Test address canvassing operation, the Bureau hired fewer listers than it assumed it needed at two sites and hired more at the other site. In West Virginia, 60 percent of the required field staff was hired and in Washington, 74.5 percent of the required field staff was hired. Nevertheless, the operation finished on schedule at both these sites. In contrast in Rhode Island the Bureau hired 112 percent of the required field staff and finished early.[7]

According to Bureau officials, both the West Virginia and Washington state test sites started hiring field staff later than expected because of uncertainty surrounding whether the Bureau would have sufficient funding to open all three test sites for the 2018 End-to-End Test. When a decision was made to open all three sites for the address canvassing operation only, that decision came late, and Bureau officials told us that once they were behind in hiring and were never able to catch up because of low unemployment rates and the short duration of the operation.[8] According to Bureau officials, their approach to hiring for the 2018 End-to-End Test was similar to that used for the 2010 and 2000 Censuses. In both censuses the Bureau's goal was to recruit and hire more workers than it needed because of immutable deadlines and attrition.

After the 2010 Census we reported that the Bureau had over recruited; conversely, for the 2000 Census the Bureau had recruited in the midst of one of the tightest labor markets in three decades.[9] Thus we recommended, and the Bureau agreed to evaluate current economic factors that are associated with and predictive of employee interest in census work, such as national and regional unemployment levels, and use these available data to determine the potential temporary workforce pool and adjust its recruiting approach. The Bureau implemented this recommendation, and used unemployment and 2010 Census data to determine a base recruiting goal at both the Los Angeles, California and Houston, Texas 2016 census test sites. Specifically, the recruiting goal for Los Angeles was reduced by 30 percent.

Bureau officials told us that it continues to gather staffing data from the 2018 End-to-End Test that will be important to consider looking forward to 2020. Although address canvassing generally finished on

---

[7] In Rhode Island, the Bureau had to redo some address listing after the data were lost as discussed later in the report, but was still within the planned time frame.

[8] Remaining operations for the 2018 End-to-End Test, including non-response follow-up, will be conducted at the Providence County, Rhode Island test site only.

[9] GAO, *2010 Census: Data Collection Operations Were Generally Completed as Planned, but Long-standing Challenges Suggest Need for Fundamental Reforms*, GAO-11-193 (Washington, D.C.: Dec. 14, 2010).

schedule even while short staffed, Bureau officials told us they are carefully monitoring recruiting and hiring data to ensure they have sufficient staff for the test's next census field operation non-response follow-up, when census workers go door-to-door to follow up with housing units that have not responded. Non-response follow-up is set to begin in May 2018. According to test data as of March 2018, the Bureau is short of its recruiting goal for this operation which is being conducted in Providence County, Rhode Island. The Bureau's goal is to recruit 5,300 census workers and as of March 2018, the Bureau had only recruited 2,732 qualified applicants to fill 1,166 spots for training and deploy 1,049 census workers to conduct non-response follow-up. Bureau officials told us they believe that low unemployment is making it difficult to meet its recruiting goals in Providence County, Rhode Island, but they are confident they will be able to hire sufficient staff without having to increase pay rates.

Recruiting and retaining sufficient staff to carry out operations as labor-intensive as address canvassing and nonresponse follow-up for the 2020 Census is a huge undertaking with implications for cost and accuracy. Therefore, striking the right staffing balance for the 2020 Census is important for ensuring deadlines are met and costs are controlled.

Resolving Challenges from the Address Canvassing Test Will Better Position the Bureau for the 2020 Census

The Bureau Does Not Have Procedures to Ensure All Collected Address Canvassing Data Are Retained

Bureau officials told us that during the test 11 out of 330 laptop computers did not properly transmit address and map data collected for 25 blocks. The lister-collected address file and map data are supposed to be electronically transmitted from the listers' laptops to the Bureau's data processing center in Jeffersonville, Indiana. The data are encrypted and remain on the laptop until the laptops are returned to the Bureau where the encrypted data are deleted. Prior to learning that not all data had properly transmitted off the laptops, data on seven of the laptops was deleted. Data on the remaining four laptops were still available. In Providence, Rhode Island, where the full test will take place, the Bureau recanvassed blocks where data were lost to ensure that the address and map information for nonresponse follow-up was correct. Recanvassing blocks increases costs and can lead to credibility problems for the Bureau when listers visit a home twice.

Going into address canvassing for the End-to-End Test, Bureau officials said they knew there was a problem with the LiMA software used to update the Bureau's address lists and maps. Specifically, address and map updates would not always transfer when a lister transmitted their completed work assignments from the laptop to headquarters. Other census surveys using LiMA had also encountered the same software problem. Moreover, listers were not aware that data had not transmitted because there was no system-generated warning. Bureau officials are working to fix the LiMA software problem, but told us that the software problem has been persistent across other census surveys that use LiMA and they are not certain it will be fixed.

Bureau officials told us that prior to the start of address canvassing they created an alert report to notify Bureau staff managing the operation at headquarters if data were not properly transmitted. When transmission problems were reported, staff was supposed to remotely retrieve the data that were not transmitted. This workaround was designed to safeguard the data but according to officials was not used. Bureau officials told us that they do not know whether this was because the alert reports were not viewed by responsible staff or whether the alert report to notify the Bureau staff managing the operation was not triggered. Bureau officials told us they recognize the importance of following procedures to monitor alert reports, and acknowledge that the loss of data on seven of the laptops may have been avoided had the procedures that alert reports get triggered and monitored been followed; however, officials did not know why the procedures were not followed.

For 2020, if the software problem is not resolved, then officials said the Bureau plans to create two new alert reports to monitor the transmission of data. One report would be triggered when the problem occurs and a second report would capture a one-to-one match between data on the laptop and data transmitted to the data center so that discrepancies would be immediately obvious. While these new reports should help ensure that Bureau staff are alerted when data has not properly transmitted, the Bureau has not determined and addressed why the procedures that required an alert report get triggered and then reviewed by Bureau staff did not work as intended. Standards for Internal Control require that organizations safeguard data and follow policies and procedures to achieve their objectives. Thus, either fixing the LiMA software problem, or if the software problem cannot be fixed, then determining and addressing why procedures that alert reports get triggered and monitored were not followed would position the Bureau to help prevent future data losses.

More Useful and Accurate Monitoring Data for Field Supervisors Would Strengthen Management of Operations

To effectively manage address canvassing, the Bureau needs to be able to monitor the operation's progress in near real time. Operational issues such as listers not working assigned hours or falling behind schedule need to be resolved quickly because of the tight time frames of the address canvassing and subsequent operations. During the address canvassing test, the Bureau encountered several challenges that hindered its efforts to efficiently monitor lister activities as well as the progress of the address canvassing operation.

System Alerts Were Not Consistently Used by Supervisors

The Bureau provides data-driven tools for the census field supervisors to manage listers, including system alerts that identify issues that require the supervisor to follow-up with a lister. For the address canvassing operation, the system could generate 14 action codes that covered a variety of operational issues such as unusually high or low productivity (which may be a sign of fraud or failure to follow procedures) and administrative issues such as compliance with overtime and completion of expense reports and time cards.

During the operation, over 8,250 alerts were sent to CFSs or about 13 alerts were sent per day per CFS. Each alert requires the CFS to take action and then record how the alert was resolved. CFSs told us and the Bureau during debriefing sessions that they believed many of the administrative alerts were erroneous and they dismissed them. For example, during our site visit one CFS showed us an alert that incorrectly identified that a timecard had not been completed. The CFS then showed us that the lister's timecard had indeed been properly completed and submitted. CFSs we spoke to said that they often dismissed alerts related to expense reports and timecards and did not pay attention to them or manage them. Bureau officials reported that one CFS was fired for not using the alerts to properly manage the operation.

To assist supervisors, these alerts need to be reliable and properly used. Bureau officials said that they examined alerts for errors after we told them about our observation. They reported that they did not find any errors in the alerts. They believe that CFSs may not fully understand that the alerts stay active until they are marked as resolved by the CFS. For example, if a CFS gets an alert that a lister has not completed a timecard the alert will remain active until the CFS resolves the alert by stating the time card was completed. The Bureau's current CFS manual does not address that by the time a CFS sees the alert a lister may have already taken action to resolve it. Because this was a reoccurring situation, CFSs told us they had a difficult time managing the alerts.

Standards for Internal Control call for an agency to use quality information to achieve objectives. Bureau officials acknowledge that it is a problem that some CFSs view the alerts as erroneous and told us they plan to address the importance of alerts in training. We spoke to Bureau officials about making the alerts more useful to CFSs, such as by differentiating between critical and noncritical alerts and streamlining alerts by perhaps combining some of them. Bureau officials told us they would monitor the alerts during the 2018 End-to-End Test's nonresponse follow-up operation and make adjustments if appropriate. However, while the Bureau told us it will monitor alerts for the non-response follow-up operation, the Bureau does not have a plan for how it will examine and make alerts more useful.

Ensuring alerts are properly followed up on is critical to the oversight and management of an operation. If the CFSs view the alerts as unreliable, they could be likely to miss key indicators of fraud such as unusually high or low productivity or an unusually high or low number of miles driven. Moreover, monitoring overtime alerts and the submission of daily time cards and expense reports is also important to ensure that overtime is appropriately approved before worked and that listers get paid on time.

The Bureau's Management Dashboard Did Not Always Display Accurate Information

Another tool the Bureau uses to monitor operations is its Unified Tracking System (UTS), a management dashboard that combines data from a variety of Census systems, bringing the data to one place where the users can run or create reports. It was designed to track metrics such as the number and percentage of blocks assigned and blocks completed as well as the actual expenditures of an operation compared to the budgeted expenditures. However, information in UTS was not always accurate during address canvassing. For example UTS did not always report the correct number of addresses assigned and completed by site. As a result, Bureau managers reported they did not rely on UTS and instead used data from the source systems that fed into it. Bureau officials agreed that inaccurate data is a problem and that this workaround was inefficient as users had to take extra time to go to multiple systems to get the correct data.

Bureau officials reported problems importing information from the feeder systems into UTS because of data mismatches. They said that address canvassing event codes were not processed sequentially, as they should have been, which led to inaccurate reporting.[10] Bureau officials told us that they did not specify that the codes needed to be processed in chronological order as part of the requirements for UTS. Bureau officials said UTS passed the requisite readiness reviews and tests. However, Bureau officials also acknowledged that some of these problems could have been caught by exception testing which was not done prior to production.[11]

To resolve this issue for 2020, Bureau officials stated they are developing new requirements for UTS to automatically consider the chronological order of event codes. The Bureau told us they are working on these UTS requirements and will provide us with documentation when they are complete. They also said the Bureau plans to implement a process which compares field management reports with UTS reports to help ensure that the reports have the same definitions and are reporting accurate information. Standards for Internal Control call for an organization's data be complete and accurate and processed into quality information to achieve their objectives. Thus, finalizing UTS requirements for the address canvassing reporting should help increase efficiency for the 2020 Census by avoiding time consuming workarounds.

The Bureau Does Not Have Documented Procedures to Address Broadband Internet Service Coverage Gaps

The Bureau has taken significant steps to use technology to reduce census costs. These steps include using electronic systems to transmit listers' assignments and address and map data. However, during the address canvassing test, several listers and CFSs at the three test sites experienced problems with Internet connections primarily during training. The West Virginia site, which was more rural than the other sites,

---

[10] Bureau officials reported that there was no sequencing identifier built into events from feeder systems resulting in UTS processing some events out of order and at times incorrectly updating the operation's status.

[11] Exception testing is a type of program-level/integration testing that focuses on system behavior and the handling of exception scenarios across business processes.

experienced the most problems with Internet connectivity. All six West Virginia CFSs reported Internet connectivity problems during the operation. As a work around, CFSs told us that a couple of their listers transmitted their work assignments from libraries where they could access the Internet.

Bureau officials stated that the laptops in the 2018 End-to-End Test only used two broadband Internet service providers, which may have contributed to some of the Internet access issues. Bureau officials added that despite the reported Internet connectivity issues, the 2018 End-to-End Test for address canvassing finished on schedule and without any major problems. While this might be true for the test, we have previously reported that minor problems can become big challenges when the census scales up to the entire nation.[12] Therefore, it is important that these issues get resolved before August 2019 when in-field address canvassing for the 2020 Census is set to begin.

The Bureau is analyzing the cellular network coverage across all 2020 Census areas using coverage maps and other methods to determine which carrier is appropriate (including a backup carrier) for geographic areas where network coverage is limited. According to Bureau officials, they anticipate identifying the cellular carriers for each of its 248 area census offices by the summer of 2018. The officials said they are considering both national and regional carriers to provide service in some geographic areas because the best service provider in a certain geographic area may not be one of the national providers, but a regional provider. In those cases, listers and other staff in those areas will receive devices with the regional carrier. According to Bureau officials, for the 2020 Census, the ability to access multiple carriers should provide field staff with better connectivity around the country.

We also found that there was no guidance for listers and CFSs on what to do if they experienced Internet connectivity problems and were unable to access the Internet. Bureau officials told us that staff in the field can use different methods to access the Internet, such as using home wireless

---

[12] GAO, *2010 Census: Planning and Testing Activities are Making Progress,* GAO-06-465T (Washington D.C.: Mar. 1, 2006).

networks or mobile hotspots located at libraries, or coffee shops to transmit data. However, the Bureau did not provide such instructions to listers. In addition, the Bureau also does not define what constitutes a secure Internet public connection. Ensuring data are safeguarded is important because census data are confidential. Bureau officials told us that the Bureau plans to provide instructions to field staff on what to do if they are unable to access census systems and what constitutes a secure Internet connection for the next 2018 End-to-End Test field operation, non-response follow-up. However, the Bureau has not finalized or documented these instructions. Standards for Internal Control call for management to design control activities, such as providing instructions to employees to achieve objectives. Finalizing these instructions to field staff will help ensure listers have complete information on how to handle problems with Internet connectivity and that data are securely transmitted.

The Bureau Has Not Identified Alternative Sites for Listers to Take Online Training When Access to the Internet Is Unavailable

Some listers had difficulty accessing the Internet to take online training for address canvassing. This is the first decennial census that the Bureau is using online training, in previous decennials training was instructor-led in a class room. According to the Bureau, in addition to the Bureau provided laptop, listers also needed a personal home computer or laptop and Internet access at their home in order to complete the training. However, while the Bureau reported that listers had access to a personal computer to complete the training, we found some listers did not have access to the Internet at their home and were forced to find workarounds to access the training.

According to American Community Survey data from 2015, among all households, 77 percent had a broadband Internet subscription. Bureau officials told us they are aware that not all households have access to the Internet and that the Bureau's field division is working on back-up plans for accessing online training.

Specifically, Bureau officials told us for 2020 they plan to identify areas of the country that could potentially have connectivity issues and plan to identify alternative locations such as libraries or community centers where Internet connections are available to ensure all staff has access to training. However, they have not finalized those plans to identify locations for training sites. Standards for Internal Control call for management to design control activities, such as having plans in place to achieve objectives. Finalizing these plans to identify alternative training locations will help ensure listers have a place to access training.

Conclusion

The Bureau's re-engineered approach for address canvassing shows promise for controlling costs and maintaining accuracy. However, the address canvassing operation in the 2018 End-to-End test identified the need to reexamine assumptions and make some procedural and technological improvements. For example, at a time when plans for infield address canvassing should be almost finalized, the Bureau is in the process of evaluating workload and productivity assumptions to ensure sufficient staff are hired and that enough laptop computers are procured. Moreover, Bureau officials have not finalized (1) procedures for reassigning work from one lister to another to prevent the unnecessary duplication of work assignments, (2) instructions for using the Internet when connectivity is a problem to ensure listers have access to training and the secure transmission of data to and from the laptops, and (3) plans for alternate training locations. To ensure address and map data are not lost during transmission, Bureau officials will also need to either (1) fix the problem with the LiMA software used to update the address and map files or (2) determine and address why procedures that alert reports be triggered and monitored were not followed.

Finally, the Bureau has made progress in using data driven technology to manage address canvassing operations. However, ensuring data used by supervisors to oversee and monitor operations are both useful and accurate will help field supervisors take appropriate action to address supervisor alerts and will help managers monitor the real-time progress of the address canvassing operation. With little time remaining it will be important to resolve these issues. Making these improvements will better ensure address canvassing for the actual enumeration, beginning in August 2019, fully functions as planned and achieves desired results.

RECOMMENDATIONS FOR EXECUTIVE ACTION

We are making the following seven recommendations to the Department of Commerce and the Census Bureau:

- Secretary of Commerce should ensure the Director of the U.S. Census Bureau continues to evaluate and finalize workload estimates for in-field address canvassing as well as evaluates the factors that impacted productivity rates during the 2018 End-to-End Test and, if necessary, make changes to workload and productivity assumptions before the 2020 Census in-field address canvassing operation to help ensure that assumptions that impact staffing and the number of laptops to be procured are accurate. (Recommendation 1)
- Secretary of Commerce should ensure the Director of the U.S. Census Bureau finalizes procedures for reassigning blocks to prevent the duplication of work. (Recommendation 2)
- Secretary of Commerce should ensure the Director of the U.S. Census Bureau finalizes backup instructions for the secure transmission of data when the Bureau's contracted mobile carriers are unavailable. (Recommendation 3)

- Secretary of Commerce should ensure the Director of the U.S. Census Bureau finalizes plans for alternate training locations in areas where Internet access is a barrier to completing training. (Recommendation 4)
- Secretary of Commerce should ensure the Director of the U.S. Census Bureau takes action to either fix the software problem that prevented the successful transmission of data, or if that cannot be fixed, then determine and address why procedures that alert reports be triggered and monitored were not followed. (Recommendation 5)
- Secretary of Commerce should ensure the Director of the U.S. Census Bureau develops a plan to examine how to make CFS alerts more useful so that CFSs take appropriate action, including alerts a CFS determines are no longer valid because of timing differences. (Recommendation 6)
- Secretary of Commerce should ensure the Director of the U.S. Census Bureau finalizes UTS requirements for address canvassing reporting to ensure that the data used by census managers who are responsible for monitoring real-time progress of address canvassing are accurate before the 2020 Census. (Recommendation 7)

AGENCY COMMENTS AND OUR EVALUATION

We provided a draft of this chapter to the Department of Commerce. In its written comments, reproduced in appendix I the Department of Commerce agreed with our recommendations. The Census Bureau also provided technical comments that we incorporated, as appropriate.

As agreed with your offices, unless you publicly announce the contents of this chapter earlier, we plan no further distribution until 30 days from the report date. At that time, we are sending copies of this chapter to the Secretary of Commerce, the Under Secretary of Economic Affairs, the

Acting Director of the U.S. Census Bureau, and interested congressional committees.

Robert Goldenkoff
Director, Strategic Issues.

List of Requesters

The Honorable Ron Johnson
Chairman

The Honorable Claire McCaskill
Ranking Member
Committee on Homeland Security and Governmental Affairs
United States Senate

The Honorable Gary Peters
Ranking Member
Subcommittee on Federal Spending Oversight
and Emergency Management
Committee on Homeland Security and Governmental Affairs
United States Senate

The Honorable Thomas R. Carper
United States Senate

The Honorable Trey Gowdy
Chairman

The Honorable Elijah E. Cummings
Ranking Member
Committee on Oversight and Government Reform
House of Representatives

APPENDIX I: COMMENTS FROM THE DEPARTMENT OF COMMERCE

UNITED STATES DEPARTMENT OF COMMERCE
The Secretary of Commerce
Washington, D.C. 20230

May 29, 2018

Mr. Robert Goldenkoff
Director, Strategic Issues
U.S. Government Accountability Office
441 G Street, NW
Washington, DC 20548

Dear Mr. Goldenkoff:

The U.S. Department of Commerce appreciates the opportunity to comment on the U.S. Government Accountability Office's (GAO) draft report titled *2020 Census: Actions Needed to Improve In-Field Address Canvassing Operation* (GAO-18-414).

The Department agrees with the findings and recommendations in this draft report, as noted in the enclosed comments. Once the GAO issues the final version of this report, the Department will prepare an action plan to document the steps we will take regarding the final recommendations.

Sincerely,

Wilbur Ross

Department of Commerce's Comments on
GAO Draft Report titled *2020 Census: Actions Needed to Improve In-Field Address Canvassing Operation* (GAO-18-414)

The Department of Commerce has reviewed the draft report and offers the following responses:

- **Recommendation 1**: Secretary of Commerce should ensure the Director of the U.S. Census Bureau continues to evaluate and finalize workload estimates for in-field address canvassing as well as evaluates the factors that impacted productivity rates during the 2018 End-to-End Test and, if necessary, make changes to workload and productivity assumptions before the 2020 Census in-field address canvassing operation to help ensure that assumptions that impact staffing and the number of laptops to be procured are accurate.

Commerce Response: The Department of Commerce agrees with this recommendation and will prepare an action plan upon issuance of the final report.

- **Recommendation 2:** Secretary of Commerce should ensure the Director of the U.S. Census Bureau finalizes procedures for reassigning blocks to prevent the duplication of work.

Commerce Response: The Department of Commerce agrees with this recommendation and will prepare an action plan upon issuance of the final report.

- **Recommendation 3**: Secretary of Commerce should ensure the Director of the U.S. Census Bureau finalizes backup instructions for the secure transmission of data when the Bureau's contracted mobile carriers are unavailable.

Commerce Response: The Department of Commerce agrees with this recommendation and will prepare an action plan upon issuance of the final report.

- **Recommendation 4:** Secretary of Commerce should ensure the Director of the U.S. Census Bureau finalizes plans for alternate training locations in areas where Internet access is a barrier to completing training.

Commerce Response: The Department of Commerce agrees with this recommendation and will prepare an action plan upon issuance of the final report.

- **Recommendation 5:** Secretary of Commerce should ensure the Director of the U.S. Census Bureau takes action to either fix the software problem that prevented the successful transmission of data, or if that cannot be fixed, determine and address why procedures that alert reports be triggered and monitored were not followed.

Commerce Response: The Department of Commerce agrees with this recommendation and will prepare an action plan upon issuance of the final report.

- **Recommendation 6:** Secretary of Commerce should ensure the Director of the U.S. Census Bureau develops a plan to examine how to make Census Field Supervisor (CFS) alerts more useful so that CFSs take appropriate action, including alerts that a CFS determines are no longer valid because of timing differences.

Commerce Response: The Department of Commerce agrees with this recommendation and will prepare an action plan upon issuance of the final report.

- **Recommendation 7:** Secretary of Commerce should ensure the Director of the U.S. Census Bureau finalizes Unified Tracking System requirements for address canvassing reporting to ensure that the data used by census managers who are responsible for monitoring real-time progress of address canvassing are accurate before the 2020 Census.

Commerce Response: The Department of Commerce agrees with this recommendation and will prepare an action plan upon issuance of the final report.

In: A Closer Look at the 2020 Census
Editor: Sille M. Schou

ISBN: 978-1-53616-508-1
© 2019 Nova Science Publishers, Inc.

Chapter 12

2020 CENSUS: CONTINUED MANAGEMENT ATTENTION NEEDED TO ADDRESS CHALLENGES AND RISKS WITH DEVELOPING, TESTING, AND SECURING IT SYSTEMS[*]

United States Government Accountability Office

ABBREVIATIONS

Bureau	U.S. Census Bureau
CEDCaP	Census Enterprise Data Collection and Processing
CIO	chief information officer
Commerce	Department of Commerce
FISMA	Federal Information Security Management Act of 2002 and Federal Information Security Modernization Act of 2014

---

[*] This is an edited, reformatted and augmented version of the United States Government Accountability Office Report to Congressional Requesters, Publication No. GAO-18-655, dated August 2018.

FITARA	Federal Information Technology Acquisition Reform Act
IT	information technology
NIST	National Institute of Standards and Technology
OMB	Office of Management and Budget
POA&M	plan of action and milestones
PII	personally identifiable information

WHY GAO DID THIS STUDY

One of the Bureau's most important functions is to conduct a complete and accurate decennial census of the U.S. population. The decennial census is mandated by the Constitution and provides vital data for the nation. The Bureau plans to significantly change the methods and technology it uses to count the population with the 2020 Census, such as by offering an option for households to respond to the survey via the Internet. In preparation for the 2020 Census, the Bureau is conducting a test of all key systems and operations (referred to as the 2018 End-to-End Test), which began in August 2017 and runs through April 2019.

GAO was asked to review the Bureau's IT readiness for the 2020 Census. This chapter (1) determines the Bureau's progress in developing and testing systems for the 2018 End-to-End Test and (2) describes the challenges and risks that the Bureau has faced in implementing and securing these systems. To do this, GAO reviewed key documentation, including plans for system development and testing, and outcomes of key IT milestone reviews and security assessments.

WHAT GAO RECOMMENDS

Over the past decade, GAO has made 93 recommendations specific to the 2020 Census to address the issues raised in this and other products. As of August 2018, the Bureau had implemented 61 recommendations, and had taken initial steps—including developing action plans—to implement the other 32 recommendations. GAO is not making additional recommendations in this chapter.

WHAT GAO FOUND

The Census Bureau (Bureau) has continued to make progress in developing and testing information technology (IT) systems for the 2020 Census. Specifically, as of June 2018, the Bureau had completed all development activities for 36 of the 44 systems needed to support the 2018 End-to-End Test, and was in the process of completing these activities for the remaining 8 systems. In addition, the Bureau had completed all system and integration testing activities for 20 of the 44 systems, and was in the process of conducting these activities for the remaining 24 systems.

Nevertheless, the Bureau continues to face significant challenges and risks in its efforts to manage the schedules, contracts, costs, and cybersecurity of its 2020 Census systems.

- *Schedule management*: The Bureau's schedule for developing systems to support the 2018 End-to-End Test has experienced delays. These delays have compressed the time available for system and integration testing, and several systems experienced problems during the 2018 End-to-End Test. In addition, the Bureau is currently revising the system development and testing schedule for the 2020 Census as a result of challenges experienced and lessons learned while completing these activities during the 2018 End-to-End Test. Continued schedule management challenges may compress the time available for the remaining system and integration testing and increase the risk that systems will not function as intended.
- *Contractor oversight*: Among other challenges, the Bureau is still filling vacancies in the government program management office that is overseeing its key integration contractor. In June 2018,

Bureau officials reported that 33 of the office's 58 federal employee positions were vacant. This adds risk that the office may not be able to provide adequate oversight of contractor cost, schedule, and performance.

- *IT cost growth*: The Bureau reported that its estimated IT costs had grown from $3.41 billion in October 2015 to $4.97 billion in December 2017—an increase of $1.56 billion. This increase was due, in large part, to the addition of technical integration services and updated costs for other major contracts (such as the contract for mobile devices). The amount of cost growth since the October 2015 estimate raises questions as to whether the Bureau has a complete understanding of the IT costs associated with the 2020 Census.
- *Cybersecurity*: The Bureau has made progress by completing the security assessments for 33 of the 44 systems needed to support the 2018 End-toEnd Test. However, as of June 2018, the Bureau had identified nearly 3,100 security weaknesses that will need to be addressed in the coming months. Because the 2020 Census involves collecting personal information from over a hundred million households across the country, it will be important that the Bureau addresses system security weaknesses in a timely manner and ensures that risks are at an acceptable level before systems are deployed.

With the 2020 Census less than 2 years away, it is critical that the Bureau address these challenges and risks to ensure that its IT systems are developed, tested, and secured in time to support the count of the nation's population.

August 30, 2018
Congressional Requesters

Conducting the decennial census of the U.S. population is mandated by the Constitution and provides vital data for the nation. The information that the census collects is used to apportion the seats of the House of Representatives; redraw congressional districts; allocate billions of dollars each year in federal financial assistance; and provide a social, demographic, and economic profile of the nation's people to guide policy decisions at each level of government. Further, businesses use census data to market new services and products and to tailor existing ones to demographic changes.

For 2020, a complete count of the nation's population is an enormous undertaking. The U.S. Census Bureau (Bureau), a component of the Department of Commerce (Commerce), is seeking to control the cost of the census while it implements several innovations and manages the processes of acquiring and developing information technology (IT) systems. However, in recent years, we have identified challenges that raise serious concerns about the Bureau's ability to conduct a cost-effective count of the nation, including issues with the agency's research, testing, planning, scheduling, cost estimation, systems development, and cybersecurity practices. We also added the 2020 Census to GAO's high-risk list in February 2017.[1]

Currently, the Bureau is conducting the 2018 End-to-End Test, which began in August 2017 and runs through April 2019. This effort is the Bureau's final opportunity to test all key systems and operations in a census-like environment to ensure readiness for the 2020 Census.

Given the importance of the IT systems to the 2018 End-to-End Test and the 2020 Census, you asked us to review the Bureau's IT readiness for the 2020 Census. Our specific objectives were to (1) determine the progress that the Bureau has made in developing and testing the critical IT systems for the 2018 End-to-End Test, and (2) describe the challenges and risks that the Bureau has faced in implementing and securing these systems.

---

[1] GAO, *High-Risk Series: Progress on Many High-Risk Areas, While Substantial Efforts Needed on Others*, GAO-17-317 (Washington, D.C.: Feb. 15, 2017). GAO maintains a high-risk program to focus attention on government operations that it identifies as high risk due to their greater vulnerabilities to fraud, waste, abuse, and mismanagement or the need for transformation to address economy, efficiency, or effectiveness challenges.

To determine the progress in developing and testing systems for the 2018 End-to-End Test, we updated information related to our recent work on the Bureau's system development and testing efforts.[2] To do this, we reviewed relevant Bureau documentation on the 44 IT systems in the 2018 End-to-End Test, including the 2020 Census Operational Plan, the Bureau's system integration and implementation plan, outcomes of key IT milestone reviews, and requirements traceability matrices. We also interviewed agency officials, including the Chief Information Officer (CIO), the Associate Director for Decennial Census Programs, and officials from the Bureau's technical integration contractor.

To describe the challenges and risks that the Bureau has faced in implementing and securing these systems, we reviewed Bureau documentation, including risk and issue registers, meeting minutes from 2020 Census executive review meetings, and presentations from bimonthly meetings from the Bureau's technical integration contractor. We also reviewed documentation discussing the Bureau's progress in mitigating or addressing the risks and challenges, including plans for 2020 Census system development and testing, deliverables from key contractors (including the technical integration contractor), the basis of estimate documentation for the 2020 Census cost estimate developed in December 2017, results of 2020 Census executive review board meetings, outcomes from security assessments, and the Bureau's list of plans of action and milestones (POA&Ms). In addition, we interviewed relevant agency officials, including the CIO and the Chief Information Security Officer.

---

[2] For example, GAO, 2020 Census: Actions Needed to Mitigate Key Risks Jeopardizing a Cost-Effective and Secure Enumeration, GAO-18-543T (Washington, D.C.: May 8, 2018); 2020 Census: Continued Management Attention Needed to Mitigate Key Risks Jeopardizing a Cost-Effective and Secure Enumeration, GAO-18-416T (Washington, D.C.: Apr. 18, 2018); 2020 Census: Actions Needed to Mitigate Key Risks Jeopardizing a Cost-Effective Enumeration, GAO-18-215T (Washington, D.C.: Oct. 31, 2017); 2020 Census: Continued Management Attention Needed to Oversee Innovations, Develop and Secure IT Systems, and Improve Cost Estimation, GAO-18-141T (Washington, D.C.: Oct. 12, 2017); 2020 Census: Sustained Attention to Innovations, IT Systems, and Cost Estimation Is Needed, GAO-17-584T (Washington, D.C.: May 3, 2017); and Information Technology: Better Management of Interdependencies between Programs Supporting 2020 Census Is Needed, GAO-16-623 (Washington, D.C.: Aug. 9, 2016).

We conducted this performance audit from August 2016 to August 2018 in accordance with generally accepted government auditing standards. Those standards require that we plan and perform the audit to obtain sufficient, appropriate evidence to provide a reasonable basis for our findings and conclusions based on our audit objectives. We believe that the evidence obtained provides a reasonable basis for our findings and conclusions based on our audit objectives.

BACKGROUND

For the 2020 Census, the Bureau is significantly changing how it intends to conduct the census, in part by re-engineering key census-taking methods and infrastructure, and making use of new IT applications and systems. For example, the Bureau plans to offer an option for households to respond to the survey via the Internet and enable field-based enumerators[3] to use applications on mobile devices to collect survey data from households. In December 2017, the Bureau estimated the total cost of the redesigned 2020 Census to be about $15.6 billion, more than $3 billion higher than it estimated in October 2015.

To inform the design of the 2020 Census operations and systems, the Bureau held several major operational tests. These tests included (1) the 2016 Census tests in Texas and California, which evaluated, among other things, the efficiency of non-response follow-up[4] using contractor-provided mobile devices; and (2) the 2017 Census Test—a nationwide sample of how individuals respond to Census questions using paper, the Internet, or the phone—which evaluated key new IT components, such as the Internet self-response system and the use of a cloud-based infrastructure.

---

[3] Enumerators are Census Bureau employees who travel from door-to-door throughout the country to try to obtain census data from individuals who do not respond through other means, including the Internet, on paper, or by phone.

[4] In non-response follow-up, if a household does not respond to the census by a certain date, the Bureau will conduct an in-person visit by an enumerator to collect census data using a mobile device provided by the Bureau.

Currently, the Bureau is conducting the 2018 End-to-End Test, which began in August locations—Rhode Island, West Virginia, and Washington state. The Bureau is currently testing its non-response operation in Rhode Island.[5] This operation began in May 2018 and is scheduled to conclude in August 2018.

The Bureau Plans to Rely Heavily on IT for the 2018 End-to-End Test and the 2020 Census

The Bureau plans to rely heavily on both new and legacy IT systems and infrastructure to support the 2018 End-to-End Test and the 2020 Census operations. For example, the Bureau's plans call for deploying and using 44 systems in the 2018 End-to-End Test. Eleven of these systems are currently being developed or modified as part of an enterprise-wide initiative called Census Enterprise Data Collection and Processing (CEDCaP).[6] This initiative is a large and complex modernization program intended to deliver a system-of-systems to support all of the Bureau's survey data collection and processing functions, rather than continuing to rely on unique, survey-specific systems with redundant capabilities.

As part of the 2018 End-to-End Test, the Bureau plans to incrementally test, deploy, and use the 44 systems from December 2016 through the end of the test in April 2019.[7] These systems are to be deployed in 14 groups based on the operations that they support in the test, including address canvassing, self-response (i.e., Internet, phone, or paper), field enumeration, and tabulation and dissemination. A system may be

---

[5] The Bureau originally planned to perform the entire 2018 End-to-End Test in all three locations. However, in May 2017, the Bureau scaled back the operational scope of the test and, of the three planned test sites, the Bureau would fully implement the test in the Rhode Island site only.

[6] The Bureau is pursuing enterprise-wide technology solutions intended to support other major surveys the Bureau conducts as well, such as the American Community Survey and the Economic Census.

[7] Prior to deployment in the 2018 End-to-End Test, the systems are to undergo various forms of testing, including system-level testing to ensure that the system meets business requirements, and integration testing to validate (among other things) the interfaces between systems.

deployed for one operation in the 2018 End-to-End Test (such as address canvassing), and then be deployed again for a subsequent operation in the test (such as field enumeration).

Following the 2018 End-to-End Test, the Bureau has additional system development and testing activities planned leading up to the 2020 Census. Specifically, Bureau officials said they expect that the 44 systems used in the 2018 End-to-End Test will need to undergo further development and testing due to, among other things, the need to add functionality that was not part of the end-to-end test, scale system performance to support the number of respondents expected during the 2020 Census, and to address system defects identified during the 2018 End-to-End Test. Bureau officials also reported that they plan to use an additional 8 systems that were not included in the 2018 End-to-End Test—for a total of 52 systems—to carry out the 2020 Census operations.[8]

As of June 2018, the Bureau planned to deploy the 52 systems for the 2020 Census in four groups, or operational releases, to support the key operations in the 2020 Census: (1) recruiting and hiring; (2) address canvassing; (3) self-response, non-response follow-up, and fraud detection; and (4) reporting and coverage measurement.[9] The systems are grouped according to the operations that they support during the 2020 Census. For example, the third operational release—which includes the most systems—has 47 systems to be used for self-response (including via the Internet), non-response follow-up, and fraud detection.

In addition to its systems and applications, the Bureau is designing, configuring, and managing the IT infrastructure needed for the 2020 Census. The Bureau's 2020 Census infrastructure includes: (1) an on premises data center being managed by the Bureau; (2) an on premises data center being managed by the Bureau's technical integration contractor; (3) a cloud-based infrastructure using Amazon Web Services being managed

---

[8] Several of these systems are for the coverage measurement operation, which was removed from the scope of the 2018 End-to-End Test. Coverage measurement evaluates the quality of the census data by estimating the census coverage based on a post-enumeration survey.

[9] Similar to the 2018 End-to-End Test, a system being used in the 2020 Census may be deployed multiple times (with additional or new functionality) if that system is needed for more than one of these operations.

by the technical integration contractor; (4) hardware located at the National Processing Center for printing and mailing systems; and (5) hardware managed and located elsewhere for those systems that are provided as software-as-a-service.[10]

THE BUREAU HAS MADE PROGRESS IN DEVELOPING AND TESTING ITS IT SYSTEMS FOR THE 2018 END-TO-END TEST

The Bureau has made progress in developing and testing the IT systems for the 2018 End-to-End Test. In this regard, it has finished developing a majority of the 44 systems in the test. Specifically, as of June 2018, the Bureau had completed all development activities for 36 of the 44 systems in the test, and was in the process of completing these activities for the remaining 8 systems. Figure 1 summarizes the development status for the 44 systems planned for the 2018 End-to-End Test, as of June 2018.

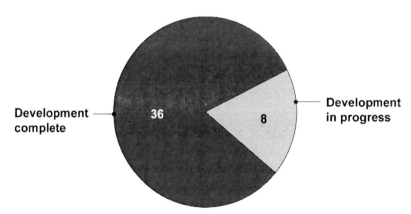

Source: GAO analysis of Census Bureau data. | GAO-18-655.

Figure 1. Development Status for the 44 Systems in the Census Bureau's 2018 End-to-End Test, as of June 2018.

---

[10] Software-as-a-service involves purchasing commercial software that is operated and maintained by a commercial vendor. Examples of systems that the Bureau has acquired as software-as-a-service include Census Questionnaire Assistance (the phone response system), and Recruiting and Assessment.

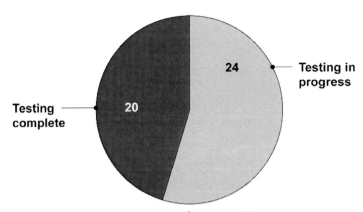

Source: GAO analysis of Census Bureau data. | GAO-18-655.

Figure 2. Testing Status for the 44 Systems in the Census Bureau's 2018 End-to-End Test, as of June 2018.

In addition, as of June 2018, the Bureau had completed all testing activities (e.g., system and integration testing) for 20 of the 44 systems included the 2018 End-to-End Test, and was in the process of conducting these tests for the remaining 24 systems. Figure 2 summarizes the status of testing for the 44 systems in the 2018 End-to-End Test. Further, appendix I provides additional details about the status of the development and testing activities for these systems.

In total, as of June 2018, the Bureau had completed all development and testing activities to support 10 of the 14 operations in the 2018 End-to-End Test, such as in-field address canvassing and response processing.[11] For the remaining 4 operations—field enumeration, group quarters enumeration, fraud detection, and reporting—system development and/or testing activities were in process, but had not been completed. Figure 3 depicts the total number of systems supporting each operation, the number of systems that have completed development and testing, and the status of the operation.

---

[11] As stated previously, the 44 systems in the test are to be deployed multiple times in a series of operations (such as group quarters enumeration). That is, a system may be deployed for one operation in the 2018 End-to-End Test (such as address canvassing), and be deployed again for a subsequent operation in the test (such as group quarters enumeration). As such, additional development and testing is to occur each time a system is deployed.

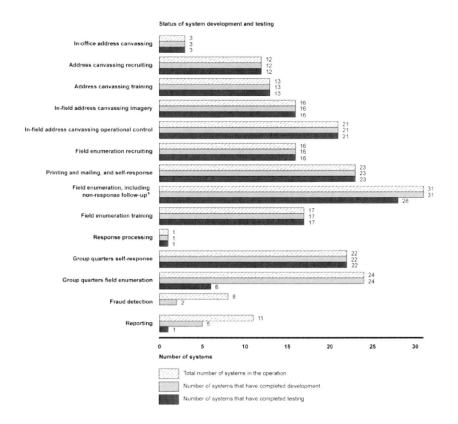

Source: GAO analysis of Census Bureau data. | GAO-18-655.

[a] In addition to non-response follow-up, field enumeration also includes operations such as update/leave and coverage improvement. In update/leave, listers update a housing unit's address and leave a questionnaire to allow the household to self-respond. The goal of coverage improvement is to resolve erroneous enumerations (such as people counted in the wrong place or more than once) and omissions.

Figure 3. Development and Testing Status for System Operations in the Census Bureau's 2018 End-to-End Test, as of June 2018.

THE BUREAU CONTINUES TO FACE CHALLENGES AND RISKS IN IMPLEMENTING ITS IT SYSTEMS FOR THE 2020 CENSUS

Even as the Bureau has made progress in its system development and testing activities, it continues to face challenges in managing and overseeing the development and testing of its IT systems for the 2018 End-to-End Test and the 2020 Census. Specifically, we have noted challenges in the Bureau's efforts to manage the schedules, contracts, costs, governance and internal coordination, and cybersecurity of its systems.

Schedule Management

The Bureau has faced significant challenges in managing its schedule for developing and testing systems for the 2018 End-to-End Test. Further, due, in part, to these challenges, the Bureau is replanning key IT milestones for the 2020 Census.

In May 2018, we reported that the Bureau had delayed by several months key IT milestone dates (e.g., dates to begin system integration testing) for a majority of the 14 operations in the 2018 End-to-End Test.[12] For example, the Bureau moved the test readiness review date for the fraud detection operation from April 2018 to July 2018—a delay of 3 months. These delays have compressed the time the Bureau has had for integration testing before the systems are deployed in the 2018 End-to-End Test.

Several of the systems subsequently experienced problems during the end-to-end test, including the mobile device applications being used by enumerators for the non-response follow-up[13] operation of the test.[14] For

---

[12] GAO-18-543T.

[13] In non-response follow-up, if a household does not respond to the census by a certain date, the Bureau will send out employees to visit the home. The Bureau's plan is for these enumerators to use a census application, on a mobile device provided by the Bureau, to capture the information given to them by the in-person interviews.

[14] As mentioned previously, the non-response follow-up operation of the End-to-End Test is being performed in Rhode Island and began in May 2018 and is scheduled to conclude in August 2018.

example, Bureau officials reported that enumerators have experienced problems with the sensitivity of the mobile devices' touch screen. More specifically, in certain cases, the mobile device application did not identify that the enumerator had made a selection on the touch screen until after the enumerator attempted to select it multiple times.

In addition, we previously reported that the delays in system development and testing had reduced the time available to conduct the security reviews and approvals for the systems being used in the 2018 End-to-End Test.[15] Officials in the Bureau's Office of Information Security stated that the original plan was to have at least 6 to 8 weeks to perform security assessments for each system. However, given the compressed time frames, Bureau officials informed us that, in some instances, they have had 5 to 8 days to complete certain assessments. This resulted in systems being deployed before the security of all system components were assessed.[16] We concluded that, going forward, it would be important for these security assessments to be completed in a timely manner and that risks be at an acceptable level before the systems are deployed.

Due in part to IT development and testing schedule challenges that it has identified during the 2018 End-to-End Test, the Bureau is in the process of revising the milestone dates for the additional system development and testing that is to occur after the 2018 End-to-End Test and before the 2020 Census. As noted earlier, the Bureau plans to develop, test, and deploy the 52 systems in the 2020 Census in four operational releases.

According to the Bureau's plans, the agency originally planned to complete development for its first 2020 Census operational release (for recruiting and hiring) in May 2018. However, in June 2018, Bureau officials reported that the Bureau did not meet the May 2018 delivery date for the 2020 Census recruiting and hiring operational release. Additionally, the agency originally planned to complete integration and testing for this operational release by July 2018. However, in July 2018, Bureau officials

---

[15] GAO-18-543T.
[16] According to the Bureau's Chief Information Security Officer, components that do not have all controls assessed are to be tracked until the assessments are completed, even if it is after the system deploys.

reported that this milestone had been delayed to August 2018. The Bureau's original milestone dates for the operational releases, reflecting the system development completion status for recruiting and hiring, are shown in table 1.

Bureau officials reported that they intend to revise the development and testing milestone dates for all four operational releases for the 2020 Census, but that they do not expect the final deployment dates to change. The officials further noted that they are planning to incorporate lessons learned to date from the 2018 End-to-End Test as part of the replanning efforts. However, Bureau officials had not yet identified a specific time frame for completing these efforts.

Table 1. The Census Bureau's Original Milestone Dates for Operational Releases for the 2020 Census, as of July 2018

Operational release name	Number of systems in the operational release	Expected completion date for system development	Expected completion date for integration and test	Expected deployment date
1. Recruiting and hiring	21	May 2018 (Not met)	July 2018 (Not met)	September 2018
2. Address canvassing	29	November 2018	March 2019	May 2019
3. Self-response, non-response follow-up, and fraud detection	47	February 2019	June 2019	November 2019
4. Reporting and coverage measurement	25	October 2019	February 2020	July 2020

Source: GAO analysis of Census Bureau data. | GAO-18-655.

Managing the schedule for system development and testing is also important because the Bureau plans to conduct system performance and scalability testing after the 2018 End-to-End Test and prior to the 2020

Census.[17] Specifically, in February 2018, the Bureau established an approach to conducting performance and scalability testing that began in February 2018 (with system design reviews and analyses) and is expected to be completed in October 2019.

As of July 2018, the Bureau reported that it had completed design reviews and analysis for 11 systems (such as the operational control system) and had developed performance test plans for 8 systems. Figure 4 summarizes the Bureau's performance and scalability test plans.

As planning for the 2020 Census continues, it will be important for the Bureau to provide adequate time for system development and testing activities. This will help ensure that the time available for security assessments is not reduced as it has been, thus far, during the 2018 End-to-End Test. We have previously reported that, without adequate time for completing these security assessments, the Bureau will be challenged in ensuring that risks are at an acceptable level before the systems are deployed for the 2020 Census.

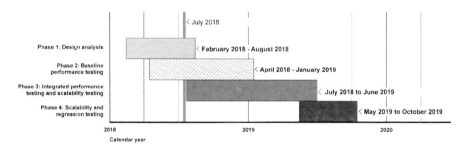

Source: GAO analysis of Census Bureau data. | GAO-18-655.

Figure 4. The Census's Bureau's Expected Performance and Scalability Test Plans for the 2020 Census, as of July 2018.

---

[17] Performance testing is the process of determining how a system behaves under a specific workload (e.g., number of users). Scalability testing is a subset of performance testing to determine a system's effectiveness in handling an increasing number of users.

Contract Management

The Bureau also faces challenges in managing its significant contractor support. The Bureau is relying on contractor support in many areas to prepare for the 2020 Census. For example, it is relying on contractors to develop a number of systems and components of the IT infrastructure. These activities include (1) developing the IT platform (as part of the CEDCaP program) that is intended to be used to collect data from households responding via the Internet and telephone, and for non-response follow-up activities; (2) procuring the mobile devices and cellular service to be used for non-response follow-up; and (3) deploying the IT and telecommunications hardware in the field offices. According to Bureau officials, contractors are also providing support in areas such as fraud detection, cloud computing services, and disaster recovery.

In addition to the development of technology, the Bureau is relying on a technical integration contractor to integrate all of the key systems and infrastructure. The Bureau awarded a contract to integrate the 2020 Census systems and infrastructure in August 2016. The contractor's work was to include evaluating the systems and infrastructure and acquiring the infrastructure (e.g., cloud or data center) to meet the Bureau's scalability and performance needs. It was also to include integrating all of the systems, supporting technical testing activities, and developing plans for ensuring the continuity of operations. Since the contract was awarded, the Bureau has modified the scope to also include assisting with operational testing activities, conducting performance testing for two Internet self-response systems, and providing technical support for the implementation of the paper data capture system.

However, the Bureau continues to face staffing challenges that could impact its ability to manage and oversee the technical integration contractor. Specifically, the Bureau is managing the integration contractor through a government program management office, but this office is still filling vacancies. In June 2018, Bureau officials reported that 33 of the office's 58 federal employee positions were vacant. This means that the Bureau has only filled 2 of these positions since we originally reported about this risk in

October 2017. These vacancies increase the risk that the program management office may not be sufficiently staffed to provide adequate oversight of contractor cost, schedule, and performance.

The development and testing schedule delays during the preparations for the 2018 End-to-End Test raise concerns about the Bureau's ability to effectively perform contractor management. As we reported in November 2016, a greater reliance on contractors for these components of the 2020 Census requires the Bureau to focus on sound management and oversight of the key contracts, projects, and systems.[18]

It Cost Growth

The Bureau faces challenges in controlling IT cost growth. Specifically, the Bureau's October 2015 cost estimate included about $3.41 billion in total IT costs for fiscal years 2012 through 2023. These included costs for, among other things, system engineering, test and evaluation, and infrastructure, as well as for a portion of the CEDCaP program.[19] However, in October 2017, we reported[20] that IT costs would likely be at least $4.8 billion, due to increases in costs associated with the CEDCaP program[21] and certain IT contracts (including those associated with technical integration and mobile devices).

In December 2017, the Bureau reported that its estimated IT costs had grown from $3.41 billion to $4.97 billion—an increase of $1.56 billion. Figure 5 identifies the Bureau's estimate of total IT costs associated with the 2020 program as of December 2017.

---

[18] GAO, Information Technology: Uncertainty Remains about the Bureau's Readiness for a Key Decennial Census Test, GAO-17-221T (Washington, D.C.: Nov. 16, 2016).

[19] The 2020 Census program pays for the portion of costs for the CEDCaP program that relate to 2020 Census operations. According to the October 2015 estimate, the portion of CEDCaP costs associated with the 2020 Census was estimated at $328 million of the $548 million total program estimate.

[20] GAO-18-215T.

[21] In May 2017, the Bureau reported that the CEDCaP program's cost estimate was increasing by about $400 million—from its original estimate of $548 million in 2013 to a revised estimate of $965 million in May 2017.

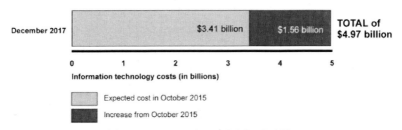

Source: GAO analysis of Census Bureau data. | GAO-18-655.

Figure 5. Total Information Technology Costs Estimated by the Census Bureau, as of December 2017.

The cost increases were due, in large part, to the Bureau (1) updating the cost estimate for the CEDCaP program, (2) including an estimate for technical integration services, and (3) updating costs related to other major contracts (such as mobile device as a service).[22] Table 2 describes the IT costs that comprised the Bureau's cost estimate as of December 2017.

Table 2. Total 2020 Census Information Technology (IT) Costs Estimated by the Census Bureau, by Cost Category, as of December 2017

IT cost category	Expected cost
Technical integration services	$1,492
Census questionnaire assistance	$817
Other IT services, such as day-to-day IT support	$808
Census Enterprise Data Collection and Processing (CEDCaP) costs related to the 2020 Census	$509[a]
Decennial device as a service	$489
Field IT deployment	$450
Other non-CEDCaP systems, such as recruitment and personnel systems	$401
Total	$4,966

Source: GAO analysis of Census Bureau data. | GAO-18-655.

[a] The 2020 program pays for a portion of the costs for the CEDCaP program. As of May 2017, the Census Bureau estimated that the entire cost of the CEDCaP program would be about $965 million.

---

[22] As part of mobile device as a service, the Bureau plans to provide mobile devices (including mobile phones, tablets, and laptops) and cellular service to field staff to support operations such as address canvassing and non-response follow-up.

IT cost information that is accurately reported and clearly communicated is necessary to help ensure that Congress and the public have confidence that taxpayer funds are being spent in an appropriate manner. However, the amount of cost growth since the October 2015 estimate raises questions as to whether the Bureau has a complete understanding of the IT costs associated with the 2020 program. We have ongoing work reviewing the extent to which the Bureau's December 2017 cost estimate is reliable.

Governance and Internal Coordination

Effective governance can drive change, provide oversight, and ensure accountability for results. Further, effective IT governance was envisioned in the statutory provisions enacted in 2014 and referred to as the Federal Information Technology Acquisition Reform Act (FITARA),[23] which strengthened and reinforced the role of the departmental CIO. The component CIO (such as the Bureau's CIO) also plays a role in effective IT governance, as the component is subject to the oversight and policies of the parent department implementing FITARA.

Our work has noted that officials in Commerce's Office of the Secretary have increased their oversight of the Bureau's preparations for the 2020 Census by holding regular meetings to discuss contracts, expected costs, and risks, among other topics.[24] For example, Bureau officials in the Decennial Directorate told us that they have recently begun meeting with the Secretary of Commerce on a monthly basis, and with the Under Secretary of Commerce for Economic Affairs on a weekly basis, to discuss 2020 Census issues. Moreover, the department's Acting CIO has also been involved in overseeing the Bureau's IT system readiness.

The Bureau has also appointed two new assistant directors within the Decennial Directorate. Each of these individuals is responsible for

---

[23] Carl Levin and Howard P. 'Buck' McKeon National Defense Authorization Act for Fiscal Year 2015, Pub. L. No. 113-291, div. A, title VIII, subtitle D, 128 Stat. 3292, 3438-50 (Dec. 19, 2014).
[24] GAO-18-543T.

overseeing aspects of the 2020 Census program, to include schedules, contracts, and system development. In addition, Bureau officials told us that the CIO (or a designated representative) is to be a member of the governance boards that oversee all of the operations and technology for the 2020 Census, in order to ensure executive-level oversight of the key systems and technology.

Nevertheless, in August 2016, we reported on challenges that the Bureau has had with IT governance and internal coordination, including weaknesses in its ability to monitor and control IT project costs, schedules, and performance.[25] We made eight recommendations to the Secretary of Commerce to direct the Bureau to, among other things, better ensure that risks are adequately identified and schedules are aligned. The department agreed with our recommendations. As of June 2018, the Bureau had fully implemented five of the recommendations and had taken initial steps toward implementing the other three recommendations.

Given the schedule delays and cost increases previously mentioned, and the vast amount of development, testing, and security assessments left to be completed, we remain concerned about executive-level oversight of systems and security. Moving forward, it will be important that the CIO and other Bureau executives continue to use a collaborative governance approach to effectively manage risks and ensure that the IT solutions meet the needs of the agency within cost and schedule.

Cybersecurity

In November 2016, we described the significant challenges that the Bureau faced in securing systems and data for the 2020 Census, and we noted that tight time frames could exacerbate these challenges.[26] Two such challenges were (1) ensuring that individuals gain only limited and appropriate access to the 2020 Census data, including personally identifiable information (PII), such as name, personal address, and date of

---
[25] GAO-16-623.
[26] GAO-17-584T.

birth; and (2) making certain that security assessments were completed in a timely manner and that risks were at an acceptable level.[27] Protecting PII, for example, is especially important because a majority of the 44 systems to be used in the 2018 End-to-End Test contain such information, as reflected in figure 6.[28]

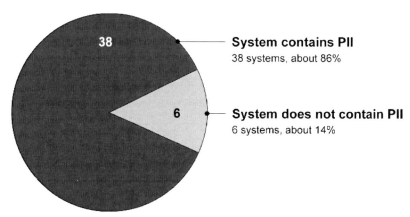

Source: GAO analysis of Census Bureau data. | GAO-18-655.

Figure 6. Personally Identifiable Information (PII) in Census Bureau Systems Included in the 2018 End-to-End Test, as of June 2018.

To address these and other challenges, federal law specifies requirements for protecting federal information and information systems, such as those systems to be used in the 2020 Census. Specifically, the Federal Information Security Management Act of 2002 and the Federal Information Security Modernization Act of 2014 (FISMA) require executive branch agencies to develop, document, and implement an agency-wide program to provide security for the information and information systems that support operations and assets of the agency.[29]

---

[27] GAO-17-221T.

[28] According to officials in the Bureau's Office of Information Security, 26 systems contain data that is protected from disclosure under Title 13 of the U.S. Code. This law protects information provided by the public for the Bureau's censuses and surveys and requires that the Bureau keep it confidential. 13 U.S.C. § 9. The Bureau may not disclose or publish any private information that identifies an individual or business, such as names, addresses, Social Security numbers, and telephone numbers.

[29] The Federal Information Security Modernization Act of 2014, Pub. L. No. 113-283, 128 Stat. 3073 (Dec. 18, 2014) largely superseded the Federal Information Security Management Act

Accordingly, the National Institute of Standards and Technology (NIST) developed risk management framework guidance for agencies to follow in developing information security programs.[30] In addition, the Office of Management and Budget's (OMB) revised Circular A-130 on managing federal information resources required agencies to implement the NIST risk management framework to integrate information security and risk management activities into the system development life cycle.[31]

In accordance with FISMA, NIST guidance, and OMB guidance, the Bureau's Office of the CIO established a risk management framework. This framework requires system developers to ensure that each of the Bureau's systems undergoes a full security assessment, and that system developers remediate critical deficiencies. In addition, according to the framework, system developers are to ensure that each component of a system has its own system security plan that documents how the Bureau intends to implement security controls. As a result of this requirement, system developers for a single system might develop multiple system security plans which all have to be approved as part of the system's complete security documentation.

According to the Bureau's framework, each of the 44 systems in the 2018 End-to-End Test will need to have complete security documentation (such as system security plans) and an approved authorization to operate prior to its use in the 2018 End-to-End Test.[32] In May 2018, Bureau officials reported that they had recently updated their policies related to obtaining an authorization to operate. Specifically, once a system

---

of 2002, enacted as Title III, E-Government Act of 2002, Pub. L. No. 107-347, 116 Stat. 2899, 2946 (Dec. 17, 2002).

[30] NIST, Guide for Applying the Risk Management Framework to Federal Information Systems: A Security Life Cycle Approach, SP 800-37, Revision 1 (Gaithersburg, Md.: February 2010).

[31] OMB, Revision of OMB Circular A-130, Managing Federal Information as a Strategic Resource (Washington, D.C.: July 28, 2016).

[32] According to the Bureau's framework, systems are to obtain security authorization approval from the authorizing official in order to operate. Specifically, the authorizing official evaluates the security authorization package and provides system authorization if the overall risk level is acceptable. In addition, according to the Bureau's IT security program policy, the issuance of an authorization to operate for a system requires support of both the technical authorizing official (i.e., the CIO) and the business authorizing official responsible for funding and managing the system (i.e., the Associate Director for Decennial Census Programs).

undergoes a security assessment and receives an authorization, the system moves into continuous monitoring.[33] According to the Bureau's Chief Information Security Officer, authorized systems do not need a formal reauthorization unless the risk posture of the system changes; this could occur, for example, if the system undergoes significant new development.

As of June 2018, most of the systems in the 2018 End-to-End Test had received an authority to operate. Specifically, according to the Bureau:

- Thirty-three of the 44 systems in the test had obtained an authorization to operate and were under continuous monitoring.
- Eight systems had obtained an authorization, but will need to be reauthorized due to additional significant planned development or changes to the infrastructure environment (e.g., from a data center to a cloud-based environment).
- Three systems do not yet have an authorization to operate for the 2018 End-to-End Test.

Figure 7 summarizes the authorization to operate status for the systems being used in the 2018 End-to-End Test, as reported by the Bureau.

According to the Bureau's framework, security assessment findings that need to be remediated are tracked in a plan of action and milestones (POA&M). Specifically, the POA&M provides a description of the vulnerability identified in the security assessment as a result of a control weakness. As of June 2018, the Bureau had nearly 3,100 open POA&Ms to remediate issues identified during security assessments performed for the 2018 End-to-End Test. Of these nearly 3,100 POA&Ms, 43 were considered "very high risk" or "high risk" weaknesses. Further, over 2,700 of the POA&Ms were related to the infrastructure components being developed by the technical integration contractor. Officials from the

---

[33] According to the Bureau's risk management framework, once a system obtains an authorization, it is transitioned to the continuous monitoring process where the authorizing official can provide ongoing authorization for system operation as long as the risk level remains acceptable.

Bureau and the technical integration contractor reported that they are currently working to address these POA&Ms.

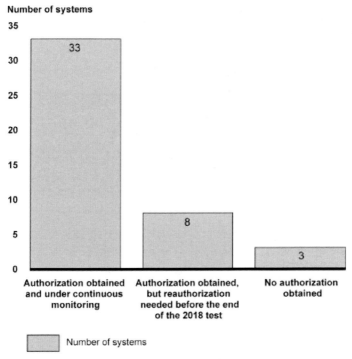

Source: GAO analysis of Census Bureau data. | GAO-18-655.

Figure 7. Authorization to Operate Status for the 44 Systems Being Used in the Census Bureau's 2018 End-to-End Test, as of June 2018.

Further, because several of the systems that will be a part of the 2018 End-to-End Test and the 2020 Census are not yet fully developed, the Bureau has not finalized all of the security controls to be implemented; assessed those controls; developed plans to remediate control weaknesses; and determined whether there is time to fully remediate any deficiencies before the systems are needed for the test. Also, as discussed earlier, the Bureau is facing system development and testing challenges that are delaying the completion of milestones and compressing the time available for security testing activities.

In addition, while the large-scale technological changes (such as Internet self-response) increase the likelihood of efficiency and effectiveness gains, they also introduce many cybersecurity challenges. The 2020 Census also involves collecting PII on over a hundred million households across the country, which further increases the need to properly secure these systems. Thus, it will be important that the Bureau provides adequate time to perform these security assessments, completes them in a timely manner, and ensures that risks are at an acceptable level before the systems are deployed.

Moving forward, the Bureau's continued attention to addressing the challenges and risks that we have identified in its efforts to manage the schedules, contracts, costs, governance and internal coordination, and cybersecurity of its IT is critical. Over the past decade, we have made 93 recommendations specific to the 2020 Census to help address, among other things, the Bureau's implementation and management of IT, scheduling, and cost estimation. The Bureau has generally agreed with those recommendations and has taken action to address 61 of them. However, as of July 2018, the remaining 32 recommendations had not been fully implemented, although the Bureau had taken initial steps— including developing action plans—to address them. Continued management attention to fully implementing these recommendations is essential for a cost-effective and secure enumeration.

AGENCY COMMENTS AND OUR EVALUATION

Commerce provided written comments on a draft of this chapter. In its comments, reprinted in appendix II, Commerce stated that it did not have any substantive disagreements with the findings in the report. The department further stated that, while it had made progress over the past year as a result of increased management focus in the areas of cost estimation, scheduling, IT security, contract management, and governance, much work remains to prepare and implement the IT systems for the 2020

Census. Commerce also provided technical comments, which we addressed, as appropriate.

We are sending copies of this chapter to the Secretary of Commerce, the Acting Director of the U.S. Census Bureau, and interested congressional committees.

Nick Marinos
Director,
Cybersecurity and Data Protection Issues

List of Requesters

The Honorable Ron Johnson
Chairman

The Honorable Claire McCaskill
Ranking Member
Committee on Homeland Security and Governmental Affairs
United States Senate

The Honorable Gary Peters
Ranking Member
Subcommittee on Federal Spending Oversight
and Emergency Management, Committee on Homeland Security
and Governmental Affairs
United States Senate

The Honorable Trey Gowdy
Chairman

The Honorable Elijah E. Cummings
Ranking Member
Committee on Oversight and Government Reform
House of Representatives

The Honorable Mark Meadows
Chairman

The Honorable Gerald E. Connolly
Ranking Member
Subcommittee on Government Operations
Committee on Oversight and Government Reform
House of Representatives

The Honorable Will Hurd
Chairman

The Honorable Robin L. Kelly
Ranking Member
Subcommittee on Information Technology
Committee on Oversight and Government Reform
House of Representatives

The Honorable Thomas R. Carper
United States Senate

APPENDIX I: STATUS OF DEVELOPMENT AND TESTING FOR SYSTEMS IN THE 2018 END-TO-END TEST, AS OF JUNE 2018

As part of the 2018 End-to-End Test, the Census Bureau (Bureau) plans to incrementally test, deploy, and use the 44 systems from December 2016 through the end of the test in April 2019. These operations include address canvassing, self-response (i.e., Internet, phone, or paper), field enumeration, and tabulation and dissemination. According to the Bureau, a single system may be deployed multiple times throughout the test (with additional or new functionality) if that system is needed for more than one of these operations.

Table 3 describes the status of development and testing, and describes if a portion of functionality has been deployed for each system in the 2018 End-to-End Test. The table also describes key system deployment dates and the delay in these dates since August 2017.

Table 3. Development, Testing, and Deployment Status for the 44 Systems in the Census Bureau's 2018 End-to-End Test, as of June 2018

System name and description	Status of development	Status of testing	Expected/ actual first deployment date[a] (delay since August 2017)	Expected/ actual final deployment date[a] (delay since August 2017)	Has at least a portion of the system's functionality been deployed?
1. Block Assessment, Review and Classification Application Interactive review tool that is designed to assist an analyst in assessing a set of geographic work units.	Complete	Complete	December 2016	n/a	Yes
2. One Form Designer Plus Tool that creates paper forms including decennial questionnaires, letters, envelopes, notices of visit, language guides, and other Decennial field and public materials.	Complete	Complete	March 2017	n/a	Yes

Table 3. (Continued)

System name and description	Status of develop-ment	Status of testing	Expected/ actual first deployment date[a] (delay since August 2017)	Expected/ actual final deployment date[a] (delay since August 2017)	Has at least a portion of the system's functionality been deployed?
3. Census Document System Web-based system for requesting forms design services, publications and graphics services, and printing services.	Complete	Complete	March 2017	September 2017	Yes
4. MOJO Recruiting Dashboard System that provides a dashboard to show recruiting metrics.	Complete	Complete	March 2017	June 2018	Yes
5. Listing and Mapping Application Single instrument that enables field users to capture and provide accurate listing and mapping updates to the Master Address File/ Topologically Integrated Geographic Encoding and Referencing Database.	Complete	Complete	July 2017	April 2018 (1-month delay)	Yes

System name and description	Status of development	Status of testing	Expected/ actual first deployment date[a] (delay since August 2017)	Expected/ actual final deployment date[a] (delay since August 2017)	Has at least a portion of the system's functionality been deployed?
6. Mobile Case Management Tool that provides mobile device-level survey case management and dashboards, and manages data transmissions and other applications on the mobile device.	Complete	Complete	July 2017	April 2018 (1-month delay)	Yes
7. MOJO Optimizer/Modeling Service to optimize the field workers' routes.	Complete	Complete	August 2017	April 2018 (1-month delay)	Yes
8. Integrated Logistics Management System to manage logistics and resource planning.	Complete	Complete	August 2017	July 2018	Yes
9. Matching and Coding Software System that allows for clerical matching and geocoding during Non-ID Processing.	Complete	Complete	February 2018	n/a	Yes
10. Real Time Non-ID Processing System that matches addresses in real-time, geocodes	Complete	Complete	February 2018	n/a	Yes

Table 3. (Continued)

System name and description	Status of development	Status of testing	Expected/ actual first deployment date[a] (delay since August 2017)	Expected/ actual final deployment date[a] (delay since August 2017)	Has at least a portion of the system's functionality been deployed?
addresses in real-time, and geo-locates housing units using web map services.					
11. Concurrent Analysis and Estimation System that stores data and uses it to execute statistical models in support of survey flow processing, analysis, and control.	Complete	Complete	March 2018	n/a	Yes
12. Enterprise Censuses and Surveys Enabling (ECaSE) – Internet Self-Response (ISR) Tool that supports self-response data collection via the Internet for respondents and by call center agents on behalf of respondents.	Complete	Complete	March 2018 (1-month delay)	n/a	Yes
13. Census Questionnaire Assistance Provides call center capability for self-response	Complete	Complete	March 2018 (1-month delay)	April 2018 (1-month delay)	Yes

System name and description	Status of development	Status of testing	Expected/ actual first deployment date[a] (delay since August 2017)	Expected/ actual final deployment date[a] (delay since August 2017)	Has at least a portion of the system's functionality been deployed?
and assists respondents with responding to and completing census questionnaires.					
14. Census Hiring and Employment Check Administrative system that automates the clearance processing of all personnel at Census Bureau Headquarters, the Bureau of Economic Analysis, the Regional Offices, the National Processing Center, and two Computer-Assisted Telephone Interview sites.	Complete	Complete	March 2017	June 2018 (4-month delay)[b]	Yes
15. Decennial Physical Access System that is used to generate badges for certain employees, including enumerators, listers, and Census Field	Complete	Complete	March 2018	June 2018	Yes

Table 3. (Continued)

System name and description	Status of development	Status of testing	Expected/ actual first deployment date[a] (delay since August 2017)	Expected/ actual final deployment date[a] (delay since August 2017)	Has at least a portion of the system's functionality been deployed?
Supervisors.					
16. Census Human Resources Information System Web-based personal information tool providing personnel and payroll information on desktops.	Complete	Complete	March 2017	July 2018	Yes
17. Commerce Business System that collects and reports labor hours and costs for the activities that the National Processing Center performs.	Complete	Complete	March 2017	July 2018	Yes
18. Decennial Service Center Suite of systems to handle all IT service requests initiated by field staff.	Complete	Complete	March 2017	July 2018	Yes
19. Desktop Services Suite of systems that includes chat.	Complete	Complete	March 2017	July 2018	Yes
20. 2020 Website for the 2018 End-to-End Test.	Complete	Complete	June 2018	January 2019	Yes

System name and description	Status of development	Status of testing	Expected/ actual first deployment date[a] (delay since August 2017)	Expected/ actual final deployment date[a] (delay since August 2017)	Has at least a portion of the system's functionality been deployed?
21. Unified Tracking System Data warehouse that is to combine data from a variety of Census systems, bringing the data to one place where the users can run or create reports to analyze survey and resource performance.	Complete	In progress	December 2016	July 2018	Yes
22. Master Address File/ Topologically Integrated Geographic Encoding and Referencing System Database that contains, manages, and controls a repository of spatial and non-spatial data used to provide extracts to define census operations, provide maps, and support Web applications.	Complete	In progress	December 2016	October 2018	Yes

Table 3. (Continued)

System name and description	Status of development	Status of testing	Expected/ actual first deployment date[a] (delay since August 2017)	Expected/ actual final deployment date[a] (delay since August 2017)	Has at least a portion of the system's functionality been deployed?
23. Automated Tracking and Control Tool that provides customer, employee, and workflow management by automating business and support activities. It provides outbound call tracking for Geographic Partnership Programs and material tracking and check-in.	Complete	In progress	February 2018	July 2018	Yes
24. Intelligent Postal Tracking Service Mail tracking system developed by the Census Bureau and the U.S. Postal Service to trace individual mail pieces during transit.	Complete	In progress	February 2018	July 2018	Yes
25. Decennial Applicant, Personnel and Payroll Systems System that supports personnel and	Complete	In progress	March 2017	July 2018 (11-month delay)[b]	Yes

System name and description	Status of development	Status of testing	Expected/ actual first deployment date[a] (delay since August 2017)	Expected/ actual final deployment date[a] (delay since August 2017)	Has at least a portion of the system's functionality been deployed?
payroll administration for temporary, intermittent Census Bureau employees participating in the 2018 End-to-End Test.					
26. Recruiting and Assessment Tool that provides capabilities for applicant recruiting and the applicant pre-selection assessment process.	Complete	In progress	March 2017	July 2018 (5-month delay)[b]	Yes
27. Identity Management System System used to ensure that the right individuals have access to the right resources at the right times for the right reasons.	Complete	In progress	March 2017	January 2019	Yes
28. ECaSE –Field Operational Control System that manages field assignments, reviews and approves field worker's time and expense, and tracks field worker's	Complete	In progress	July 2017	July 2018 (4-month delay)[b]	Yes

Table 3. (Continued)

System name and description	Status of development	Status of testing	Expected/ actual first deployment date[a] (delay since August 2017)	Expected/ actual final deployment date[a] (delay since August 2017)	Has at least a portion of the system's functionality been deployed?
performance.					
29. Geospatial Services Tool that provides vintage imagery service, internal current imagery service, public current imagery service, and mapping services.	Complete	In progress	July 2017	July 2018	Yes
30. Service Oriented Architecture Enterprise software architecture model used for designing and implementing communication between mutually interacting software applications in a service-oriented architecture.	Complete	In progress	July 2017	January 2019 (6-month delay)	Yes
31. ECaSE Operational Control System that manages the data collection universe for all enumeration operations, maintains operational workloads, and provides alerts to	Complete	In progress	August 2017	July 2018 (4-month delay)[b]	Yes

System name and description	Status of development	Status of testing	Expected/actual first deployment date[a] (delay since August 2017)	Expected/actual final deployment date[a] (delay since August 2017)	Has at least a portion of the system's functionality been deployed?
management.					
32. National Processing Center Printing Service that provides printing services for low-volume forms and merges static form and variable data, such as printing a standard form with unique addresses.	Complete	In progress	August 2017	July 2018	Yes
33. ECaSE – Enumeration Tool that captures survey responses collected by door-to-door enumeration, records contact attempts, and collects employee availability and time and expenses.	Complete	In progress	March 2018 (1-month delay)	July 2018 (4-month delay)[b]	Yes
34. Integrated Computer Assisted Data Entry Tool that captures paper responses from questionnaires.	Complete	In progress	March 2018 (1-month delay)	July 2018	Yes

Table 3. (Continued)

System name and description	Status of development	Status of testing	Expected/ actual first deployment date[a] (delay since August 2017)	Expected/ actual final deployment date[a] (delay since August 2017)	Has at least a portion of the system's functionality been deployed?
35. Census Image Retrieval Application that provides secure access to census data and digital images of the questionnaires from which the data were captured.	Complete	In progress	March 2018 (1-month delay)	January 2019 (11-month delay)[b]	Yes
36. Centurion Tool that provides an external interface for the upload of group quarters electronic response data.	Complete	In progress	July 2018 (4-month delay)	n/a	No
37. Sampling, Matching, Reviewing, and Coding System System that is to support quality control for field operations.	In progress	In progress	August 2017	October 2018 (7-month delay)[b]	Yes
38. Control and Response Data System that is to provide a sample design and universe determination for the Decennial Census.	In progress	In progress	February 2018	January 2019 (3-month delay)	Yes
39. Census Data Lake Repository	In progress	In progress	March 2018 (1-month delay)	January 2019	Yes

System name and description	Status of development	Status of testing	Expected/ actual first deployment date[a] (delay since August 2017)	Expected/ actual final deployment date[a] (delay since August 2017)	Has at least a portion of the system's functionality been deployed?
for response data that is to provide data access to reporting and analytics applications.					
40. Decennial Response Processing System that is to perform data processing on the raw response data and stores the final processed response data for long-term storage.	In progress	In progress	March 2018 (1-month delay)	January 2019	Yes
41. Production Environment for Administrative Records Staging, Integration and Storage Tool that is to manage Administrative Records and provides services associated with those records.	In progress	In progress	March 2018 (1-month delay)	January 2019 (10-month delay)[b]	Yes
42. Fraud Detection System that is to identify fraudulent responses either in real-time or post data collection.	In progress	In progress	October 2018 (8-month delay)	n/a	No

Table 3. (Continued)

System name and description	Status of development	Status of testing	Expected/ actual first deployment date[a] (delay since August 2017)	Expected/ actual final deployment date[a] (delay since August 2017)	Has at least a portion of the system's functionality been deployed?
43. Center for Enterprise Dissemination Services and Consumer Innovation Tool that will provide search and access to tabulated Census data.	In progress	In progress	January 2019	n/a	No
44. Tabulation Tool that is to receive post-processed response data and produces tabulated statistical data.	In progress	In progress	January 2019	n/a	No

Source: GAO analysis of Census Bureau data. | GAO-18-655.

Legend:

n/a = not applicable. These systems are only being deployed one time, so the first deployment date also represents the final deployment date.

[a] The dates listed for June 2018 or earlier should be considered actual dates.

[b] According to officials within the Bureau's 2020 Census Systems Engineering and Integration office, the delay in the final deployment date for this system is due to a change in the timing of the operations it is supporting for the 2018 End-to-End Test.

APPENDIX II: COMMENTS FROM THE DEPARTMENT OF COMMERCE

August 17, 2018

Mr. David Powner
Director
Information Technology Management Issues
U.S. Government Accountability Office
441 G Street, NW
Washington, DC 20548

Dear Mr. Powner:

The U.S. Department of Commerce appreciates the opportunity to comment on the U.S. Government Accountability Office's (GAO) draft report, *"2020 Census: Continued Management Attention Needed to Address Challenges and Risks with Developing, Testing, and Securing IT Systems"* (GAO-18-655). We have no substantive disagreements with the findings in this report.

While we agree that much work remains to prepare and implement our information technology (IT) systems for the 2020 Census, we appreciate GAO's recognition of the substantial progress we have made over the past year as a result of increased management focus in the areas of cost estimation, scheduling, IT security, contract management, and governance. These include:

- An extensive and independent review at the Secretary's request of the lifecycle cost estimate for the entire 2020 Census, including all key assumptions, methods, and risk analyses for both IT and non-IT operations.

- Executing a detailed schedule development effort from July – December 2017 with the baselining of the schedule on December 14, 2017. The baselining has been followed by weekly statusing and monitoring of the schedule. Currently, we are working with Operations, Systems, and Testing Project Managers to incorporate the converted systems releases into the baselined Integrated Master Schedule by October 31, 2018.

- We completed security authorizations for all 43 systems currently operational and in use for the 2018 Census Test. The 44th and final system to be used in the 2018 Census Test is scheduled for authorization prior to its scheduled use in October of this year.

- We are continuously working with the Federal intelligence community and private-sector companies to strengthen our cybersecurity posture and to improve our incident response capabilities. We have implemented all Federal requirements and industry best practices, including use of both Federal and private-sector third parties to test our cyber defenses.

- Over the past year, we have increased our contract oversight and monitoring efforts with the addition of a weekly meeting where Decennial senior leadership meets to review contract performance status. Contract performance issues presented at this leadership status meeting are addressed to reduce risk to 2020 operations. In addition, we implemented monthly reporting on the 2020 Major Contracts using an EVM or EVM-like processes to track performance against cost and schedule, which are presented during a monthly status meeting with Secretary Ross.
- Revising 2020 Census governance to operationalize the processes as we transition from Research & Testing to Peak Operations. The revised approach provides clear decision escalation, reduces meeting burden, and improves communication of decisions to all stakeholders.

We have also enclosed our technical comments on this draft report.

Sincerely,

Wilbur Ross

INDEX

#

14th Amendment, vii, ix, 1, 3, 35

A

accountability, 103, 191, 216, 225, 338
agencies, 7, 16, 30, 54, 55, 63, 65, 71, 76, 87, 88, 94, 97, 108, 118, 134, 150, 158, 171, 173, 216, 260, 264, 272, 340, 341
agency actions, 64
American Community Survey, viii, 2, 3, 5, 7, 13, 39, 44, 52, 63, 253, 311, 326
appropriations, ix, 3, 8, 27, 32, 33, 38, 59, 66
assessment, xi, 32, 75, 107, 109, 110, 111, 112, 113, 125, 129, 132, 133, 136, 148, 160, 168, 169, 173, 184, 185, 188, 192, 193, 195, 196, 197, 198, 199, 203, 212, 213, 215, 216, 217, 242, 245, 265, 275, 276, 341, 342, 355
assessment tools, 148
audit, 75, 126, 144, 145, 171, 180, 187, 188, 215, 222, 247, 254, 284, 292, 325
authentication, 238
authority, 13, 38, 51, 55, 58, 62, 65, 110, 132, 235, 251, 261, 262, 263, 342
automation, 145, 156, 214, 272
awareness, 20, 111, 127, 132, 134, 164

B

benefits, 55, 117, 134, 142, 158, 176, 177
breakdown, 193, 204, 212, 221, 230, 237, 240, 245
budget cuts, 298
Bureau of the Census, viii, 2, 3
business processes, 309
businesses, ix, 36, 75, 323

C

census accuracy, vii, 4
census addresses, viii, 2, 14, 127, 137
Census Bureau, vi, viii, ix, 2, 3, 4, 5, 6, 7, 8, 9, 10, 11, 12, 13, 14, 15, 16, 17, 18, 19, 20, 21, 22, 23, 24, 25, 26, 27, 28, 32, 33, 35, 36, 38, 39, 40, 41, 43, 44, 51, 52, 61, 62, 63, 69, 71, 72, 78, 79, 81, 83, 84, 88, 92, 95, 104, 107, 121, 122, 123, 124, 126, 130, 131, 135, 139, 141, 142, 144,

147, 149, 151, 155, 156, 157, 159, 162, 177, 178, 184, 186, 190, 192, 194, 195, 200, 206, 208, 211, 213, 214, 217, 218, 220, 221, 222, 223, 224, 226, 227, 231, 232, 233, 235, 237, 241, 242, 243, 244, 249, 250, 252, 255, 259, 281, 282, 283, 289, 291, 295, 300, 301, 313, 314, 315, 319, 321, 323, 325, 328, 329, 330, 333, 334, 337, 340, 343, 345, 346, 347, 351, 354, 355, 360
census counts, vii, 1, 3, 118
census coverage, vii, 4, 10, 11, 12, 129, 327
census information, viii, 2, 17, 26, 51
census offices, x, 18, 27, 130, 139, 140, 143, 145, 149, 150, 153, 178, 193, 281, 310
census operations, xi, 28, 38, 84, 129, 146, 167, 169, 183, 186, 238, 327, 336, 353
census planning, viii, 2
census questionnaire, v, 4, 24, 26, 43, 45, 47, 50, 51, 52, 53, 54, 58, 61, 62, 99, 107, 126, 128, 137, 143, 145, 189, 211, 242, 252, 328, 337, 350, 351
census responses, viii, 2, 18, 20, 21, 22
challenges, x, xiii, 10, 14, 23, 30, 44, 49, 50, 57, 58, 70, 73, 91, 97, 99, 100, 110, 128, 142, 161, 165, 166, 167, 168, 176, 179, 188, 251, 264, 273, 274, 280, 292, 296, 306, 310, 320, 321, 322, 323, 324, 331, 332, 335, 336, 339, 340, 343, 344
citizenship, 39, 40, 43, 44, 47, 49, 50, 52, 53, 54, 55, 56, 57, 58, 59, 61, 63, 65, 66, 98, 99, 253
classroom, 21, 146, 148, 167, 169, 171, 172, 173, 266
computer, 21, 129, 141, 148, 167, 170, 172, 239, 294, 311
Congress, iv, viii, ix, 1, 2, 3, 4, 5, 6, 7, 8, 9, 10, 12, 14, 17, 19, 24, 25, 26, 27, 28, 33, 35, 36, 45, 50, 51, 53, 54, 55, 58, 59, 62, 63, 64, 66, 98, 186, 215, 338

Constitution, vii, viii, ix, xii, 1, 3, 35, 43, 45, 47, 50, 51, 58, 62, 186, 214, 320, 322
construction, 153, 154, 176, 179, 186, 200
contingency, x, 30, 70, 71, 72, 73, 74, 76, 81, 82, 83, 84, 85, 86, 87, 88, 89, 90, 91, 92, 93, 94, 95, 96, 98, 99, 100, 101, 102, 103, 104, 105, 106, 120, 121, 123, 124, 185, 189, 198, 213, 228, 229, 237, 239, 240, 241
cost, viii, x, xi, xii, 2, 4, 5, 6, 7, 8, 9, 10, 12, 14, 16, 20, 21, 29, 30, 36, 63, 72, 73, 76, 77, 81, 87, 88, 91, 94, 96, 101, 102, 109, 118, 120, 140, 141, 142, 143, 144, 151, 152, 165, 167, 173, 175, 176, 177, 180, 184, 187, 188, 189, 191, 192, 194, 195, 199, 201, 202, 211, 212, 213, 214, 215, 216, 217, 218, 219, 220, 221, 223, 224, 225, 226, 227, 228, 229, 230, 231, 232, 233, 234, 235, 236, 237, 238, 239, 240, 241, 242, 244, 245, 246, 247, 249, 252, 289, 290, 293, 296, 300, 301, 304, 322, 323, 324, 325, 336, 337, 338, 339, 344
cost controls, 233
cost saving, 152, 293
cost-benefit analysis, 63
cost-driven, 233
cyber-attack, 229, 240
cybersecurity, 71, 88, 96, 97, 98, 321, 323, 331, 344

D

data center, 27, 29, 306, 327, 335, 342
data collection, 16, 18, 19, 25, 29, 37, 40, 126, 127, 130, 131, 146, 147, 148, 167, 172, 173, 189, 224, 228, 233, 239, 242, 250, 251, 257, 258, 259, 260, 276, 277, 280, 281, 283, 292, 326, 350, 356, 359
data processing, 96, 304, 359
data set, 18
database, 23, 127, 291

Index

deadlines, x, xi, 4, 58, 72, 140, 142, 153, 154, 176, 183, 186, 194, 212, 216, 303, 304
decennial census data, vii, 1, 3, 15
Department of Commerce, v, ix, xi, 3, 35, 40, 49, 54, 56, 57, 58, 59, 61, 62, 69, 70, 72, 98, 107, 117, 121, 122, 135, 139, 141, 168, 177, 181, 184, 185, 189, 195, 200, 209, 211, 212, 214, 242, 244, 248, 250, 279, 281, 285, 288, 313, 314, 316, 319, 323, 361
Department of Defense, 175
Department of Health and Human Services, 66
Department of Homeland Security, 69, 97
Department of Justice, 39, 43, 44, 49, 52, 63, 98, 118, 134
detection, 27, 75, 108, 109, 113, 117, 119, 125, 133, 134, 135, 327, 329, 331, 333, 335
detection system, 75, 109, 113, 117, 119, 125, 135
draft, xi, 84, 85, 87, 93, 94, 122, 177, 184, 200, 242, 260, 267, 276, 279, 281, 314, 344

E

employees, ix, 3, 14, 30, 51, 116, 119, 128, 133, 135, 144, 145, 146, 158, 161, 163, 167, 169, 170, 171, 173, 180, 251, 254, 267, 268, 291, 294, 295, 311, 325, 331, 351, 355
employment, 7, 158, 161, 162, 163, 165, 269
employment status, 269
enforcement, 39, 44, 52, 54, 55, 56, 118, 134, 151
engineering, 27, 93, 241, 325, 336
environment, 30, 104, 111, 112, 132, 214, 254, 264, 273, 323, 342
equipment, 154, 161, 184, 193, 195, 268, 299
estimation process, 30, 217, 221, 225, 230, 234
evidence, xi, 50, 53, 54, 56, 57, 58, 75, 126, 145, 180, 188, 206, 208, 212, 215, 223, 225, 245, 247, 254, 272, 284, 292, 325

F

facilitated communication, 111
faith, 16, 53, 56, 57
Federal Bureau of Investigation, 161
federal funds, vii, ix, 1, 3, 28, 36, 51
federal government, 13, 30, 46, 72, 76, 94, 153, 170, 216, 242, 244, 290
Federal Government, 84, 85, 114, 144, 152, 170, 180, 260, 262, 264, 272, 287, 298
federal law, 13, 45, 51, 97, 340
Federal Register, 22
field staff, x, 18, 20, 21, 23, 37, 130, 140, 141, 143, 144, 148, 154, 155, 156, 163, 167, 169, 170, 171, 172, 173, 179, 196, 271, 272, 281, 289, 292, 302, 303, 310, 311, 337, 352
fieldwork, viii, 2, 15, 18, 32, 37, 96, 145, 146, 251, 252, 254, 257, 267, 268, 270
fiscal year, 72, 103, 143, 189, 214, 221, 233, 252, 290, 300, 336
flexibility, 32, 99, 153, 188, 204, 278, 279
Fourteenth Amendment, 45, 46, 50
fraud, x, 27, 30, 70, 72, 73, 74, 76, 107, 108, 109, 110, 111, 112, 113, 115, 116, 117, 118, 119, 120, 121, 122, 123, 125, 131, 132, 133, 134, 135, 136, 307, 308, 323, 327, 329, 331, 333, 335
fraud risk, x, 70, 72, 73, 74, 76, 107, 108, 109, 110, 111, 112, 113, 114, 115, 116, 117, 118, 119, 120, 121, 123, 125, 131, 132, 133, 134, 135, 136
fuel prices, 220

funding, ix, 2, 4, 9, 24, 28, 33, 34, 38, 47, 204, 215, 220, 228, 229, 233, 240, 245, 303, 341

funds, 24, 33, 38, 59, 77, 108, 338

G

governance, 73, 123, 331, 338, 339, 344

governments, ix, 34, 36, 158

growth, xi, 212, 215, 244, 247, 322, 336, 338

guidance, 9, 59, 71, 73, 119, 123, 133, 135, 152, 180, 218, 233, 234, 235, 244, 246, 247, 250, 251, 261, 263, 264, 265, 272, 277, 279, 280, 281, 310, 341

H

hiring, x, xii, 27, 88, 102, 140, 141, 142, 143, 145, 146, 155, 156, 157, 158, 161, 162, 163, 164, 176, 178, 179, 194, 269, 288, 289, 292, 299, 301, 303, 304, 327, 332, 333

historical data, 219, 225, 239

House of Representatives, vii, ix, 1, 3, 35, 45, 51, 75, 123, 178, 194, 201, 243, 244, 282, 290, 315, 323, 345, 346

households, xii, xiii, 10, 12, 15, 17, 18, 21, 31, 37, 119, 128, 131, 135, 145, 146, 155, 165, 187, 189, 191, 238, 250, 252, 257, 275, 279, 293, 311, 320, 322, 325, 335, 344

housing, viii, 2, 5, 6, 9, 10, 13, 14, 17, 19, 20, 21, 22, 23, 25, 36, 37, 38, 44, 84, 88, 93, 128, 129, 154, 156, 169, 189, 191, 213, 214, 224, 239, 250, 254, 255, 256, 257, 258, 261, 266, 267, 269, 270, 274, 275, 277, 279, 280, 291, 292, 293, 294, 295, 297, 299, 300, 304, 330, 350

housing information, viii, 2

human resources, 179

I

imagery, viii, 2, 15, 23, 36, 93, 239, 293, 294, 295, 356

improvements, 200, 212, 213, 225, 242, 312, 313

individuals, 51, 80, 85, 91, 94, 97, 98, 103, 106, 107, 108, 128, 133, 155, 158, 160, 165, 166, 262, 325, 338, 339, 355

inflation, 8, 72, 143, 214, 225, 245

information technology, x, 19, 28, 70, 73, 88, 96, 188, 213, 214, 218, 228, 232, 247, 273, 296, 320, 321, 323

information technology systems, x, 70, 73, 188, 296

infrastructure, 27, 29, 40, 100, 130, 145, 166, 240, 241, 253, 325, 326, 327, 335, 336, 342

integration, 23, 27, 29, 71, 88, 92, 99, 100, 109, 110, 117, 241, 309, 321, 322, 324, 326, 327, 329, 331, 332, 333, 335, 336, 337, 342

integrity, 88, 96, 108, 109, 132, 134, 135, 152, 191, 199, 205

internet, x, xiii, 16, 20, 22, 23, 25, 37, 38, 40, 70, 73, 93, 96, 99, 100, 107, 112, 127, 131, 137, 161, 168, 169, 170, 219, 228, 238, 242, 253, 256, 264, 289, 291, 293, 309, 310, 311, 312, 314, 320, 325, 326, 327, 335, 344, 346, 350

issues, vii, xii, 28, 50, 57, 58, 66, 73, 98, 105, 111, 120, 129, 143, 171, 187, 188, 197, 203, 225, 228, 229, 250, 251, 253, 254, 261, 262, 263, 264, 265, 270, 271, 273, 280, 281, 282, 283, 296, 298, 306, 310, 312, 313, 320, 323, 338, 342

IT readiness, xiii, 320, 323

J

job performance, 148, 177

job position, 162, 163

L

labor market, 41, 239, 303
language barrier, 31, 161, 166, 176, 252, 262, 264, 271, 275
language diversity, 23
language skills, 158, 271
languages, 16, 22, 41, 126, 157, 166
laptop, 170, 295, 300, 304, 305, 306, 311, 312
law enforcement, 119, 150, 151
laws and regulations, 65
leadership, 57, 76, 162, 164, 267
learning, 6, 148, 172, 177, 305
legislation, 7, 8, 9, 33, 58, 98
legislative boundaries, ix, 35
local community, 157
local government, 15, 51, 127, 299
logistics, 130, 145, 167, 232, 349

M

majority, 11, 46, 49, 52, 54, 81, 128, 162, 165, 169, 240, 328, 331, 340
management, x, xi, 5, 6, 9, 15, 16, 17, 18, 21, 22, 25, 27, 30, 32, 64, 70, 72, 73, 83, 84, 85, 86, 88, 91, 95, 97, 100, 102, 103, 105, 106, 107, 108, 109, 111, 116, 120, 121, 123, 124, 126, 130, 143, 145, 176, 184, 185, 188, 193, 194, 195, 196, 198, 199, 200, 202, 204, 212, 213, 214, 215, 218, 223, 225, 226, 232, 233, 234, 240, 245, 247, 260, 261, 262, 263, 265, 266, 269, 271, 280, 283, 284, 290, 292, 296, 298, 308, 309, 311, 312, 321, 335, 336, 341, 344, 349, 354, 357
mapping, 23, 158, 190, 204, 238, 298, 348, 356

materials, 57, 126, 127, 129, 147, 148, 157, 167, 185, 194, 196, 347
measurement, 15, 225, 327, 333
media, 16, 21, 37, 156, 159, 166
methodology, 75, 112, 144, 187, 203, 215, 219, 223, 230, 245, 300
metropolitan areas, 23
mobile device, 20, 23, 27, 29, 30, 37, 96, 146, 241, 298, 322, 325, 331, 335, 336, 337, 349
mobile phone, 337

N

national origin, 52, 166
natural disasters, 104, 188, 229, 240, 296
nonprofit organizations, vii, ix, 1, 3, 36, 75
nursing, 25, 253, 255, 269, 274, 293

O

Office of Management and Budget, 22, 69, 74, 76, 90, 124, 158, 212, 216, 233, 320, 341
Office of the Inspector General, 140, 168
operations, xi, xii, xiii, 8, 14, 15, 24, 25, 26, 27, 28, 29, 30, 31, 32, 34, 38, 40, 71, 73, 77, 84, 88, 93, 99, 100, 104, 110, 117, 118, 125, 126, 127, 128, 129, 130, 132, 142, 143, 144, 145, 146, 149, 154, 155, 156, 158, 164, 166, 167, 168, 169, 171, 172, 175, 176, 179, 183, 184, 186, 190, 195, 213, 218, 219, 224, 229, 238, 250, 253, 254, 255, 256, 257, 262, 271, 273, 280, 282, 283, 284, 293, 295, 299, 303, 304, 306, 308, 313, 320, 323, 325, 326, 327, 329, 330, 331, 335, 336, 337, 339, 340, 346, 353, 356, 358, 360
opportunities, 26, 159, 177, 198, 204
organizational culture, 109, 110, 132

outreach, 16, 25, 26, 36, 37, 93, 153, 164, 166
oversight, 3, 10, 11, 17, 18, 24, 25, 26, 27, 28, 30, 33, 38, 51, 63, 102, 132, 213, 215, 233, 234, 308, 321, 336, 338, 339
overtime, 307, 308

P

payroll, xii, 156, 164, 241, 250, 255, 263, 268, 284, 352, 355
performance indicator, 255
performance measurement, 199
policy, 55, 62, 63, 64, 65, 66, 75, 290, 323, 341
population, vii, viii, ix, xi, xii, 1, 2, 3, 5, 10, 11, 12, 16, 22, 25, 35, 36, 37, 39, 43, 44, 45, 46, 47, 51, 52, 72, 104, 127, 128, 129, 142, 183, 186, 189, 214, 252, 255, 257, 258, 259, 275, 293, 320, 322, 323
population census, vii, ix, 1, 3, 35, 45
population group, 11, 16, 22, 37
population size, vii, 1, 3
private information, 340
private sector, 94
productivity rates, 156, 175, 238, 292, 299, 301, 302, 313
programming, 216, 276
progress reports, 254, 284, 290
project, 77, 184, 185, 187, 191, 192, 193, 194, 195, 196, 197, 198, 199, 202, 203, 204, 205, 231, 233, 234, 339
public assistance, 158
public concern, 104

Q

questionnaire, viii, 2, 4, 11, 16, 22, 24, 26, 37, 43, 45, 47, 50, 51, 52, 53, 54, 58, 61, 99, 107, 127, 128, 145, 146, 160, 242, 293, 330, 337

R

recommendations, iv, 70, 97, 121, 122, 174, 185, 186, 187, 200, 203, 212, 232, 250, 281, 288, 313, 314, 320, 339, 344
recruiting, x, 10, 27, 140, 141, 142, 143, 145, 146, 148, 154, 155, 156, 157, 158, 159, 160, 161, 162, 163, 164, 165, 166, 176, 178, 179, 194, 196, 303, 304, 327, 332, 348, 355
redistricting, vii, xi, 1, 3, 5, 28, 44, 45, 46, 72, 128, 129, 143, 183, 186, 293
regional unemployment, 303
reliability, xi, 119, 185, 187, 199, 200, 203, 212, 215, 218, 230, 244, 292
requirements, 30, 59, 63, 65, 71, 77, 81, 85, 104, 126, 150, 151, 152, 153, 175, 235, 236, 238, 241, 263, 272, 288, 290, 309, 314, 324, 326, 340
researchers, vii, ix, 1, 3, 36
resource allocation, 195, 215
resource availability, 197
resource management, 65
resources, 4, 7, 24, 76, 78, 81, 91, 96, 109, 115, 116, 117, 133, 135, 163, 176, 177, 185, 186, 188, 191, 193, 194, 195, 197, 198, 199, 202, 204, 205, 206, 207, 208, 214, 216, 221, 230, 232, 233, 242, 255, 275, 341, 355
risk assessment, 74, 107, 109, 110, 111, 112, 113, 116, 117, 118, 125, 131, 132, 185, 186, 198, 200
risk management, x, 69, 70, 71, 73, 74, 76, 77, 78, 79, 80, 81, 83, 84, 85, 86, 87, 88, 89, 90, 91, 92, 94, 95, 96, 100, 101, 102, 103, 104, 105, 106, 108, 109, 110, 111, 116, 117, 120, 121, 123, 124, 125, 132, 133, 134, 135, 188, 239, 296, 341, 342
risk profile, 111, 112, 113, 116, 133, 134, 135

S

schedule delays, 84, 336, 339
scope, 44, 51, 53, 75, 100, 144, 187, 188, 191, 193, 199, 205, 215, 224, 233, 259, 260, 326, 327, 335
Secretary of Commerce, viii, ix, 1, 3, 35, 39, 49, 51, 54, 58, 61, 62, 64, 66, 121, 122, 141, 177, 186, 200, 212, 229, 232, 242, 243, 281, 282, 313, 314, 338, 339, 345
security, ix, x, xiii, 3, 23, 27, 28, 30, 41, 70, 73, 88, 94, 96, 97, 117, 119, 126, 135, 161, 188, 296, 320, 322, 324, 332, 334, 339, 340, 341, 342, 343, 344
socioeconomic data, viii, 2
software, 158, 169, 194, 198, 219, 245, 288, 290, 298, 305, 306, 312, 314, 328, 356
structure, 109, 110, 131, 145, 193, 204, 221, 230, 237, 245, 246, 269, 283
supervisor, 23, 62, 64, 66, 160, 163, 168, 250, 262, 263, 272, 273, 274, 281, 306, 313
supervisors, xii, 18, 156, 161, 167, 171, 250, 251, 252, 255, 260, 261, 262, 263, 268, 271, 272, 276, 278, 280, 281, 283, 292, 298, 306, 307, 313

T

technical assistance, 97
technical comments, 122, 177, 242, 250, 281, 288, 314, 345
technical support, 100, 335
techniques, 80, 81, 113, 133, 204, 230, 239
technological change, 344
technology, viii, ix, xiii, 2, 3, 4, 10, 11, 18, 21, 23, 29, 30, 37, 93, 143, 145, 156, 158, 167, 180, 219, 262, 291, 293, 309, 313, 320, 326, 335, 339

telephone, viii, 2, 15, 16, 17, 21, 22, 26, 93, 107, 128, 152, 219, 242, 256, 258, 293, 335, 340
telephone numbers, 340
temporary workforce, x, 41, 140, 143, 229, 303
test procedure, 251, 260, 278
test scores, 168, 265
testing, viii, ix, xiii, 2, 3, 4, 20, 21, 22, 28, 40, 59, 73, 97, 99, 100, 167, 174, 179, 188, 194, 221, 253, 254, 256, 259, 260, 263, 264, 267, 269, 273, 277, 279, 280, 283, 284, 295, 296, 309, 320, 321, 323, 324, 326, 327, 328, 329, 331, 332, 333, 334, 335, 336, 339, 343, 347, 348, 349, 350, 351, 352, 353, 354, 355, 356, 357, 358, 360
time constraints, 197, 204
time frame, 29, 70, 71, 72, 83, 84, 87, 97, 115, 119, 120, 121, 143, 150, 176, 189, 214, 252, 256, 290, 297, 299, 303, 306, 332, 333, 339
training, x, xii, 21, 23, 32, 73, 123, 140, 141, 142, 143, 144, 145, 147, 148, 153, 167, 168, 169, 170, 171, 172, 173, 174, 175, 176, 177, 178, 179, 196, 250, 251, 261, 263, 264, 265, 272, 273, 276, 278, 280, 281, 283, 288, 291, 297, 304, 307, 309, 311, 312, 314
transmission, 305, 306, 312, 313, 314

U

U.S. Constitution, vii, ix, 1, 3, 35, 43, 45, 50, 186, 214
U.S. Department of Commerce, ix, 35, 40
U.S. history, 6, 189
U.S. residents, ix, 2, 4, 12
unemployment rate, 41, 146, 164, 165, 289, 303

United States, v, vi, vii, viii, ix, x, xii, 1, 3, 4, 6, 11, 12, 13, 14, 19, 27, 35, 36, 39, 40, 50, 53, 58, 61, 62, 66, 69, 98, 112, 122, 128, 139, 165, 183, 189, 201, 211, 243, 249, 279, 287, 288, 291, 293, 315, 319, 345, 346

United States Code, viii, 1, 3, 62

updating, viii, 2, 72, 93, 107, 115, 119, 121, 128, 199, 205, 233, 234, 241, 258, 289, 301, 302, 309, 337

V

voting, 39, 43, 44, 46, 52
voting majority, 46

W

workers, xii, 25, 36, 41, 129, 143, 145, 146, 155, 156, 174, 189, 288, 293, 303, 304, 349

workflow, 354

workforce, x, 140, 143, 146, 157, 229, 251, 253, 258, 261, 274, 283, 303

workload, xii, 17, 18, 19, 20, 23, 37, 112, 118, 128, 147, 149, 175, 239, 257, 259, 266, 267, 279, 280, 284, 288, 289, 292, 295, 299, 300, 301, 302, 312, 313, 334

Related Nova Publications

KEY CONGRESSIONAL REPORTS FOR FEBRUARY 2019. PART III

EDITOR: Mandy Todd

SERIES: Congressional Policies, Practices and Procedures

BOOK DESCRIPTION: This book is a comprehensive compilation of all reports, testimony, correspondence and other publications issued by the Congressional Research Service during the month of March, grouped according to topics.

HARDCOVER ISBN: 978-1-53615-997-4
RETAIL PRICE: $230

KEY CONGRESSIONAL REPORTS FOR MARCH 2019. PART I

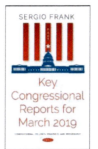

EDITOR: Sergio Frank

SERIES: Congressional Policies, Practices and Procedures

BOOK DESCRIPTION: This book is a comprehensive compilation of all reports, testimony, correspondence and other publications issued by the Congressional Research Service during the month of March, grouped according to topics. This book is focused on the following topics:
· Information Security & Technology
· Military Technology

HARDCOVER ISBN: 978-1-53615-976-9
RETAIL PRICE: $160

To see a complete list of Nova publications, please visit our website at www.novapublishers.com

Related Nova Publications

KEY CONGRESSIONAL REPORTS FOR FEBRUARY 2019. PART II

EDITOR: Mandy Todd

SERIES: Congressional Policies, Practices and Procedures

BOOK DESCRIPTION: This book is a comprehensive compilation of all reports, testimony, correspondence and other publications issued by the Congressional Research Service during the month of February, grouped according to topics. This book is focused on the following topics:
· Business
· Finance

HARDCOVER ISBN: 978-1-53615-737-6
RETAIL PRICE: $195

KEY CONGRESSIONAL REPORTS ON INTERNATIONAL AFFAIRS

EDITOR: Hattie Ross

SERIES: Congressional Policies, Practices and Procedures

BOOK DESCRIPTION: This book is a comprehensive compilation of all reports, testimony, correspondence and other publications issued by the Congressional Research Service on U.S. International Relations during the month of February.

HARDCOVER ISBN: 978-1-53615-733-8
RETAIL PRICE: $230

To see a complete list of Nova publications, please visit our website at www.novapublishers.com